D0506119

MoM

How to Restore & Improve your

VICTORIAN
HOUSE

Alan Johnson

DAVID & CHARLES
Newton Abbot   London

British Library Cataloguing in Publication Data

Johnson, Alan
  How to restore and improve your Victorian
  house.
  1. Dwellings—Remodelling—Amateurs' manuals
  I. Title
  643'.7   TH4816

  ISBN 0-7153-8334-5

First published 1984
Second impression 1984
Third impression 1988

Typeset by Typesetters (Birmingham) Ltd,
and printed in Great Britain
by Butler & Tanner Limited, Frome and London
for David & Charles (Publishers) plc
Brunel House   Newton Abbot   Devon

Contents

Acknowledgements

I would particularly like to thank Richard Kay for drawing many of the illustrations to Chapters 4, 7, 8 and 10; Robin Bishop for providing three of the colour photographs which appear on the cover; Joan Hodge for very carefully typing the text from my often indecipherable scrawl, and my wife Liz who not only tolerated the discomfort resulting from the renovation of a Victorian house, but also bravely endured the consequences of her husband's insistence upon writing a book about it! Also I am grateful to Christopher Pick for encouraging me to pursue the idea for this book.

It is only fair to add that for facts related to the historical background of Victorian housing, I have leaned quite heavily on Dr Stefan Muthesius' admirable book, *The English Terraced House*, which I warmly commend to those readers who wish to learn more about the evolution of the wide variety of types of Victorian dwellings.

For Liz

Foreword

At least a third of Britain's 18.1 million dwellings were erected before 1919. The nineteenth century, in particular, was a period of prolific house-building. Between 1801 and 1911, 6 million houses were built, more than 2½ million of these being erected between the years 1870 and 1911.

These statistics alone would justify the publication of a book which describes the construction and restoration of Victorian houses, if it was not equally plain that many of the popular DIY handbooks advocate the removal of the very features which distinguish Victorian and Edwardian houses from those of the succeeding inter-war and post-war periods in the name of 'modernisation'.

This book has been written expressly to counteract this attitude, in the belief that the removal or concealment of characteristically 'Victorian' features impoverishes the general environment and tends to reduce the interest of the individual householder in preserving or enhancing his or her property.

Strictly speaking, Victorian houses are those dwellings erected between the years 1837 and 1901, but because construction techniques for domestic buildings did not change significantly during the period between the accession of Queen Victoria and the end of World War I, this book regards all houses built between 1837 and 1918 as 'Victorian'. It was only after 1918, with the commencement of large-scale private and public house-building, that radical changes occurred in the materials and methods of domestic construction. Therefore this book concentrates on the anatomy and restoration of Victorian houses – how they were assembled in traditional materials – brick and stone, wood, slates and tiles. This account is particularly relevant to British buildings, though certain information – notably the description of timber-framed buildings contained in Chapter 3 – is relevant to the construction of period houses in the USA and former British colonies.

Avid antiquarians are likely to be disappointed that I have not entirely rejected modern materials and methods of building construction in favour of the revival of antique methods. In Chapters 1–10, current materials and techniques are described which will perform as well as, or better than, the results of the original Victorian methods, whilst the advantages of adopting modern methods and products in making major alterations or additions to Victorian houses are explained in Chapter 11, Alterations and Improvements. I have adopted this approach not only because it would be foolish to recommend obsolete materials and techniques where tried and tested modern products are more readily available and more easily installed than the original items, but also because the advice on restoration which is provided by architectural textbooks relies upon a knowledge of traditional materials and the related crafts which would be very difficult and time-consuming for the average DIY handyman to acquire.

I hope, therefore, that this book will be both a practical aid to DIY-minded owners of Victorian houses and a stimulus to those householders who currently lack such skills to investigate the construction of their houses with a view to learning techniques for the repair, maintenance and preservation of these venerable buildings.

Alan Johnson
Kingston upon Thames

Historical Background

The Victorian period witnessed an acceleration of the changes in British society which the Industrial Revolution of the eighteenth century had initiated. It was an age dominated by an enlarging middle class which sought improved standards and new architectural qualities in their houses. Surviving Victorian houses display a great diversity of internal layouts and architectural styles: to understand the forces which shaped the appearance of even the 'typical' terraced house it is necessary to know a little about the development of nineteenth-century housing.

Although the building, on a large scale, of houses for sale or rent had commenced in Georgian times, after 1820 the rapid advance of industrialism greatly assisted this activity. The concentration of steam-powered industries in the manufacturing towns generated a need for great numbers of new dwellings to house the workers who had migrated from rural areas. Initially, densely packed courtyard developments of poorly built terraced houses assembled from locally produced brick and Welsh slate were erected around the industrial cores of the factory towns. These developments proceeded in the absence of an overall plan. Little care was given to sanitation and landscaping, whilst clear access, natural lighting and ventilation received no thought at all.

. The resultant squalor quite quickly aroused the concern of social reformers, and public health legislation initiated by the Health of Towns Act of 1848 conceived a series of housing acts from 1875 which prescribed minimum distances between dwellings, the inclusion of damp-proof courses in walls to prevent damp rising from the ground, and the provision of adequate natural lighting and ventilation. The model by-laws of 1877 which stemmed from the 1875 Public Health Act were very generally taken up by local authorities outside London. As a pioneer in this field, the capital continued to have its own legislation – a circumstance which to this day distinguishes building control in the inner London boroughs from the standards applied in the rest of the nation. The stipulations for minimum street widths and open areas at the back of dwellings contained in these model by-laws explain the conspicuous uniformity of layout of much late-nineteenth-century terraced housing in entirely unrelated areas of the country. Only the industrial towns of West Yorkshire continued to sanction the building of the 'back-to-back' houses which had been a favourite form in the early, crowded courtyard developments. Not until the 1920s did the terraced house succumb to the semi-detached type which populates so many pre-World War II suburbs, even

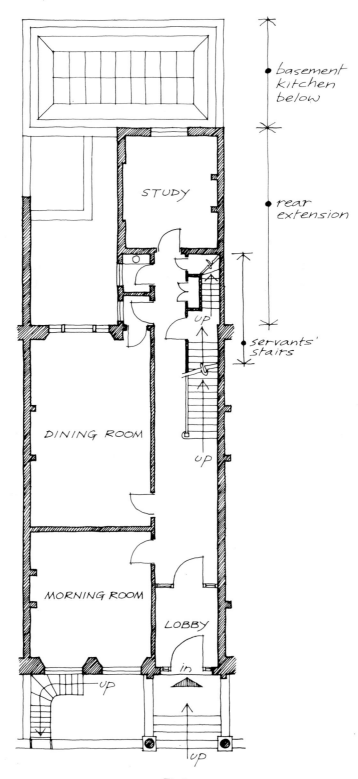

basement
kitchen
below

rear
extension

STUDY

servants'
stairs

UP

DINING ROOM

UP

UP

MORNING ROOM

LOBBY

in

UP

UP

Fig 1

though the essential layout of the pre-war 'semi' had been worked out by the late 1880s. Thus it is fair to say that 'Victorian' housing extends at least as far forward as 1914 – to World War I and the fourth year of George V's reign.

The plan of the nineteenth-century terraced house is essentially that of the small Georgian town house. It is two rooms deep and one room wide. Enlargements of this simple scheme were achieved by adding one or more storeys to the basic two-storey structure in the form of basements or upper floors, or providing extra space in a narrow 'back extension'. The frontage of the house rarely exceeded 8m (26ft 3in), and a 4m (13ft) width between party walls was conventional in the smallest houses. This planning principle held good even in the largest terraced houses erected in London in the middle of the nineteenth century. Though a South Kensington 'town mansion' of 1860 could contain twenty rooms on six storeys, the main body of the house accommodated only two main rooms per floor (Fig 1 and Plate 1); ancillary spaces were housed in a rear extension. Yet apart from the differences in construction and layout which resulted from compliance with new building regulations, technological and social developments as well as changing fashions caused Victorian houses to differ from their Georgian ancestors.

New industries and improved transport in the shape of a rapidly growing rail network facilitated the mass production and easy dispersal of new and traditional building materials. The building of large areas of terraced housing in formerly remote regions became a practical proposition. The introduction of steam saws at the quarries meant that ornamental carved stone window sills, lintels and brackets could be quickly and cheaply produced. Cast iron and terracotta began to be used in Victorian houses following their adoption in other types of buildings. Vast quantities of Welsh slates were delivered by rail to almost all areas of Britain to form the impervious roof covering for countless thousands of homes. The introduction after 1840 of wood-working machinery into joiners' shops stimulated the mass production of standard items like internal doors and sash windows, whilst the machines invented to grind and press brick clay more precisely encouraged the mass production of hard and durable bricks, which quickly displaced the unreliable products of a multitude of local brick fields.

The changing social system spawned as many distinctive features in Victorian houses as these technological advances. Until the beginning of the twentieth century 90 per cent of all British dwellings were rented from private landlords. The houses were owned by builders or speculators for whom the position of landlord provided a safe if unspectacular income. A typical annual rent was about 10 per cent of the purchase price of the house (which would itself be 10 per cent more than the building cost). The rent yielded a profit of about 5 per cent for the landlord. Almost all houses were built as a speculation – that is, the builder did not have a specific tenant in mind when construction commenced, and consequently, throughout the nineteenth century about 10 per cent of houses stood empty. When the supply of houses significantly exceeded demand, rents had to be lowered.

Plate 1 The front elevation of a South Kensington town mansion, *c*1860 (*Author*)

The speculators ranged from aristocrats to local builders of quite modest means. In London, the aristocrats, as the traditional landowners, developed Bloomsbury, St Marylebone, Mayfair, Belgravia, Pimlico and Chelsea as residential areas from the eighteenth century onwards. Outside central London and in the suburbs of provincial towns, the old estates were more likely to be broken up into small 'parcels' so that a tract of farm or parkland would be developed by a large number of speculative builders. Though the price of land rarely exceeded 20 per cent of the building cost, the economics of Victorian building and the necessity of complying with the by-laws could ensure that terraced houses erected in quite separate areas by different builders were strikingly similar. The marginal profits from residential development caused the bankruptcy of speculative builders to be a regular event. However, the other parties to a development – the original landowner, the solicitor who arranged the builder's finance and the investors who provided the funds – were much less likely to lose money, because a bankruptcy normally demanded the resale of the land or half-finished dwellings, deferring rather than eliminating the profits from the development.

Who were the inhabitants of these houses? Since Victorian Britain was controlled by the attitude and enterprise of the middle class, outside central London – where the initiative for development had been taken by the aristocracy – most of the developers of speculative housing came from this group, and so, generally speaking, did the customers for their products. The vast majority of surviving Victorian houses are located in the suburbs or the countryside. Before they were depopulated by the pressure for commercial redevelopment, the centres of British cities contained the homes of the poor. Though the growing population of Victorian bankers, merchants, manufacturers and clerks carried on their businesses in the city centres, they did not desire to live among the poor. The suburbs were healthier, quieter and more attractive. The middle-class professionals – solicitors, surveyors, doctors and teachers – who greatly increased in numbers during the last decades of the nineteenth century, concurred with this judgement and the residential suburbs consequently sprawled further and further out of town. Of course, the working class still made up by far the largest part of the population, but those who did not live in ancient city-centre slum dwellings made their homes in the primitive early Victorian pre-by-law housing which was not completely cleared from the inner-city areas until the 1960s.

As a collective description of the inhabitants of 'typical' Victorian houses, the term 'middle class' should not be interpreted too narrowly. It covers a wide range of people from rich, self-made industrialists to humble shipping clerks or skilled artisans earning annual incomes barely sufficient to maintain 'respectability.' None of the stigma which today attaches to the renting of property applied in the nineteenth century. Many of the very largest town mansions in South Kensington were rented by their plutocratic tenants for around £500 per annum. In addition to the tenant's family, up to twelve servants would also live on the premises. At the bottom end of the middle

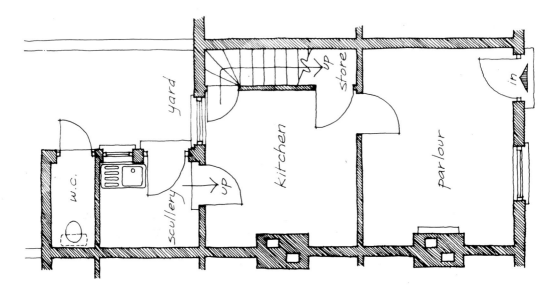

Fig 2

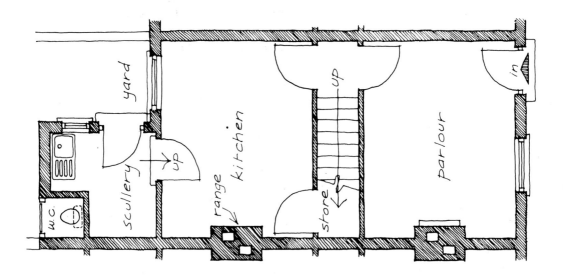

Fig 3

class, common clerks with an annual income of £100 would pay £30 per year to rent a six-room house. They were distinguished from the higher-earning professionals by their inability to afford even one resident servant. A good illustration of the respectability of renting is given by the fact that the fictional Mr Pooter of George and Weedon Grossmith's *Diary of a Nobody* (1894) rented his middle-sized villa in Holloway, North London.

Thus the vast majority of surviving Victorian houses were built for a middle-class clientele, and though it is generally accepted that ageing houses attract a series of occupants of successively diminishing social status, the attraction of Victorian houses for the current generation of the middle class seems to contradict this rule. Building society statistics show that more first-time buyers seek mortgages for pre-1919 properties than for post-war or inter-war dwellings combined. Clearly this phenomenon is partly because of the social and economic benefits which are believed to flow from home ownership. This has caused a demand for freehold property which has been met partly by the virtual elimination of private tenancies from the stock of Victorian houses. Yet the change of attitude towards home-ownership does not entirely explain the popularity of pre-1920 houses. The appeal of these buildings may also be due to the type of accommodation they offer and to the qualities of their architecture. Plainly, these products of the Victorian attitude to society, technology and art deserve closer investigation.

Although the basic plan of the Victorian terrace house had much in common with that of its Georgian forebear, throughout the nineteenth century there emerged a bewildering range of variations upon this standard scheme, and by the turn of the century the principle of the one-room wide 'two-up and two-down' was almost universally shunned in new speculative housing developments. The back-to-back houses of West Yorkshire were a 'rogue' type which never accorded with the standard scheme. Only the refusal of particular local authorities to adopt certain aspects of the model by-laws relating to open space and ventilation prevented the standard layout from displacing the less-civilised back-to-back. However, the eventual rejection of the standard plan in favour of a more four-square arrangement for the houses which populated the Edwardian suburbs resulted more from changing fashions than new building regulations.

A version of the standard scheme which can be found in many areas of England and Wales places the staircase between the two main rooms of the ground floor. In the smallest houses there is no lobby giving direct access to the stair from the entrance door – visitors have to cross the front living room or 'parlour' to reach the foot of the stair (Fig 2). A kitchen or scullery was sited in the back extension which also accommodated a water closet or earth closet accessible only from the outside. Another familiar version of the two-up and two-down terraced house placed the staircase alongside the rear room (Fig 3). Slightly larger houses of the first type – those with a 'lateral' staircase – generally incorporated a two-storey back extension, giving on the first floor a third bedroom accessible only from the rear room. Downstairs there might be

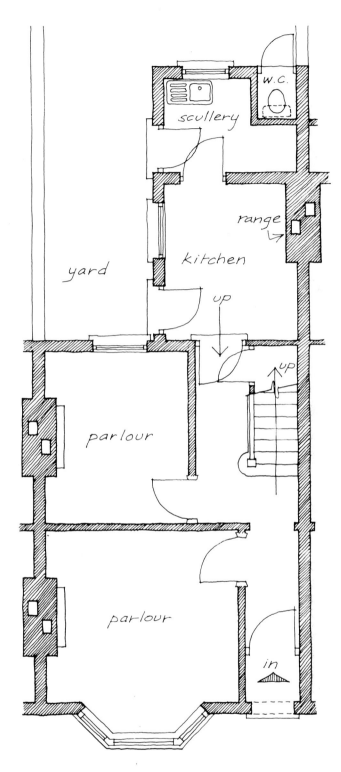

Fig 4

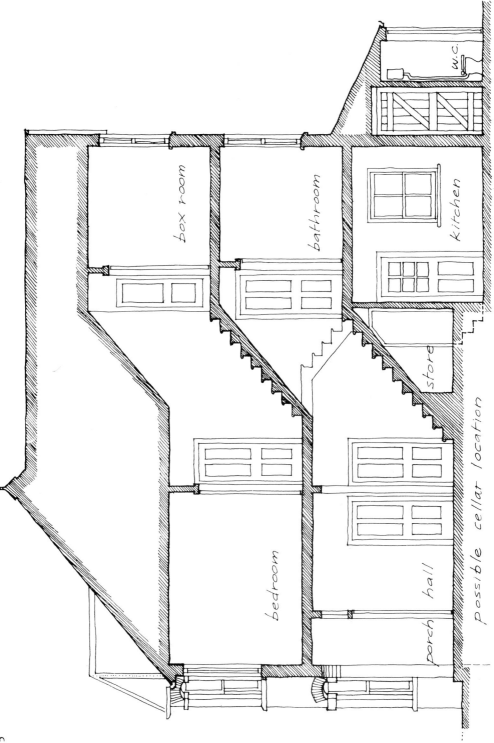

Fig 5

space enough to include a hallway which enhanced the privacy of the living rooms. Houses of this type were still being erected around 1900 and even then it was not considered essential to include a bathroom in the living accommodation. Although this plan is most suitable for terraced houses, in north-east Surrey entire estates of small detached and semi-detached houses were erected which were planned in this manner.

The proper response to growing demands for greater privacy in narrow-frontage terrace houses was the siting of the staircase alongside the party wall rather than at right angles to it. If the frontage exceeded 4.9m (16ft), it was feasible to include a passageway adjacent to the straight-flight stair to give private access to the rooms in the back extension. The zone between this passage and the party wall was just wide enough to accommodate a rear living room of useful size (Fig 4). This plan is very common in London, an important variation on the theme being the 'split level' house in which the ancillary rooms of the back extension are accessible from mezzanine levels of the 'dog leg' staircase. Rear extensions planned on this principle may rise higher than the rooms of the main accommodation and this disposition of levels causes any cellar space to be situated under the ground-floor front room (Fig 5). Smaller versions of this 'classic' middle-sized house omitted the passage flanking the straight-flight stair so that it was necessary to cross the rear living room to gain access to the scullery.

House-hunters in East London may have been puzzled by dwellings apparently displaying two front entrance doors to the street which otherwise appear to be conventional Edwardian houses. These are examples of the London 'cottage flat': two-storey terraced dwellings which incorporate ground- and first-floor flats separately accessible from the street (Plate 2). This type of building is well-known in the north-east of England where, from the mid-nineteenth century onwards, highly elaborate arrangements were often adopted to provide individual front and rear entrances and separate backyards for vertically contiguous 'Tyneside flats'. Rather in contrast to this northern ingenuity, purpose-built low-rise flats were introduced to the capital only around 1900.

At about the same time, the back extension seems to have disappeared from many of the medium-sized houses then being erected in the outer London suburbs. No doubt the loss of increasingly valued privacy, which resulted from the coupling of the rear extensions of adjacent terraced or semi-detached houses under one roof, was a reason for its demise. Yet this new planning principle was also consistent with the concurrent desire of many architects to imbue their designs with the simple shapes characteristic of traditional rural dwellings. Thus all the accommodation was condensed into a plain rectangular wide-frontage plan which produced essentially flat front and rear elevations (Fig 6). The ancillary rooms of the back extension, which had long been associated with 'service' and which were therefore rarely visited by those wealthy tenants whose terraced town mansions shared this arrangement, were finally integrated into the body of the house. Access to the formerly neglected

Plate 2 The front elevation of a pair of 'cottage flats' in East London. Note the twin entrance doors (*Author*)

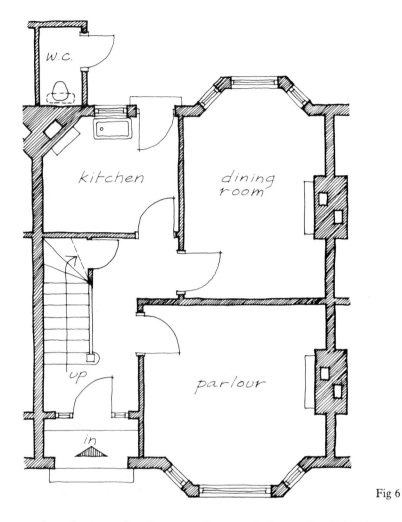

W.C.

kitchen

dining room

parlour

up

in

Fig 6

yard or back garden became direct and the back of the house was at last 'designed' with almost as much care as the front.

What was the original price of a Victorian house? Its cost could vary considerably according to its size and embellishments, but a cheap house was very cheap indeed. The town mansions of South Kensington each cost about £4,000 to build in 1860, yet even after the turn of the century the architectural magazines continued to promote architectural competitions for the design of a '£100 cottage'. The common two-up and two-down terraced house of 1870 certainly cost less than £100 to build, and a two-storey London terraced house of 1900 still cost only £150, though building in the capital was traditionally 20 per cent more expensive than elsewhere. The three-storey, split-level terraced houses of the 1880s which proliferate in the inner London suburbs each absorbed about £300 of the builder's funds.

The last, but not the least important distinction between Victorian houses and those of previous periods lies in their architectural treatment. It is a common misconception that the character of art and architecture was uniform

Plate 3 Early Victorian terraced houses in Pimlico. Their street façades hardly differ from those of late Georgian town houses (*Author*)

throughout the entire Victorian period. The image of sitting rooms cluttered with overstuffed furniture and draped with voluminous curtains, the walls teeming with ornately framed paintings, holds good for only a phase of the Victorian age. In 1837, at the start of Victoria's reign, architecture continued to express the qualities of lightness and elegance which were characteristic of the Regency phase of Georgianism (Plate 3). The introduction of new and versatile building materials such as cast iron undoubtedly assisted a reaction

Plate 4 Gothic arches and diapered (diamond-pattern) decorative brickwork make this South London villa a good example of the 'High Victorian' style (*Author*)

against Regency taste, and by the 1850s an awkward and angular neo-Gothic style popularized by increased church building started to appear in 'bespoke' houses (Plate 4). Pointed arches and multi-coloured (or 'polychromatic') brickwork began to replace the flat stuccoed surfaces of Regency exteriors. A claustrophobic cramming of multitudes of overly ornate, mass-produced furnishings and fittings into interiors flouted the breadth and simplicity of Georgian design rather in the way that the strict morality of the Victorians rejected Georgian liberalism. This was the era of the overstuffed furniture, the heavy hangings and the potted aspidistra in the window bay which is so well remembered as typical of Victorianism. Certainly it was a suitable style for the first generation of self-made and self-righteous merchants and manufacturers who inhabited these spiky, church-like houses. As the fashion for Gothic forms established itself, so the more easily reproduced features of these 'High Victorian' villas were grafted on to modest speculative houses, though it is unusual to find conspicuously Gothic features – such as pointed arches – in small Victorian houses (Plate 5). The fact that a long period elapsed before the fashion affected low-price, speculative housing is evidenced by the appearance of vaguely Gothic features (carved stone column capitals, etc) in middle-sized terraced houses in London only in the late 1870s and early 1880s.

For the generation who inherited the wealth created by the early Victorian

Plate 5 The entrances of these late-Victorian semi-detached houses in Teddington, Middlesex, are spanned by Gothic arches. Yet the designers of contemporary urban houses in fashion-conscious Chelsea and South Kensington had already rejected such features in favour of Baroque and Classical details. In reroofing the bay window on the right, a cheaper, but visually unsympathetic, alternative to the original style (on left) has been adopted (*Author*)

entrepreneurs, greater refinement and sophistication were needed in house design to fulfil the expectations cultivated by a public school and university education which their parents had been denied. Hence from about 1870 gentler architectural styles began to be revived (the nineteenth century was predominantly an age of revivals). Some of these historical styles were home grown, others were of foreign derivation. Popular amongst the welter of 'decadent' styles which followed the pure neo-Gothic were the 'Old English' and 'Queen Anne' revivals. These styles looked back to those phases of English architecture which followed medieval Gothic and preceded the textbook classicism of the still-denigrated Georgian period. With the appearance of the tall, lobster-red brick-faced houses of the 1870s and 1880s in Chelsea's Cadogan Estate – perhaps the most prominent examples of the later Victorian Queen Anne style (Plate 6) – there also emerged new ideas on interior design.

Plate 6 Late Victorian terraces of red-brick houses on Pont Street, Chelsea. Each house is unique, yet high and narrow elevations patterned with lofty sash windows of many panes are common to them all (*Author*)

The leaders of the 'Aesthetic Movement' who commissioned these florid and stately houses rejected much of the clutter which crowded contemporary rooms in favour of a few carefully chosen and alluring objects which also provided the isolated spots of colour. This preference was heavily influenced by a growing interest in the traditional art of Japan which was encouraged by that country's readmittance of western visitors after 1860. Under the influence of William Morris (1834–96) and his followers, designs for wall coverings, curtains and carpets again acknowledged the two-dimensional nature of these products, instead of attempting to create sculptural effects in patterns adorning flat surfaces which had been the High Victorian policy. A plainer internal environment was achieved by the generous application of white oil paint which created light rooms, contrasting directly with the gloomy interiors of High Victorianism. The Aesthetic Movement gave birth not only to the red-brick urban terraces of Chelsea and South Kensington, but also, in 1875, to a new type of suburban development at Bedford Park, Chiswick, the architectural style of which was predominantly Queen Anne. As a result of Bedford Park's success, a host of very handsome red brick and terracotta-clad houses were built in leafy late-nineteenth-century suburbs on the outskirts of many English towns. The collegiate cities of Oxford and Cambridge boast surburban developments containing many good examples of revived Queen Anne.

The profound change of attitude towards architectural style and interior decoration which took place around 1870 had a more radical effect upon Victorian domestic design than any other development of the eighty years preceding World War I. So pervasive was its influence upon the choice of furniture and furnishings used inside the house, as well as the architectural treatment of the exterior, that it has been termed the 'Domestic Revival'. Certainly most suburban houses erected in the period 1890–1914 incorporated some decoration or arrangements introduced by the *avant-garde* architects who led the Aesthetic Movement. The familiar moulded brick dressings of door and window openings and the terracotta tiles depicting sunflowers (symbolic of enlightenment and grace) are physical features derived directly from the spirit of the Domestic Revival which are to be found on many late-nineteenth-century houses. (Plate 7).

Important too for the appearance of much turn-of-the-century speculative housing were the forms adopted in the buildings of Arts and Crafts Movement architects, such as C. F. A. Voysey (1857–1941). Their desire to simplify the architecture of the modern small-to-medium sized house, involving as it did the finishing of external walls in white-painted, roughcast render, influenced the external treatment of thousands of detached and semi-detached suburban houses erected as late as 1939 (Plate 8).

Although after 1900 the decoration applied to some elements of new houses (such as internal joinery, stained glass and metal work) was tinctured with *art nouveau* (a style of architecture and interior design never very popular in Britain), it was not until after World War I that popular housing was affected by a new style which superseded the enduring influence of the Aesthetic

Plate 7 A late-Victorian red-brick villa in a London suburb. Note the characteristic 'fish-scale' tile-hanging on the bay and the 'Flemish' gable containing a panel of brickwork which has been carved with a pattern of sunflowers (*Author*)

Plate 8 An Edwardian villa with a roughcast rendered wall finish. The sham half-timbering in the gables is also characteristic of the period, but the multi-paned sashes could equally well be casements (*Author*)

Movement's Queen Anne. This was the style invented for the 1925 *Exposition des Arts Decoratifs* in Paris – Art Deco. Some features of this style were successfully grafted on to contemporary speculative semi-detached houses, the architectural treatment of which was essentially 'Old English'. We are all familiar with the fake black-and-white half-timbering of the 1930s semi which flanks an arterial road. In its general appearance it is little removed from that of the prototype semi-detached house which was developed in the 1880s, but the 'setting sun' on its garden gate harks back only to 1925.

1
Foundations

The first part of any building to be built is the foundation. This is achieved by excavating the ground to a level believed to be sufficiently firm to accept the load imposed by the complete construction of the building: walls, floors and roof. In ancient English timber-framed buildings this often meant simply digging a shallow trench in the alignment of the walls, laying a few courses of roughly hewn stone and building the wooden frame off its approximately level top surface. With the advent of brick construction, this change of materials close to ground level was dispensed with and the brickwork was carried down below the ground to form the foundation. This practice remained unchanged for most brick-built houses throughout the nineteenth century, though concrete foundations began to be accepted practice around 1900. Stone-built houses of the nineteenth and twentieth centuries are often not of solid stone construction, but are of *ashlar*, a type of composite construction which involves facing solid brickwork with slabs of stone. In this circumstance, the thickness of the external walls reverts to solid brickwork below the external ground level,

although this 'disappearance' of the stone veneer is not revealed until the ground is excavated.

The brickwork being carried down to a suitable bearing stratum, it is clear that the stability of the building is improved if the foundation is in some way widened at its base. In Victorian and Edwardian constructions entirely of brick, this was achieved by thickening the brick *footing* to around 680mm (27in) in the case of a 215mm (8½in) one-brick-thick external wall, six bricks being laid side-by-side across the bottom of the foundation trench. Through four or five courses of superincumbent brickwork 'stepping-in' above, the footing would narrow to the thickness of the external wall (Fig 7). In speculative housing, the depth of the underside of the footing from ground level might be as little as 375mm (15in) and was generally 450mm (18in), although poor ground might force the builder to dig deeper. By 1890 it was becoming common in better construction to place in the foundation trench first a strip of unreinforced concrete about 600mm (23½in) wide and perhaps 215mm (8½in) thick, off which the brick walls would be built (Fig 8). Even in this circumstance, a stepped profile of brick footing would be superimposed upon the concrete according to local regulations, which generally insisted on a 57mm (2¼in) recession of each brick course from the lowest level and an underside of footing minimally twice the thickness of the external wall. In modern construction this stepped profile has been dispensed with as the simple mass concrete strip foundation adequately distributes the load.

SUBSIDENCE

The policy of digging only a shallow trench for foundations obviously has its dangers, and these are manifested in the considerable amount of subsidence which is visible in many older

Fig 7

Fig 8

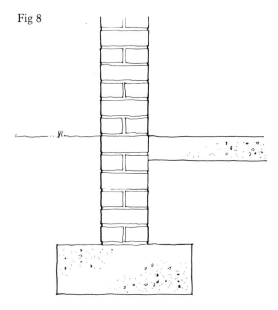

at maturity. It is common for the fine roots to reach out several hundred yards, though they are close to the ground surface. The only effective treatment for tree roots which are causing problems for foundations is the digging-out of the affected ground and the eradication of the roots.

PILED FOUNDATIONS

A rare type of foundation in domestic construction, but one which may be found where the house is sited on ground with a permanently high water-table (the general level of ground water) is the piled foundation.

This type of foundation is nowadays usually of concrete, but in Victorian times piles were almost invariably of wood. A thick wooden stake was driven into the earth to the level for a suitable sub-foundation, because it was impractical to reach and utilise this bearing stratum by the ordinary method of excavating trenches. This timber post was prevented from splitting at its base by a cast- or wrought-iron

houses. For houses in Greater London a cause of this subsidence was clearly revealed during the drought of 1976. The bearing stratum for the foundations of many houses built in the Greater London area is, or is close to, a clay substratum. The dry summer of 1976 caused the clay to dry out and shrinkage resulted, so that many shallow foundations were left partly unsupported and collapsed in consequence.

A contrary problem obtains in conditions of severe frost. Previousy saturated clayey soil becomes frozen and the clay expands, pushing parts of the foundations upwards and causing cracking of the masonry. It is clear that the dangers of clay shrinkage and expansion are reduced by digging the foundations deeper to a subsoil whose condition and moisture content is more stable under all climatic conditions, and this is a remedy to which many local authority building inspectors are turning in the case of new work. In southern England frost will not normally penetrate more than 450mm (18in) below ground level.

A further threat to the integrity of foundations is the proximity of mature trees. Tree roots quite commonly breach brick footings in their search for moisture and subsidence may result. The fact that a large tree is not cheek-by-jowl with the house may not obviate the risk. The roots of the Lombardy Poplar, for instance, will travel a great deal further horizontally than the height of the tree

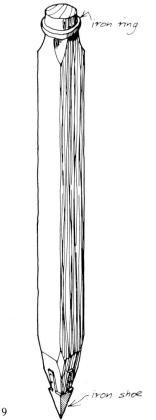

Fig 9

29

Fig 10

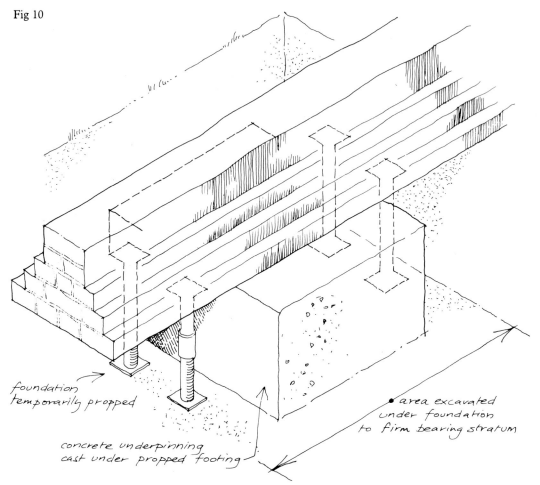

foundation
temporarily propped

concrete underpinning
cast under propped footing

area excavated
under foundation
to firm bearing stratum

shoe protecting this pointed part, and at the driven end by a metal ring fitted tightly over a chamfered profile (Fig 9).

The spacing of piles varied with the nature of the soil and the design of the superstructure, but there was unlikely to be less than 900mm (35in) between pile centres. When completely driven, the tops of the piles were cut off level and spanned by timbers, large stones or concrete, on which was built the base of the superstructure.

As timber does not decay if it is constantly saturated, timber piles were a useful foundation in continuously wet subsoils (Amsterdam is comprehensively founded on timber piles). Piles were also used in gravelly subsoils where the bearing stratum was out of the reach of conventional excavation. However, soils which are alternately wet and dry will quickly cause

timber piles to decay and subsidence will result. This is sometimes the fate of old buildings located near new buildings whose foundations penetrate far below ground level. The new foundations lower the water-table locally and the consequent drying out of the timber piles supporting the old building encourages rotting and subsidence.

UNDERPINNING

A generally known technique for arresting structural collapse resulting from subsidence is underpinning. This involves excavating around and below the subsided foundation, temporarily propping up the foundation to either side of the proposed underpinning and casting a large deep block of concrete directly below the footing, sometimes at right angles to the course of the foundation (Fig 10). The ground around is then reinstated and it is hoped that the subsidence has been arrested. The calculation of the size and extent of such underpinning is normally a task for a structural engineer, since an over-strong or over-large sub-foundation may cause subsidence elsewhere. Clearly, underpinning can be an expensive operation as it involves not only a large amount of excavation, but in the case of external walls, possibly the excavation and reinstatement of internal ground floors too, since the foundation may need to be under-pinned from both sides.

2
Basements

Many Victorian houses incorporate basements or cellars. The walls of these rooms were generally constructed in the same way as those of the upper storeys, although a thickening of solid brick walls to at least 327mm (13in) instead of the 215mm (8½in) often adopted above was common. Solid stone basement walls might be 500mm (19½in) thick and be constructed of rubble. On the completion of basement walls, it was good practice to backfill the space between the outside of the wall and the back of the foundation with gravel or sand, and the tendency of water to soak through this permeable material and drain away below would ensure a dry basement (Fig 11). However, it is common for basements to be damp, and this is often due to the normal, damp condition of surrounding earth, if local and leaking rainwater or foul drains are not suspected. Another cause of dampness in basement walls is the absorption of ground water from below by capillary attraction. Stone walls are

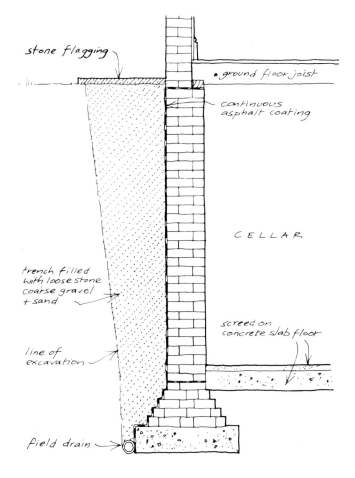

stone flagging

ground floor joist

continuous asphalt coating

CELLAR

trench filled with loose stone coarse gravel + sand

screed on concrete slab floor

line of excavation

field drain

Fig 11

particularly prone to this problem, which usually results from the omission of the damp-proof course (see section on Brickwork).

The damp condition of basement walls built too thin and directly against permanently damp earth is often worsened by the paint treatment applied to the inside surface. White limewash was a favourite treatment for cellar walls and often compounds, or even causes, the problem of dampness, since lime is hygroscopic (it attracts moisture to itself both from the air and from the masonry). If a brick surface is internally damp, the application of gloss paints produces disfiguring rashes of discoloration where the brickwork is not able to 'breathe' and allow the dampness to evaporate. Porous, water-based emulsion paints should always be applied to such raw masonry surfaces if they need decoration, and if mould growth is feared or has been present previously an emulsion paint containing a fungicidal additive should complete decorations, preceded by the application of a proprietary mould inhibitor. Good ventilation of cellar spaces will reduce the risk of dampness and decay; dry rot flourishes in warm, damp basements where there is little air movement. It will attack and infest damp brickwork and can often be eradicated only by cutting out the whole of the affected area before new materials replace it.

Fig 12

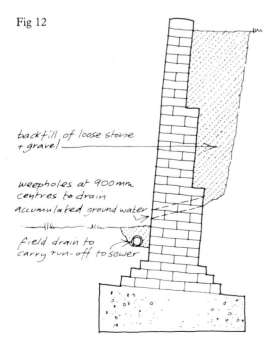

backfill of loose stone + gravel

weepholes at 900 mm centres to drain accumulated ground water

field drain to carry run-off to sewer

RETAINING WALLS

The basement walls described above are examples of retaining walls – masonry erected to retain the subsoil and to prevent the collapse of surrounding earth into the building. Retaining walls also occur in garden areas, particularly as flank walls to basement areas and their access staircases, in which circumstance they retain the garden earth. These latter walls were often cheaply and thinly constructed and can be subject to bulging from subsidence of the retained earth, or overturning, where the foot of the wall is pushed out by settlement and its top moves backward. A quite common cause of failure of these area walls is the non-provision of drainage at low level in the form of built-in pipes or 'weep-holes' in the joints to drain water from the retained earth behind. If the structure is not drained in this way, water percolating through the retained earth will in due course affect the stability of the retaining wall (Fig 12).

PAVEMENT VAULTS

Perhaps the chief purpose of the low-level retaining walls in Victorian houses is to enclose the pavement vaults associated with town houses. In urban areas where land was expensive, it was conventional to use the ground below pavements for pavement vaults or house vaults for the storage of coal and other supplies. These small, cave-like rooms were usually constructed of 327mm (13in) thick brickwork partition walls sited at 3m (10ft) centres, supporting 215mm (8½in) thick segmental arches upon which the street pavement was laid. The earth filling above these arches was commonly finished with a 75mm (3in) gravel layer on top of which the York stone pavement slabs were laid. The main job of a retaining wall is performed by the rear wall of such vaults; this was built (in plan) in the form of a segmental arch of 327mm (13in) thick brickwork to resist the mass of earth retained and the superimposed load of street traffic (Fig 13). In some cases, cast-iron columns might be substituted for the partition walls in order to achieve a wider clear space, but no precautions against damp were ever taken because the rooms were not regarded as either habitable areas or space for the storage of

33

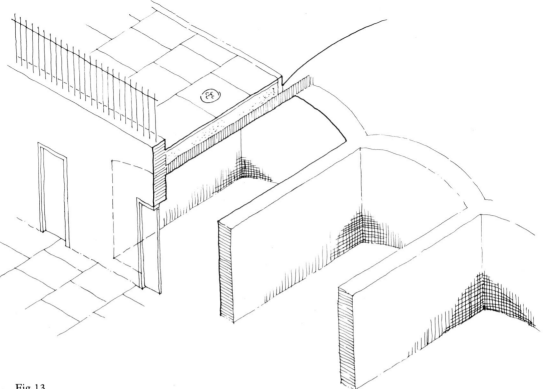

Fig 13

perishable goods. They are therefore likely to feel damp, and a street water main which is leaking locally will cause a constant stream of water to seep through a vault's walls or roof. The only practical defence against such dampness is the lining of the unfinished brickwork internally with one of the proprietary waterproof renders now available. Such an impervious lining has to be completely imperforate, for incoming moisture will always gravitate towards any gap or breach in the lining. Electricity cable entry points or incoming gas mains will provide such weak spots unless great care is taken to sleeve them in waterproof ducts.

Where there was a range of pavement vaults, one at least would incorporate a coal chute with its familiar, cast-iron cover sited in the pavement surface. Old regulations required such chutes to be brick built, of not more than 350mm (14in) internal diameter with a circular, cast-iron plate of equal diameter fitted to an iron frame firmly fixed into the paving stone. As a deterrent to thieves and practical jokers, each plate was required to be securely attached to its frame by a chain shackle, bar or other fastening!

3
External Walls

If we move higher up our Victorian house, the next element to deal with must be the external walls of the building. Clearly, these are the surfaces which hold the most interest for the architect as they are normally the chief features of the external aspect of the house. Wall finishes, even in the nineteenth century, were therefore as much subject to the changes of fashion as they were to changing ideas about how best to provide a weather-tight construction.

STUCCO

At the beginning of Queen Victoria's reign – and well into its middle years in the case of London buildings – stucco was as popular an external wall finish as it had been in Regency times. Its chief merit in terms of construction is that it provides a 'waterproof' coating for thin brick walls, thus saving on construction costs. Stucco or any other form of sand/cement render, including pebbledash and roughcast (see later sections), has the property of excluding wind-blown rain which thin brickwork alone will not resist because of its porosity. However, rainwater accumulating on the surface of unpainted render is drawn into the coating by capillary attraction and through it into the porous brickwork behind, but the amounts involved are so slight if the render has been properly applied that this combination of materials ensures that the entrapped water drains away through the brickwork at the foot of the wall. This is why unpainted rendered buildings generally look 'saturated' quite quickly as the result of a rainstorm, yet apparently dry out equally quickly when the sun comes out. Stucco, or hard plaster, is sufficiently close-grained to take a continuous paint film, and comprehensively coated with gloss paint, it will often entirely resist rain penetration, except at locations such as corners of window openings where stress-cracking of the render occurs.

The term 'stucco' was first used by Italian craftsmen to define a superior grade of plaster which they introduced. By the late nineteenth century the word was being applied as a generic term for all kinds of external plaster with a smooth finish. Part of its aesthetic appeal for the early Victorian architects was the appearance of dignity and stateliness which it granted quite cheaply to otherwise mean or poverty-stricken structures, as it is capable of being moulded into a wide variety of forms, often in imitation of stonework. As a result of its application to low-cost housing, a certain stigma was attached to the use of stucco by the start of the twentieth century, and late Victorian houses which incorporate the material as a facing were likely to be of the poorest construction compatible with the then-rudimentary building codes. At the conclusion of the nineteenth century a standard specification for stucco was one part of ordinary Portland cement to three parts of clean sharp sand. Earlier in the century, lime mortar was used instead of cement mortar. This did not prove to be durable and could still be causing problems today. It was more common to add a small amount of lime to a cement mortar mix to obtain a light colour in the stucco and to improve the elasticity of the render, and this practice should not cause problems if the workmanship was of a good standard. Other 'stone' colours were also obtained by adding 'Venetian Red' or ochre pigments to the mortar mix. In recent times the paint finish already described has often been used, but it should be remembered that the proprietary cement paints commonly recommended for external use on rendering contain cement granules which will themselves trap dirt from a city atmosphere. They are not impervious, in contrast to a well-applied gloss paint which *is* impervious. A full specification for the painting of a new stucco surface would call for two applications of undercoat before the gloss paint is applied.

Stucco elevations of expensive Victorian houses were generally decorated with elaborate cornices and mouldings. Since the fashion for stucco-fronted houses did not die out in London until the 1870s, good examples of town houses encrusted with elaborate stucco mouldings may be found in the terraces of South Kensington, Bayswater, Notting Hill and Earl's Court. These mouldings were often prefabricated in sand/cement render on a bench located on the building site. Continuous profiles were formed by running a metal or wooden template, which precisely defined the required profile, along a roughly formed bank of 'green' render. The resulting 'pre-cast' sections were cemented into place with *in situ* render which was also used to form corners and small details. Repairs to stucco are simply carried out in new cement/lime/sand render, and it may be possible to restrict the splits which occur around window openings – where the render is expected to stretch over the three planes of the elevation, window head and window reveal – by coating the new render on to expanded metal mesh laid over the brickwork. The mesh divorces the render from the brickwork, and in spanning over it will allow some internal movement in the structure before the render is affected. In London buildings it is likely that the local authority's district surveyor will require the expanded metal mesh to be of stainless steel so that it will not corrode (it is normally galvanized).

The change to a taste for 'interesting' rather than 'plain' wall surfaces which occurred during the early years of Queen Victoria's reign caused brickwork to oust stucco from the place of 'most popular wall finish' for the rest of the nineteenth century.

BRICKWORK

Countless thousands of Victorian houses were of brick construction and even in the stuccoed examples, the painted render was often reserved only for the street elevation. Rear elevations were typically of raw brickwork unless bad wall construction necessitated subsequent rendering to keep the weather out. The colour and physical properties of the bricks themselves varied widely according to the part of Britain in which they were made. In London and the south east, the yellow London stock bricks are very familiar. In the north west, a hard, almost shiny red brick which originates from Accrington in Lancashire is commonly seen in association with a more blotchy pink 'common' brick used in side and rear elevations, whilst many southern houses contain whitish facing bricks which are almost as commonplace as the yellow 'stocks'. The Potteries area of the Midlands boasts many buildings built largely of the famous Staffordshire blue brick. These colour differences are largely accounted for by the differing constituents of different brick-making clays.

Types of Brick

London stock bricks are so called because they are produced from clays local to London and come from the 'stock' or body of the 'clamp' in which they are burnt. Clamp-burning is a process of brickmaking in which a very large, elongated, flat-topped 'pyramid' of dried, unburnt bricks is built and an enduring fire consisting of a shallow bed of coke at the base of the clamp is allowed to burn continuously underneath for ten to twelve weeks. The fire having died out, the clamp is dismantled and the fully burnt stock bricks are removed from its core. The distinctive yellow of the 'London' stock is a result of the presence of magnesium and iron in the clay. The clay of the London stock brick has traditionally been mixed with ash to obtain a carbonaceous, 'self-firing' mixture and the procedure of taking the capital's chimney ash to north Kent by Thames barge to mix with the local clays to produce the characteristic stock brick continues today, though the ash is likely instead to emanate from power stations rather than domestic chimneys. *Staffordshire blue bricks* are deep blue in colour and are very dense and strong, being kiln-burnt bricks in contrast to stocks. They were often used in engineering work, including bridge and sewer building, and may be encountered in house foundations where it was good practice to use an impervious brick capable of carrying heavy loads. They are blue in colour because of the use of clay with a high iron content being fired at high temperatures.

Red builders (or 'Tudor reds' as they are often

termed nowadays) are high quality, sand-faced bricks generally used as 'rubbers', a term applied to bricks soft enough to be rubbed to the shape desired (such as 'voussoirs', or the tapering bricks forming a brick arch). Red bricks are produced from clays with a lower iron content than blue bricks and they are fired at lower temperatures.

Flettons are formed from a special type of clay discovered at Fletton in the East Midlands in the late nineteenth century. The clay has the property of being self-firing once it has been heated to about 400°C, and the resultant low cost of producing these bricks has made them the most familiar type of brick. They have a characteristic blotchy pink colouring and were much in demand for the construction of internal partition walls before the general adoption of lightweight concrete blockwork for this purpose. They are still produced in vast quantities, often for use in load-bearing brick construction, as they are very precise in size and shape. They are unsatisfactory as a facing brick for external walls unless painted and are very susceptible to frost damage.

Gault bricks are now almost unobtainable, but were made from a special clay found chiefly in the south east. They are white or whitish and very hard and durable. A certain proportion of chalk added to the brick earth gives them their colour.

Leicestershire reds and *Accrington reds* are two varieties of pressed facing bricks commonly used in the Midlands and north west of England respectively. Pressed bricks are made by placing nearly dry moulded bricks into a metal mould and subjecting them to great pressure by means of a ram or piston which tightly fits the mould. After firing, these bricks are very dense, precise and smooth-surfaced.

In Victorian times almost every small town had its local brickworks and so it is possible to describe only a few of the more common types of bricks found in nineteenth-century buildings. In addition to these main varieties, it is normal to find in Victorian houses many purpose-made bricks, often in elaborate shapes forming cornices or mouldings. The more familiar types of purpose-made or 'special' bricks are dealt with in the following sections.

Brick Bonding

Turning to the way the bricks were put together, we enter a very broad field. To ensure solid and permanent construction, good adhesion of brick-to-brick through the mortar is obtained through the bond. Perhaps the most common brick bond is *stretcher bond*, in which the vertical joints between the bricks (or 'perpends') are aligned in alternate courses (Fig 14). This is certainly the most common bond in present-day brick construction where brickwork is often used to clad a timber frame or form the outer 'leaf' of a cavity wall. In good-quality Victorian construction, solid walls 215mm (8½in) or 327mm (13in) thick were built in different kinds of bond.

Flemish bond alternates stretcher bricks with 'headers' (bricks laid 'end-on' to the outside face of the wall) which extend to the full thickness of the wall in 215mm (8½in) solid brickwork, forming a very strong construction (Fig 15).

English bond is another form of solid construction which was adopted, but it was not very general in external walls because its alternating courses of header and stretcher produce a distinct, regular 'striping' which was not considered attractive by the Victorians (Fig 16).

Fig 14 Stretcher bond

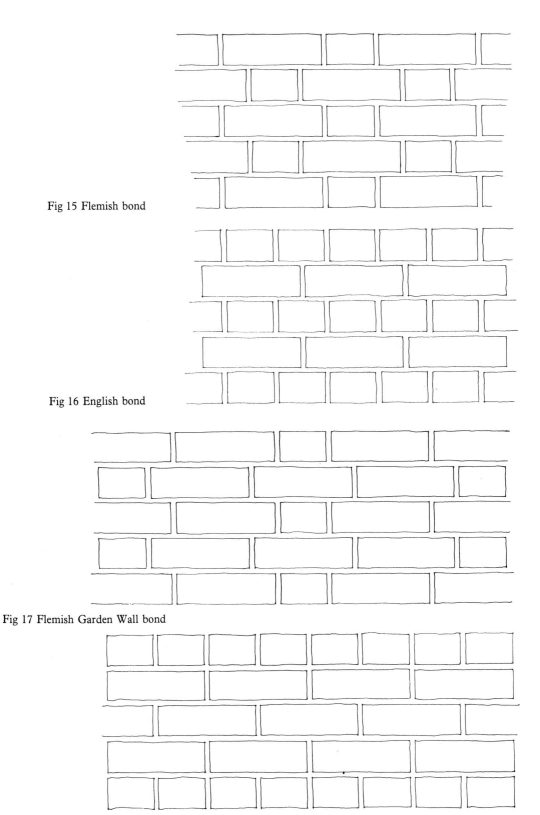

Fig 15 Flemish bond

Fig 16 English bond

Fig 17 Flemish Garden Wall bond

Fig 18 English Garden Wall bond

Forms of densely bonded construction which are quicker to construct than either Flemish or English bonds are the Garden Wall bonds, which were often used in external works as their names suggest.

Flemish Garden Wall bond is similar to Flemish bond, except that *three* stretchers are placed between each header in each course (Fig 17); it is thus a weaker bond than the full Flemish bond. *English Garden Wall bond* economises on headers by alternating three courses of stretchers with one of headers and is consequently weaker than the full English (Fig 18). The existence of these apparently solid types of brick bonding in external walls does not necessarily testify to the presence of solid (more than half-brick thick) construction. Flemish or English bond have often been used purely for decorative reasons, the 'bonded' look being obtained in an external brick skin by building 'snap' headers or 'half bats' (cut bricks) into the work in the header positions.

Brick Jointing

The way the bricks are jointed may be as important for the appearance of a wall as the pattern of the bond. A wide variety of brick joints were practised by the Victorians and our awareness of the different types is essential if the convincing restoration of an old facing, or the blending of new work with old, is to be undertaken (Fig 19). The completion of the partly filled joints of a new brick wall to give a neat mortar joint on, or close to, the face of the brickwork, is termed pointing. The eventual replacement of this mortar surface is called repointing.

In the *flush* joint, the mortar is finished on the same face as the brickwork and this treatment can produce a very flat, undifferentiated surface, particularly where the bricks are of regular and precise shape. This type of joint is rarely suitable for repointing old brickwork because the process of raking out the old mortar damages the corner of soft bricks and the very wide joints which result from flush-pointing such damaged brickwork dominate the repointed surface in an unattractive way. Much more suitable for this purpose is the *keyed* joint, which is obtained by running a short section of hosepipe or iron bucket handle along the wet mortar to give a slightly recessed profile. The *struck* or *weathered* joint is an alternative profile

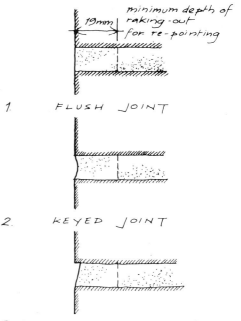

1. FLUSH JOINT

2. KEYED JOINT

3. STRUCK OR WEATHERED JOINT

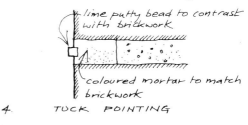

4. TUCK POINTING

Fig 19

which is formed with the bricklayer's diamond trowel. It makes the brickwork appear 'stratified' because its sloping profile causes the horizontal joints to dominate the surface, and the pleasant irregularities of old, oddly shaped bricks are thereby obscured. Nevertheless, it is an efficient shape of joint for throwing water off the wall.

The most elaborate joint is produced by *tuck pointing*, which is an old-fashioned way of making ancient brickwork look new, precise and regular. The original mortar having been raked out, the open joint is pointed up flush with a mortar which is coloured to match the general brickwork surface. Into this flush joint is inserted a thin, projecting and continuous square-section bead of white lime putty which contrasts strongly with the brick colour to suggest that the wall has been newly erected to fine tolerances. The thin putty bead of tuck pointing is easily explained: the Victorians equated thin brick joints with top-quality construction and tuck pointing was a way of making a surface look better built than it was. Though commonplace Victorian brickwork is likely to display the 10mm (⅜in) wide joints which are conventional in contemporary brick walls, the facing brickwork of the front elevations of nineteenth-century houses may boast joints of only half this thickness.

Mortars

Brickwork or stonework in house construction is almost universally accomplished with the use of mortar. In Victorian houses, except in predictably damp areas, the mortar used was almost invariably *lime mortar*. The presence of non-hydrated lime (calcium oxide, or 'quicklime') in a mortar or render mix is a cause of problems, as this substance will cause a loss of strength in the finished material and blemishes in a smooth surface. This defect is common in Victorian buildings because the lime was sold in its non-hydrated or 'unslaked' condition, and it was left to operatives on the building sites to make it suitable for use in mortar or plastering. The benefit which lime grants to a mortar is to make it slightly elastic and tolerant of small thermal or structural movements in masonry, whilst avoiding cracking.

Cement mortar is, by contrast, a material which sets hard and will not admit movements in masonry without fracturing. However, it will not break down in damp conditions as will lime mortar, which in due course loses its 'adhesive' properties. In the present day, cement mortar is almost universally used in new construction, the use of lime mortar being restricted to restoration work. Typical contemporary mixes for both types of mortar are 1:1:6 lime/cement/sand for lime mortar and 1:3 cement/sand for cement mortar.

Decorative Brickwork

Few nineteenth-century houses omit areas of decorative brickwork from their external walls, be they only brick arches over entrance porches, or red bricks contrasting with yellow stocks as the *quoins* at the external corner of outside walls. In more expensive houses it was common to find projecting horizontal string courses and cornices formed from red 'rubber' brickwork moulded into quite complicated classical profiles, with alternately projecting headers of red rubbers partly supporting the cornice in the form of classical 'dentils' (Fig 20). Bull-nosed brick mouldings or quarter-brick recessions in brickwork were often used around window openings, particularly in late-Victorian times. Perhaps one of the most common brick details in external walls was the formation of a broader base or *plinth* at the foot of the elevation by the use of 'cant' bricks (bricks moulded with a chamfer taken off one corner). In this way, recessed panels of brickwork sited between brick piers could also be included in an elevation to break up the otherwise vast expanses of undifferentiated brickwork which the Victorians abhorred (Fig 21).

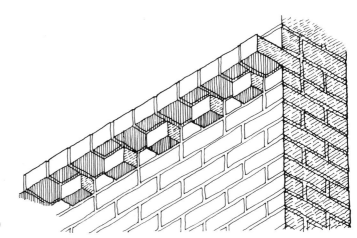

Fig 20

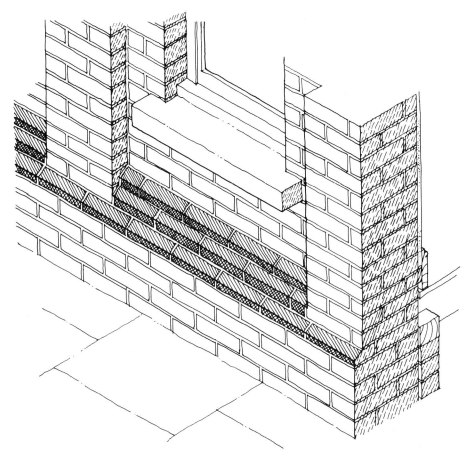

Fig 21

Damp-proof Courses

The projecting brick plinth was sometimes adopted for a constructional purpose quite separate from the intent to stabilise the base of the building. Depending on local building by-laws, from about 1870 new houses had to incorporate a damp-proof course in their external walls. The function of this dpc was to prevent the saturation of the masonry by ground water and the resultant deterioration of internal finishes. This was achieved in the nineteenth century by incorporating a horizontal layer of impervious material (asphalt, lead or slate) at a level in the external wall below the ground-floor construction. In most Victorian houses this was easy to arrange, as ground floors were almost invariably of timber boards laid on timber joists ('suspended' ground-floor construction). The joists themselves were supported on thin brick 'sleeper' walls, either built on a continuous 150mm (6in) thick concrete ground layer or a level area of

firm ground. This deep form of composite construction enabled a damp-proof course to be incorporated in the external walls at a suitable height above the external ground level to resist damp penetration (Fig 22), but on a sloping site the underside of the timber ground-floor construction might well be below the general external ground level, and consequently below the level of the dpc. This difficulty was overcome by forming a cant brick plinth at the foot of the wall, concealing two continuous horizontal dpcs linked by a vertical dpc at the rear of the external half-brick 'skin', thus ensuring continuity of the damp-proofing. The widened thickness of the wall at its base also allowed the incorporation of vertical ducts in the brickwork, linking the underfloor space with the outside air (Fig 23). Similar ducts would be incorporated even in the standard arrangement of a ground floor sited above external ground level because the chief danger of not ventilating the underfloor void is the

41

External Walls

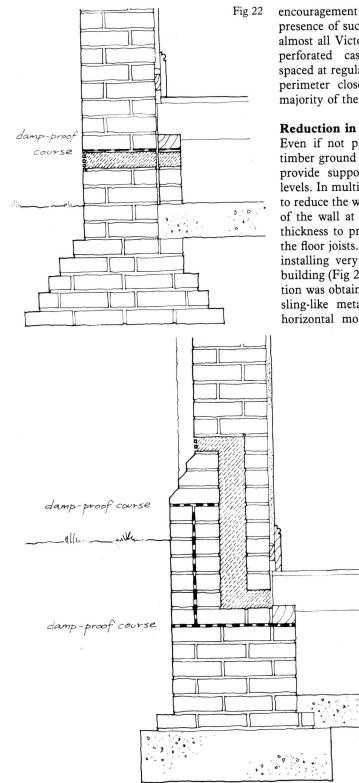

Fig 22

encouragement of dry rot in the timbers. The presence of such ducts in the external walls of almost all Victorian houses is indicated by the perforated cast-iron or terracotta gratings spaced at regular intervals round the building's perimeter close to ground level, which the majority of these houses display.

Reduction in Thickness

Even if not providing support to suspended timber ground floors, the external walls always provide support for timber floors at upper levels. In multi-storey construction it was usual to reduce the wall thickness on the internal face of the wall at each floor level by a half-brick thickness to provide a ledge on which to bear the floor joists. Clearly, this policy necessitated installing very thick walls at the base of the building (Fig 24). A more economical construction was obtained by housing the floor joists in sling-like metal joist hangers built into the horizontal mortar joints of the wall, or by

damp-proof course

damp-proof course

damp-proof course

Fig 23

corbelling or bracketing out the brickwork immediately below upper floors to provide a bearing for the joists on continuous timber wall-plates, but in low-cost construction it was normal simply to house the joists in small pockets left in the brickwork. In 215mm (8½in) brickwork, this detail leaves only a half-brick thickness separating the joist ends from the outside air, and in the long term this could lead to rotting of the joist ends from damp penetration through the single-skin brickwork,

particularly if the external mortar joints of the brickwork are open and in need of repair. It is a technique which should not be used when joists are being replaced. New joists should be located on galvanized steel joist hangers built into the brickwork.

Defects in Brickwork

The constituent bricks of a brick external wall are much less likely to break down as a result of their constant exposure to the weather than are the mortar joints which bond them together. Bricks darker than their neighbours in the wall surface are likely to have been overburnt, harder than the rest and therefore less liable to decay, whilst underburnt bricks may be recognised by their lighter colour. They may be prone to early deterioration, particularly if sited at or near to external ground level or where used as copings on top of garden walls or party walls projecting above roof surfaces. In these exposed situations, the bricks are easily saturated by driving rain even if the mortar joints are complete, and a subsequent frost will cause the bricks to 'burst' or delaminate as the entrapped water expands upon freezing. Bricks which lose their durable outer surface in this way will quite quickly deteriorate as their softer clay core is exposed to the elements. The long-term remedy is the cutting-out of the affected bricks and their replacement with new or good-quality salvaged bricks.

Other apparent defects in external brickwork include efflorescence and 'rust staining', two problems which are detrimental to the appearance of the brickwork rather than to its structural stability. In efflorescence a damp white powder appears across the surface of the bricks and the mortar joints. This occurs when the soluble salts are washed out of the brick clay and the mortar, or because of the chemical reaction of the two with rainwater. When the brick surface dries out, the salts are deposited. Efflorescence is most often encountered in new brickwork in exposed positions (such as boundary walls), though it may materialise on newly repointed old brickwork. In the course of time it will entirely disappear.

Rust staining, which produces patches of brown discoloration on external brick surfaces, is caused by the reaction of iron compounds contained in the brickwork with rainwater. Like efflorescence, the effects will diminish gradually.

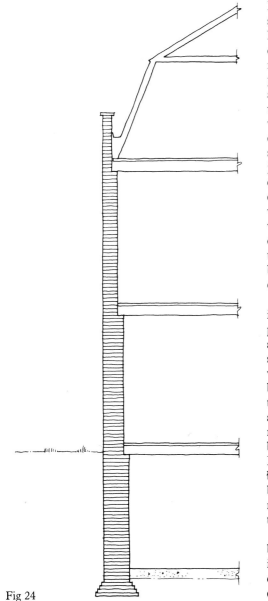

Fig 24

43

External Walls

STONE EXTERNAL WALLS

In various areas of the country and throughout the nineteenth century, houses were built with external walls of natural stone. Stonework had traditionally been regarded as superior to brick because of its renowned solidity and its association with permanence, and if their budget allowed it, the Victorians, in common with their Georgian predecessors, preferred to build external walls from solid stone. The appearance of solid stonework was sometimes achieved in ashlar construction, although this treatment was usually reserved for grander houses and public buildings.

Types of Building Stone

It is important to recognise that the majority of building stones used in the British Isles fall into the two distinct categories of limestone and sandstone. It is true that other types of building stone are found, notably *granite* which is especially prevalent in north-east Scotland, but it is unusual to find this exceptionally hard and dense stone used in the construction of modest houses, though the characteristic 'cobbles' of a Victorian mews are likely to be of granite. The *Millstone Grit* of West Yorkshire is a famous sandstone, as is Derbyshire's *Darley Dale* stone, Yorkshire's *Bolton Wood*, Edinburgh's *Craigleith*, the red sandstones of Cheshire (such as *Runcorn* stone) and Nottinghamshire (*Mansfield* stone) and the famous *York* stone which forms the slabs of so many older city pavements. British *limestones* commonly in use include the famous yellow *Bath* stone from which that city is almost exclusively built, the equally famous white *Portland* stone from Dorset's Isle of Portland and the indigenous stones of the Cotswold region. Lesser known limestones which were nevertheless much favoured during the nineteenth century include *Ketton* stone (from Leicestershire) and *Hopton Wood*, a drab-coloured carboniferous limestone from Derbyshire; *Bolsover Moor* stone also originates from this region. Its light brown tones were favoured for city buildings by the Victorians and it is easy to carve.

Slate, too, is of course a building stone, and in recent times it has been adopted for the external cladding of walls as well as its traditional use as a roofing material. In the nineteenth century it was also used as an internal floor finish, since it provides a very smooth and level surface which is impervious to spillages and hence good for kitchen and larder floors. Thick slabs of slate were also used for larder shelves, mantelpieces, cisterns and steps.

Much building stone was imported from the continent during the nineteenth century, but its consequently high cost largely prohibited its use for external walls. 'Sicilian' marble and similar metamorphic stones were generally reserved for fireplace surrounds and other internal features.

Defects in Stonework

It would be comforting to believe that the density and apparent solidity of building stone guarantees it against decay and deterioration. Unfortunately, this is not so. As in any other material, the chemical constituents of stone react with chemicals present in the atmosphere, resulting in the eventual breakdown of the material. This process was particularly acute in the industrial cities in Victorian times, where the atmosphere was loaded with the products of smoke from domestic coal fires. One ingredient of this soot was sulphuric acid, which acted on limestones and calcareous sandstones, converting the normally insoluble calcium carbonate constituent of these stones into calcium sulphate, which eventually becomes soluble and erodes the stone. Carbonic acid, present in rain containing dissolved soot, reacted with calcium carbonate, turning it into soluble calcium bicarbonate with the same results. The carved limestone cornices which adorn many elaborate Victorian buildings quite often have on their undersides sooty and decayed stone surfaces which are almost entirely composed of calcium sulphate.

The chemical compounds which polluted the air of Victorian cities are less pervasive today, but motor vehicles are the cause of much atmospheric pollution which continues to have a destructive effect upon natural stonework, particularly magnesian limestones. Many of the ancient buildings of the Oxford colleges have lost much of their elaborate carved stone ornament in the space of a few years, because of the action upon their magnesian limestone walls of an atmosphere polluted by traffic fumes.

A further cause of decay in limestones is the use of limestone and sandstone in juxtaposition where the former is subject to attack and the formation of soluble salts. If these salts are washed on to the sandstone, rapid decay of the sandstone will ensue.

Solid Stone External Walls

In house construction it is unusual to find forms of stone external walling other than the different forms of rubble, because fully 'dressed' (shaped) stonework was very expensive and gave a severe appearance, which was regarded as inappropriate for dwellings.

Rubble walls cannot be built very well if they are less than 450mm (18in) thick, and like all forms of solid masonry they should contain bond- or through-stones extending for at least two-thirds of the thickness of the wall to obtain a homogeneous construction. Rubble work is a general term for masonry in which the stones

are of various and irregular sizes, and in most cases, small. Random rubble walls were much used in country districts for centuries before Victoria's reign, and they retained some popularity in the nineteenth century (Fig 25).

Kentish Rag, a type of limestone found in Kent, is particularly suitable for this form of construction as individual stones are small, hard, irregularly shaped and difficult to dress. Good quality, random rubble walling was quite expensive because of the large amount of labour involved in dressing the beds and joints of the stones to fit close. If the joints exceed 13mm (½in) in thickness, the work is not of the best quality. This type of construction is often encountered in the ancillary buildings of country estates, such as entrance lodges.

A superior kind of rubble wall attempts to arrange the individual stones in more nearly

Fig 25

Fig 26

External Walls

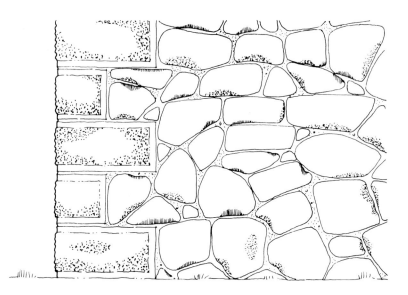

Fig 27

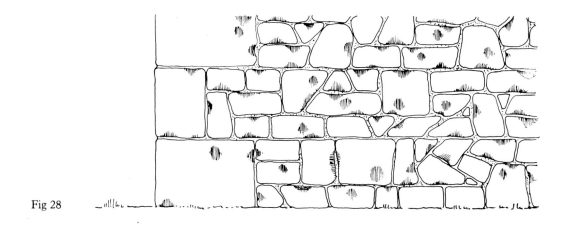

Fig 28

Fig 29

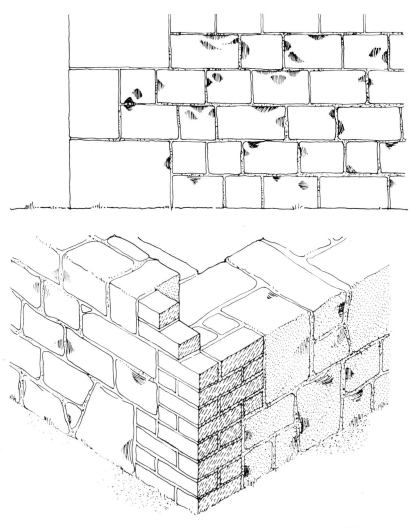

Fig 30

Fig 31

horizontal courses, the stones having been roughly squared so as to achieve this, and the wall being bonded through every 1200mm (47in) or 1500mm (59in) (Fig 26). However, most stone-built Victorian houses, particularly if located in towns, attempted some degree of formality, and more geometrically regular forms of rubble walling were adopted for these situations. The most informal of these treatments was the combination of random rubble walls with precisely squared quoins (or corner stones) of the same stone (Fig 27). Random rubble built in courses was a common treatment in some parts of the country, the aim being to achieve a true horizontal bed every 300–450mm (12–18in), these bed levels corresponding with the top and bottom surfaces of each corner stone or dressing (Fig 28). A

variation on this contains bonding blocks in each course equal to the full height of that course, and this treatment is termed *coursed header* work. *Irregular coursed* rubble is also quite common, though more mechanical in appearance. Also known as *squared and snecked* rubble, it is distinguished by having square vertical joints and horizontal beds which may run the length of separate stones, but which are not continuous for more than a few feet, being broken at any point to fit in a stone of greater depth (Fig 29). *Regular coursed* rubble gives the most uniform appearance of all, all courses being of uniform height and differing only from the stratified appearance of brick construction by the slightly irregular configuration of vertical joints which results from using stones of differing lengths (Fig 30).

Fig 32

A hybrid form of construction which is encountered in some regions is the stone wall with brick quoins. Red brick is most commonly used for this treatment, the brick quoins being often four to eight courses deep, with the dressings, band courses (at the head of each storey) and openings with arches also being formed in brickwork. In this case, all the top and bottom joints of the rubble have level beds. Such walls were built cheaply if the local stone split readily when worked, when it could be laid on its natural bed and required little dressing, or when good stone suitable for dressing for quoins was difficult to get (Fig 31).

A variation on this type of composite construction is *flint work*, often found in Sussex, Hampshire and other chalk districts where large quantities of flints are found below the beds of chalk. It is a variety of rubble work which was much used in districts where flints abounded. The walls might be built throughout in flints and be faced with small uncut stones, or the flints might be used simply as a facing. Larger stones used for facing were usually *knapped* or *polled* (split so as to show a vertical

face rather than a projecting profile), but in the best work they were roughly squared and laid in regular courses. Quoins, window and door dressings were always built in stone or brick and 'lacing' courses of stone, brick or tile were introduced at intervals of about 1800mm (71in) vertically to give longitudinal strength and to obtain visual regularity (Fig 32). An effective wall decoration was sometimes produced by using flints as panels let flush into stonework. Brickwork can be used in the same way as stone. The dark colour and smooth texture of the flints often contrasts beautifully with the stone or brick dressings to produce a chequered effect, otherwise known as diapering.

Lintels

In all types of stone construction, the stones surrounding door and window openings are necessarily regular, because the walling material at these points has to be compatible with such precisely made features as wooden doors and window frames. Therefore stone lintels and sills (respectively above and below door and window openings) are always

48

precisely shaped for their specific locations. In order to support the masonry built above and to keep themselves in place, lintels must have a bearing or area of wall in which each end of the component sits. In the present day, lintels are usually of reinforced concrete or steel, but in Victorian times external lintels were invariably of stone, though those spanning internal openings might be of timber. Generally, the lintel was a single stone with 150–215mm (6–8½in) bearing at each end into the supporting masonry. Where the span of the lintel was quite long, say 3m (10ft) over a range of windows, increasing the lintel in depth to account for a longer span would result in a

clumsy appearance, and a relieving arch was sometimes installed over the lintel to transfer most of the load away from the window head (Fig 33). In thick brickwork walls, a rough ring segmental arch was sometimes built inside the wall, thus relieving some load from the lintel on the outside face without affecting the external appearance (Fig 34). If this form of construction is encountered, it is important to remember that the arch and the lintel are interdependent and that both perform the function of supporting the wall, so that neither should be removed or substituted with any other arrangement without first obtaining the advice of a structural engineer. In the same way, the Victorians often

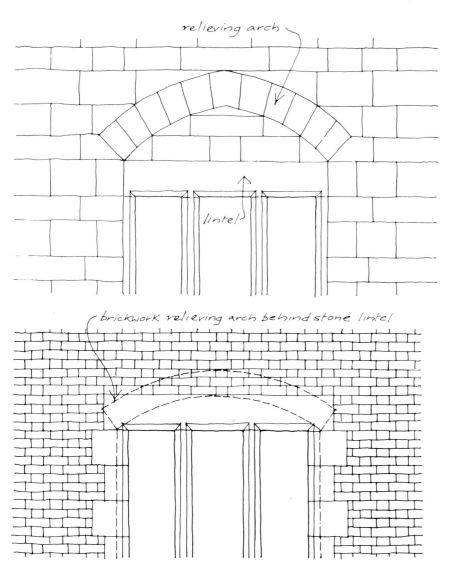

Fig 33

Fig 34

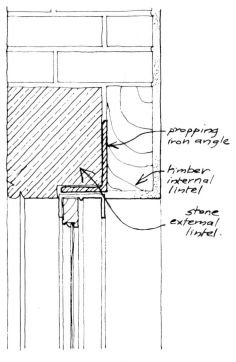

propping
iron angle

timber
internal
lintel

stone
external
lintel.

Fig 35

repaired cracked stone lintels by inserting iron beams or angles behind and below the damaged stonework, sometimes in combination with a solid timber beam backing (Fig 35). These repairs too, should not be disturbed or rebuilt until expert advice has been obtained.

An alternative means of spanning a wide opening with a solid stone lintel was the adoption of a built-up lintel formed from at least three stones, each section being joined to

its neighbour with a rebated or joggled joint so that the load from superincumbent masonry tended to compress the stones together (Fig 36). A limitation of this technique was the necessity of providing long bearings to each 'end stone' of the lintel, as these were effectively cantilevers supporting the span of the centre section.

Sills

Similar in shape to the lintel but sited at the foot of the door and window openings is the *sill*. In solid brick or masonry external walls, sills are generally of stone. They were usually arranged to project in front of the wall surface, though in some cases sills were left flush with the wall. *Lug* sills have flat ends or lugs built into the wall. Also called a *stooling* for ease of building-in, the lug surface is flat in contrast to the general top surface of the sill which is sloped or *weathered* to throw off rainwater (Fig 37).

The Victorians also used *slip* sills made equal to the width of openings and not built into the walls. Though cheaper to install than the conventional sill, they are less durable as rainwater will penetrate the exposed vertical joints at either end. Their chief merit lies in the fact that settlement of the adjoining masonry is not liable to break a slip sill, and they were therefore often used in the lower parts of heavy buildings where settlement was anticipated.

In addition to the sloping top surface of the sill, rainwater is encouraged to drain away from the profile by projecting the front surface of the sill in front of the neighbouring wall surface and providing a drip groove or throating in the

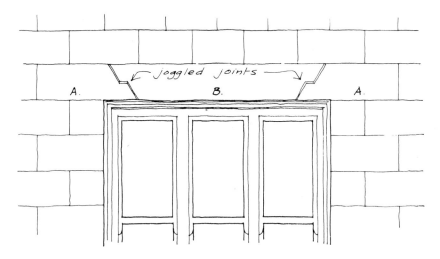

joggled joints

A.   B.   A.

Fig 36

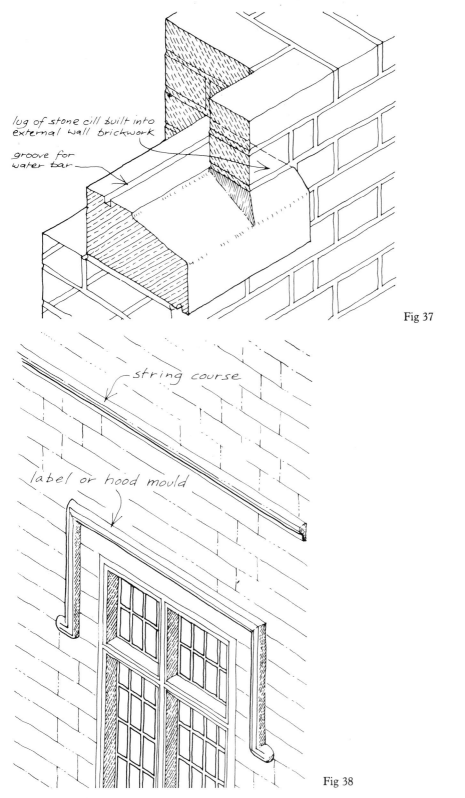

lug of stone cill built into external wall brickwork

groove for water bar

Fig 37

string course

label or hood mould

Fig 38

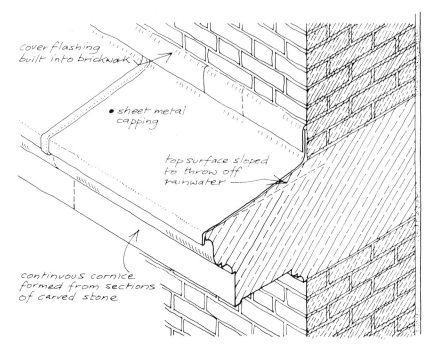

Cover flashing built into brickwork

sheet metal capping

top surface sloped to throw off rainwater

continuous cornice formed from sections of carved stone

Fig 39

underside of this projection, causing rainwater running backwards into the joint of the sill and masonry to drip off before reaching this joint. In good construction a groove for a metal water bar was also incorporated in the sill's top surface to prevent water being drawn through the gap between the stone sill and the timber window sill.

String Courses and Cornices

Continuous projecting horizontal bands of stone – usually moulded – on a building are termed string courses. A similar band formed around and above an arch is called a label or hood mould. In both instances the projection from the face of the wall is quite small (Fig 38). Moulded bands considerably deeper and more prominent than strings are called cornices. The top surfaces of all strings and cornices should have an outward and downward slope away from the wall, which is known as the weathering. Similarly, a throating or drip should be incorporated on the underside to prevent rainwater flowing down and discolouring the face of the wall below by partial washing of its surface. Cornices which project out in excess of 150mm (6in) should have their top surfaces protected by a sheet metal capping of lead, zinc or copper if gradual deterioration of

the exposed stonework is to be prevented (Fig 39).

Copings

The final stone constructional component commonly found in modest houses is the stone wall coping. To prevent the rain washing out the joints between bricks or stones at the top of parapet walls, the construction is capped with a wide stone coping (Fig 40). It should be of non-absorbent stone about 75–100mm (3–4in) wider than the wall below with its upper surface weathered and with a throating or drip on its underside where it projects in front of the wall surface. Coping stones were commonly clamped or dowelled together to prevent them becoming displaced. Where the party walls of terraced dwellings project up above the roof slope (as in the London area) or an end gable similarly projects above the roof, gable coping stones were sometimes adopted to complete the wall.

Individual gable copings could be as long as 1800mm (71in) in order to minimise the number of joints with short stones; they incorporated wedge-shaped undersides which were built into the supporting wall as bond-stones to prevent the entire run of coping from sliding off (Fig 41).

52

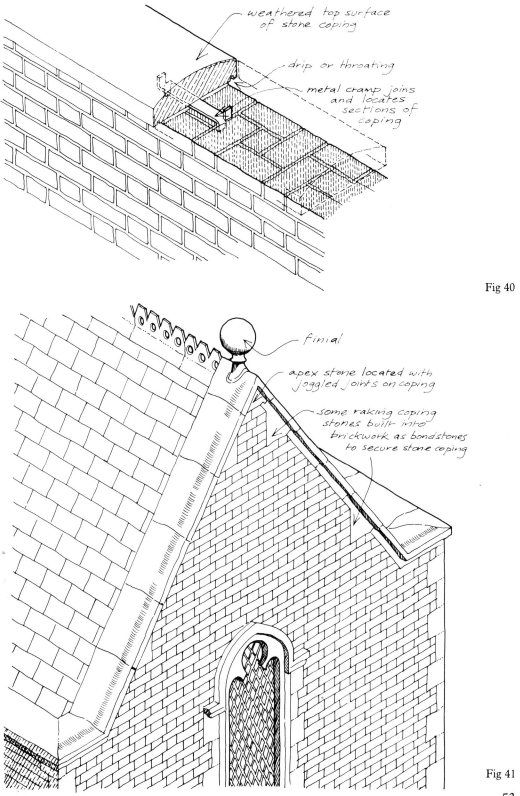

weathered top surface
of stone coping

drip or throating

metal cramp joins
and locates
sections of
coping

Fig 40

finial

apex stone located with
joggled joints on coping

some raking coping
stones built into
brickwork as bondstones
to secure stone coping

Fig 41

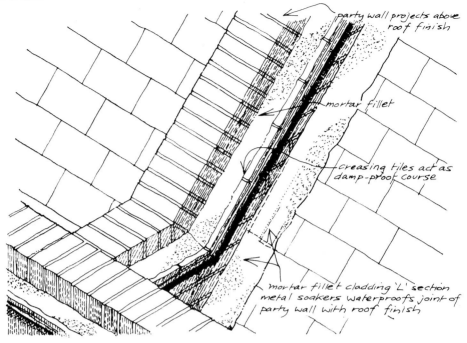

party wall projects above roof finish

mortar fillet

creasing tiles act as damp-proof course

mortar fillet cladding 'L' section metal soakers waterproofs joint of party wall with roof finish

Fig 42

Since they slope, gable copings do not need to be weathered on top, though they must project and include throatings to shed the rainwater. At the top of such a gable is fixed the apex stone which is made with a flat bed to rest solidly on the end wall. The apex is often secured to the wall below by iron ties which are concealed in the wall thickness. A decorative finial adds to its weight and reduces the chance of the stone being dislodged.

In London house construction, where the local building acts insisted upon party walls being carried up above roofs, the watertight coping of these walls was also achieved by inserting a course or courses of conventional roofing tiles, called creasing tiles, into the projecting parapet wall, the tiles projecting out to either side in front of the brickwork to form a drip for rainwater (Fig 42).

Columns and Entablatures

Porches or loggias built out from the external walls often incorporate column supports. In good-quality construction these would be of stone, though in the 'stucco period' of Victorian housing it was common for porch columns and so on to be of painted stucco. It was easy to achieve complicated classical mouldings in the stucco which was applied over a core or

armature of brickwork or timber. Circular columns naturally called for a core formed from curved bricks (Plate 9); columns constructed around a timber armature are likely to provide problems through rotting of the timber or overstressing of the wood. Stone columns were formed from several sections of stone dressed to shape and stacked up to form the base, shaft and capital of the column. The sections were joined together with cement mortar which was not allowed to emerge in the joints in order to avoid spalling (delamination of the stone). Fine joints also had an aesthetic advantage, giving the impression that the column was formed from one monolithic stone.

The section of the building supported by the columns is called the entablature. In classic architecture this comprised the architrave, frieze and cornice carried over the columns and was often surmounted by a balustrade. The porches which grace the street elevations of many stucco-fronted Bayswater and Kensington houses built as late as 1870 have made this profile very familiar to Londoners. Where the entablature is formed from solid stonework, a continuous appearance was achieved in a series of individual stones by jointing them with rebates in rather the same way as a built-up lintel was made, except that the rebates were

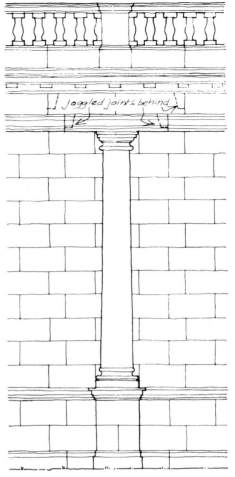

Fig 43

Plate 9 The curved bricks which make up the cores of these rendered portico columns were clearly exposed when the render coating had to be renewed (*Author*)

kept back from the face of the stone, where for the sake of order and regularity only vertical joints were exposed. This is an indication of the joinery-like precision which an expert mason can achieve, and it also suggests that stonework may conceal many complexities of construction (Fig 43).

Simpler balustrades than the familiar array of moulded or turned stone balusters supporting a continuous coping are visible above the porches or balconies of many larger town houses. Sometimes a solid parapet was adopted, which had the twin virtues of being a simple detail to construct as well as performing the necessary job of securing or 'tailing down' the projecting cornice

below. This stone feature is known as the 'blocking course' (Fig 44). More elaborate than the square profile provided by the blocking course is the well-known triangular shape of the pediment. It was frequently used as a decorative feature over door or window openings or over a portico (quite apart from decorating gables to which the shape owes its origin). Pediments over window openings are almost as commonly curved as they are triangular. In stonework they are assembled from individual shaped stones cut very accurately, with the conventional precautions taken to ensure the structural integrity of the assembled parts (inclusion of joggled joints, etc).

Much of the building stone used in modest Victorian houses was incorporated to relieve visually great masses of brickwork, and all the

55

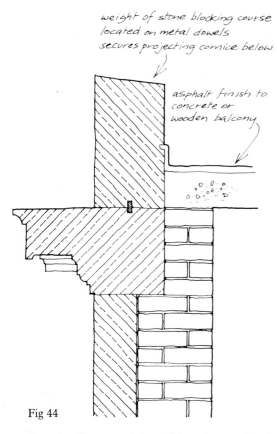

weight of stone blocking course located on metal dowels secures projecting cornice below

asphalt finish to concrete or wooden balcony

Fig 44

Ashlar

Ashlar gives a very precise appearance in stone construction and may be found in some houses, although it was an expensive technique generally reserved for public buildings. Though the term has been used in recent times to describe high-quality, solid masonry, it properly describes a composite construction of brickwork or rubble with a dressed stone facing. In this circumstance, the thickness of the ashlar face should not be less than 175mm (7in), and a quarter of the stones exposed on the external face should be built into the backing for a further 125mm (5in). Such facework was always bedded in lime mortar, though where a brick backing was employed, the bricks were laid in cement mortar to avoid shrinkage. Brick was used more extensively than stone as a backing because it is the cheaper material, and the backing was required to be at least as thick as the facing – with a minimum width of 200mm (8in). Modern textbooks on ashlar construction emphasise that the outside surface of the brickwork so bonded to the stone facing should be painted with bituminous paint to obtain a continuous vertical damp-proof course. In old construction this damp-proof membrane may have been omitted and porous stone or open joints between the stones could admit moisture to the inner skin of brickwork or rubble, causing damp staining and deterioration of internal finishes. This has occurred even in a major building of the famous architect Sir Edwin Lutyens (1869–1944), Castle Drogo at Drewsteignton in Devon, where an asphalt membrane provided between the external granite facing and the rubble backing has fractured and serious damp penetration has resulted. Clearly, Castle Drogo's exposed hilltop position intensifies this problem.

foregoing features might well have been painted from the time of their construction, as much of the stone used for window sills and lintels over window openings was soft and would be liable to rapid deterioration if left unpainted. Since gloss paintwork is impervious, it is an excellent protection for such stone against chemical attack from rainwater and frost, and should always be kept intact. Blistering of the paint film will be followed by water penetration into the porous stonework with potentially serious results.

The use of mechanical saws in the manufacture of these stone dressings produced precise shapes, which are often a match for the hand carving found in all-stone construction. In the stone-built terrace houses of Lancashire and West Yorkshire, precisely shaped and mass-produced window sills and lintels often contrast sharply with the coursed rubble of the external walls, and the contrast is all the more marked since improvement grants have returned much formerly sooty stonework to the original cream colour following external cleaning.

Preservation and Repair of Stonework

The Victorians were as aware of the short-comings of natural stonework as we are today, and various attempts to delay or prevent the decay of the stonework were made through the application of preservative coatings. There is no need to go into the Victorian methods of stone preservation, as their remedies are long out of date, but it is worth saying something about contemporary methods of stone preservation.

Much controversy surrounds the application of silicone compounds to stonework, though this has been a traditional method of stone preservation. The hardening of the outer layer of stone produced by coating the material with silicone is believed by some to accelerate deterioration of the stonework when it is saturated by rain or delaminated by a subsequent frost, since whole lumps of silicone-hardened stone are likely to fall off the still-soft core. To overcome this defect, the Building Research Establishment has developed a compound named 'Brethane' which is very effective in preventing the decay of elaborate stone mouldings (such as those at Wells Cathedral, Somerset), and it is to be hoped that before long it will be commercially available as a means of arresting deterioration of carved stonework in humbler Victorian buildings. Various epoxy-based adhesives are now available for reassembling broken stone details or resurfacing small areas of decayed stonework.

TERRACOTTA

An important substitute for brick or stone for the Victorians was terracotta. This material is of almost the same composition as clay brickwork, but for the manufacture of terracotta only good-quality fireclays were used. Manufacture of the material was very similar to brickmaking, the grog mixture which constituted a part of the terracotta (a mixture of fine sand, pulverized brick or burnt clay) being mixed with water and the ground-up fireclay before being formed into cakes prior to moulding. Like brickwork, terracotta was sometimes employed in purpose-made shapes, but where numerous pieces of the same size and shape were required, a full-size model of plaster and clay was made from which a plaster cast was taken. Into this mould the tempered clay was pressed by hand to form a hollow block or shell of clay of uniform thickness whose outside surface was a perfect impression of the mould's form. The clay in the mould was allowed to become partially dry before being removed, after which it was thoroughly dried on the drying floor of the factory at temperatures between 20°C and 25°C (70°F and 80°F). Finally the moulded block was fired in a kiln over several days. In the burning of certain clay mixtures a chemical reaction occurred which produced a hard, vitreous glaze on the surface of the terracotta, rendering the material more durable. Imperfec-

tions in or damage to this surface impair the durability of the material. A property of terracotta which has led to its replacement in the present day by ceramic tiles is the shrinkage of the constituent clay during firing. The unfired clay components were made one-twelfth larger than the desired finished size to account for this shrinkage, and some small loss of precision in the finished product resulted from this. Prior to about 1875, terracotta was available only in red and buff colours. Later in the nineteenth century a wider range of colours became available, embracing red, buff, pink, tawny and grey. Other colours were produced by the addition of chemicals, but a more reliable material resulted if the colours were restricted to those natural to the original clays. Three varieties of terracotta were manufactured – *ordinary*, with a plain, unglazed surface (which is more or less porous), *vitreous*, being covered with a slightly vitreous glaze and thus impervious to moisture, and *full-glazed* or *matt-glazed* terracotta which is normally referred to as *faience* and is recognisable by its smooth and shiny surface, achieved through the firing of a glaze or enamel on to the already-burnt material. For houses, faience was generally restricted to internal use, though it did appear externally on public buildings, notably those Victorian pubs in prominent corner locations which display large areas of bright green, maroon or even turquoise-glazed, ground-storey external walls to the street.

Terracotta is now obsolete as a constructional material. Modern architecture has not called for the detailed and elaborate moulded decoration achievable in terracotta which the Victorians so desired. The provision of impervious external surfaces has been achieved by other means – notably the use of sheet-metal cladding panels, or the mass-produced ceramic tiles already referred to. Minor repairs to the material call for very careful *in situ* reinstatement of damaged mouldings in coloured epoxy mortar, as wholesale replacement of damaged sections with purpose-made pieces can be very costly.

The chief advantage of terracotta for the Victorians was its impervious finish, which made it an ideal facing material for buildings erected in sooty industrial towns where stonework was likely to be quickly impregnated with dirt. For this reason, terracotta was often referred to as 'self-cleansing'. The possibility of cheaply producing virtually identical heavily

decorated components by semi-mass-production methods and saving weight over equivalent stone detailing were additional advantages behind terracotta which appealed to the Victorians. For these reasons it was much favoured for external balustrades and ornamental door and window dressings as well as cornices. The famous Victorian architect, Alfred Waterhouse (1830–1905), was a prime exponent of terracotta construction and his Natural History Museum at South Kensington (finished 1881) is an outstanding example of the wholesale use of the material outside and inside a very large public building.

The material also made an appearance in town houses after 1870, as a glance at the tall, neo-Flemish houses of Chelsea's Pont Street will verify. Here too, it was favoured for window sills and architraves, but entire columned and canopied porches were sometimes faced in terracotta (Plate 10).

PEBBLEDASH AND ROUGHCAST RENDERS

Towards the end of the nineteenth century and in the early years of this century, external wall renderings other than the stucco favoured by Regency and early Victorian builders became popular. The most common finishes were roughcast and pebbledash.

Roughcast is minimum two-coat work, the first 'straightening' coat being traditionally of a 1:1:6 cement/lime/sand mix. After application this was combed to provide a key and then left to dry out. A wet plastic mix of 1½ parts cement, ½ part lime, 2 parts of shingle or crushed stone and 3 parts of sand was then made up and thrown on to the wall with a hand scoop or laying-on trowel. This produces a finish of 'coated' pebble texture and it was commonly used to waterproof 215mm (8½in) solid brick external walls. It was normal for the first render coat to contain animal hair as a binding agent. 'Distemper' paintwork was often subsequently applied to the surface of the finishing coat as the use of cement in the mix resulted in a grey colour which was disliked by the Victorians.

Plate 10 Elaborate terracotta construction in an entrance porch and balcony on Pont Street, Chelsea (*Author*)

Pebbledash differs from roughcast in that a selected coarse aggregate such as spar or pea shingle, graded from 6–13mm (¼–½in) in size, was thrown on with a hand scoop when the top coat of render was still soft. Care was necessary in choosing the colour of the aggregate because, unlike rough cast, in pebbledash the self-colour of the stones remains exposed unless the material is over-painted.

It is clear that a good appearance and durability in both of these external render finishes relies very much on the skill of the tradesman. Poor adhesion of the render to the brick backing will, in the long term, cause cracking which can precipitate serious water penetration problems – rainwater being drawn into the cracks by capillary action and eventually dislodging neighbouring areas of render as well as saturating the solid wall behind. In this circumstance, there is no alternative to hacking off the affected area of render to the line of sound material, and patching in a panel of matching render before repainting.

TILE-HANGING AND SLATE-HANGING

For decorative or practical reasons, many Victorian houses in country or suburban areas have parts of their external walls clad in tile-hanging. This treatment was most commonly applied to the external surfaces of gables. After about 1870, tile-hanging was often adopted for its decorative 'rustic' effect. It generally commenced at first-floor level and continued up to the eaves or cornice of the building. In single-storey dwellings it might commence at plinth level, about 450mm (18in) above the ground. The tiles could be the plain rectangular type common in roofing, or of more complicated shape, or both types might be interspersed in bands to produce patterning (Plate 11). The late-Victorian architect, Richard Norman Shaw (1831–1912), was a great populariser of decorative tile-hanging and equally talented younger architects, such as Edwin Lutyens, inherited his enthusiasm for this treatment, applying it to their country-house designs until well into the present century. Bright red, sand-faced tiles were most often used and were fixed in various ways to the construction behind. Where the first-floor

Plate 11 A pattern in a tiled gable achieved by alternating bands of 'fish-scale' tiles with plain clay tiles (*Author*)

walling is of timber framing, tiling battens as used in roof construction were simply nailed continuously and horizontally across the wooden uprights to provide fixing 'rails' for the tiles. As such tile-hanging is vertical, a 38mm (1½in) lap of tiles (overlap) was sufficient to prevent rain driving in (this is considerably less than the overlap of tiles on low-pitched roofs). In new construction, or the renovation of old work of this type, a continuous vertical layer of bituminous felt or building paper should be installed across the timber uprights before the battens are reinstated as a further check against rainwater penetration.

Tiles were also used to clad brick external walls and the incompatibility of the brick coursing with the tiling gauge (the mortar joints

of the brickwork being at 75mm [3in] increments, in contrast to the necessarily wider spacing of the tiling battens) which prohibited direct nailing of the battens into the mortar joints, led many builders to set vertical wooden pads into the brickwork joints as grounds for fixing the battens. This technique was not generally approved even by the Victorians, and such construction may have suffered badly from decay of the timber grounds because of the simple fact that the fixings were not adequate to take the load imposed by the construction. A better method was to build bricks of coke breeze into the brick surface in every course at about 1m (3ft) centres, staggered vertically, thus providing a coarse surface to which the 50mm × 19mm (2in × ¾in) battens could be nailed. Such a cladding was normally applied to 215mm (8½in) solid brickwork to weatherproof it, but if 327mm (13in) brickwork was the background, it was feasible, although not good practice, to lay the external bricks on edge, thus obtaining brick joints at 110mm (4½in) intervals vertically to which the tiling battens could be directly fixed (Fig 45).

Windows fitted into such constructions were sealed at the edges by the application of timber mouldings to bring their frames flush with the tiling. Lead flashings and cement fillets were liberally used at heads and sills to guarantee the draining out from the tile hanging of trapped water which might otherwise attack window joinery. An alternative treatment was to set back the window frame 110mm (4½in) from the tiled face, and then to apply render to the edge of the tiles and the brickwork of the window reveal. This treatment was poor, storing up future trouble through the admission of water into the window/wall joint via cracks in the render. A timber scotia moulding was commonly used to finish the joint at the head of the wall tiling with the soffit board of the roof eaves, as this avoided having to fit precisely the tiles to the soffit (Fig 46). Where wall tiling which clads an upper storey terminates at first-floor level, it was common to adopt a 'bell-mouth' profile for the foot of the tiling to throw the rainwater off the elevation more properly with a pronounced 'drip' over the brickwork or render below. This was often achieved by corbelling out the supporting brickwork with plain or moulded bricks to give the desired profile (Fig 47).

Fig 45

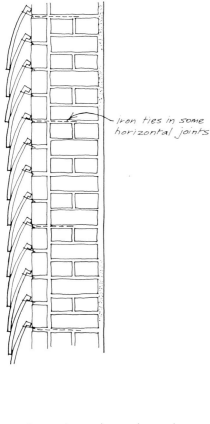

Iron ties in some
horizontal joints

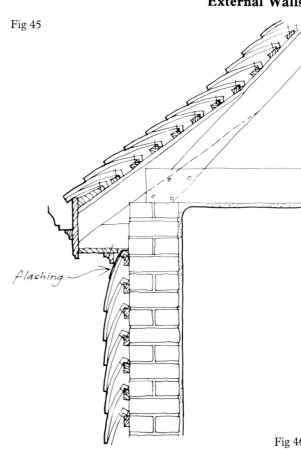

flashing

Fig 46

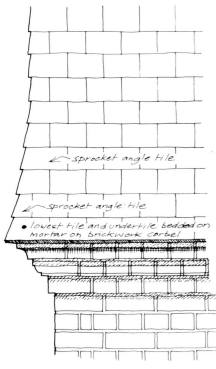

sprocket angle tile

sprocket angle tile

• lowest tile and undertile bedded on
mortar on brickwork corbel

Fig 47

Slate-hanging was applied in the same manner as tile hanging, but the unit size of slates being invariably greater than tiles, they were generally applied at a wider gauge. Perhaps because of this, they were also less commonly used for decorative purposes. A normal reason for applying slate hanging was to weatherproof a gable in a particularly exposed location, and one improvement to the appearance of such slating which was often made was the completion of the slating at the roof verges (the junctions of the roof planes with the gable) with 'Winchester cut' slates. In this treatment the underside of each slating course is 'turned up' to meet the roof verge and a neat junction of the verge with the slated gable results (Fig 48).

61

External Walls

Fig 48

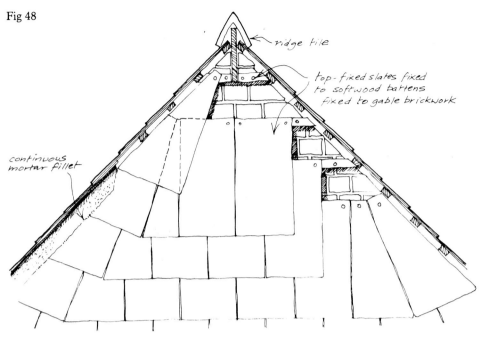

ridge tile

top-fixed slates fixed
to softwood battens
fixed to gable brickwork

continuous
mortar fillet

WOODEN EXTERNAL WALLS

Other than in temporary buildings, houses constructed entirely of wood above the foundations are uncommon in Britain. In the countries formerly constituting the British Empire, tropical countries and America, wooden-walled houses have been continuously erected throughout the last two hundred years. They can be divided into two general types: *braced-frame* and *balloon-frame* structures.

A braced-framed building is one in which each piece of the framing is carefully joined with mortice and tenon joints while the angles are held rigidly by diagonal pieces. In this way the whole skeleton is made secure and stiff in itself before any covering is applied. A balloon-frame building is one in which the structural timbers are simply butt jointed and nailed together, and the structure depends greatly on the sheathing or outer covering for its strength and stiffness.

Carpentry work in a framed building commences when the foundation is completed. First of all, a horizontal timber called the sill was laid in mortar containing animal hair on top of the foundation wall, to receive the wooden superstructure. In brace-framed buildings this sill varied from 200mm × 150mm (8in × 6in) to

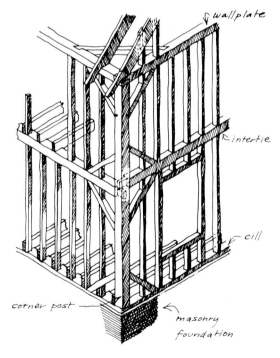

wallplate

intertie

cill

corner post

masonry
foundation

Fig 49

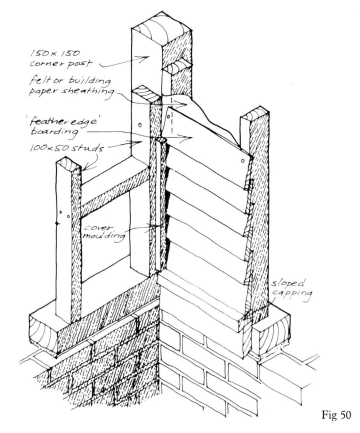

150 × 150
corner post

felt or building
paper sheathing

'feather edge'
boarding

100×50 studs

cover
moulding

sloped
capping

Fig 50

250mm × 200mm (10in × 8in) and from 150mm × 100mm (6in × 4in) to 200mm × 100mm (8in ×4in) in balloon-frame houses. It was laid 25mm (1in) inboard from the outer face of the foundation wall. Corners of this sill were halved (half the thickness of each sill section is removed, allowing the timbers to sit on top of each other without enlarging the overall sill thickness), and when the wall was longer than could be accomplished in a single piece of timber, a bevelled joint was generally used to join the lengths and prevent them from pulling apart.

Corner posts were then erected at the angles of the house (200mm × 150mm [8in × 6in] or 250mm × 200mm [10in × 8in] timber in braced frames; 150mm × 100mm [6in × 4in] or 200mm × 150mm [8in × 6in] timbers in balloon frames) and in braced frames these posts were mortised into the sill at the halved corner and into the wall plate at the eaves level of the house (Fig 49). In the simpler, balloon-framed work, the corner posts were simply butt jointed to the sill (allowed to 'rest' on it) before

being spiked to the horizontal timber and the roofplate at the head. Internal angles were formed by simply spiking a regular stud to each face of the corner post (Fig 50).

The studs, or regular timber uprights, were sometimes mortised into the sill, into the girt or intertie (the horizontal bracing timber at upper-floor level) and into the wall plate. Latterly it was more common simply to butt joint them into position except in the case of double-thickness studs at the sides of window or door openings. However, it is a principle of balloon-frame construction that the studs must extend from the sill to the wallplate in one piece if possible. Where this height was too great, separate timbers were spliced together by nailing wooden fishplates to either side of the upright and across the butt joint (Fig 51). To carry the floor joists of the first or second floors of a balloon frame, a ledger board is notched into the studs, each joint being spiked to the adjacent stud. In braced frames the upper-floor joists rest on the intertie already described. The external surface of such timber-framed houses

63

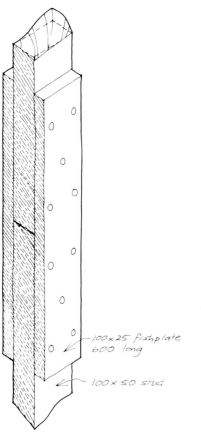

100×25 fishplate 600 long

 100×50 stud

Fig 51

was commonly of horizontal 'feather edge' boarding – in the case of the balloon frame such horizontal boarding acted as bracing and was therefore an essential structural feature. A plaster finish on the internal surface was achieved in the conventional way by applying lime plaster to timber laths (see Chapter 6).

DECORATIVE HALF-TIMBERING

In the late nineteenth century a fashion arose for reproducing the appearance of traditional Tudor or Elizabethan half-timbering on the outsides of houses. In authentic antique timber-framed buildings, the timbers exposed externally were structural members often equal to the full thickness of the outside wall (as at the sixteenth-century Little Moreton Hall in Cheshire). The gaps between these stout posts and braces were commonly filled with brickwork and the outside face of the brickwork was rendered and painted to contrast with the tarred timbers. However, in Victorian and later work, the usual aim was to obtain this appearance at low cost and this precluded the use of the massive timbers of earlier times. One means of obtaining the desired effect was the adoption of a timber-framed construction similar to the balloon frame, vertical studs being placed at

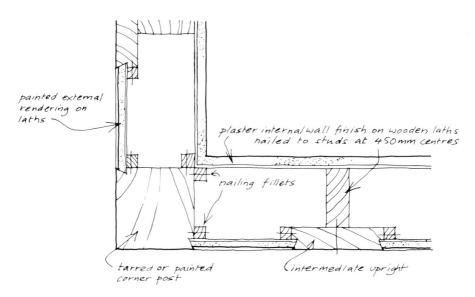

painted external rendering on laths

plaster internal wall finish on wooden laths nailed to studs at 450mm centres

nailing fillets

tarred or painted corner post

intermediate upright

Fig 52

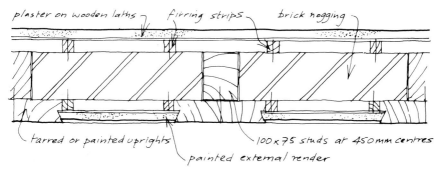

plaster on wooden laths ⌐   firring strips ⌐   brick nogging ⌐

tarred or painted uprights   100 × 75 studs at 450mm centres

painted external render

Fig 53

about 450mm (18in) intervals, with the externally exposed timber being fixed to the face of each stud. These 'cosmetic' sections were about 50mm (2in) thick and from 200–250mm (8–10in) wide on the face. Small battens were nailed to the vertical edges of these timbers to accept thin wooden laths on which the render was applied (Fig 52). An alternative and certainly more robust and weatherproof form of sham half-timber construction incorporated panels of brickwork between the vertical timber studs at the core of the wall. The outside appearance of wide, tarred timbers was obtained by the fixing of 50mm (2in) thick strips to the studs, and it was conventional for the laths supporting the external render to be fixed to small vertical battens flanking these strips. The render was often directly applied to the brickwork surface, with a consequent risk of water entering the structure at cracks caused by the shrinkage of the timber. Similarly, the internal plaster surface might be applied directly to the brickwork, though here too it was not unusual for firring strips or battens to

be fixed to the brickwork, before timber laths were laid across them and the plaster finish then applied (Fig 53). The entrapped air which resulted would improve the insulating qualities of the wall, though no one could claim that this type of construction is either thermally efficient or constructionally desirable, since its capacity to exclude wind and rain is very dependent upon the skill of the original tradesman. Present-day repairs to such construction which rely upon modern kiln-dried timber and sand/cement render, lacking respectively the durability or elasticity of the Victorians' materials, are unlikely to prove satisfactory, and care should be taken to obtain materials which are physically identical to those used in the original construction.

Following the precedent of historic buildings whose jettied-out upper storeys most prominently display their half-timbered construction, sham half-timbering in Victorian and early twentieth-century houses was almost always restricted to the upper storeys, commencing at first-floor level.

4
Roofs

Victorian houses display a wide variety of roof shapes and roof coverings. Certainly the most common shape is the *pitched* (or sloping) roof covered in slates or tiles, and of these two roofing materials, slate predominates.

Pitched roofs are usually employed even where the façade of the house suggests that it should finish with a flat roof, for in the early nineteenth century terraces were often faced with a street elevation crowned by a parapet, which conceals a 'saw-tooth' profile of alternating roof slopes. This was particularly so in London. A *valley gutter* draining the two roof slopes which cover an individual house is sited on the centre line of the accommodation, at right angles to the street, and the roof pitches rise from this line to meet the flanking party walls (Fig 54). This form of roof was favoured for Georgian terraced houses and its popularity continued until the middle of the nineteenth century, when a change in taste demanded that roof slopes should be exposed to the street rather than concealed behind parapets.

The disadvantages of the central valley gutter are obvious, and prospective purchasers of houses which are roofed in this way are advised to make a close inspection of this feature. In the first place, the central siting of the valley gutter usually denies the house a loft of useful shape. Secondly, because accumulated rainwater is concentrated over the centre of the house rather than being dispersed to its perimeter, a blockage in the gutter or a defect in its lining diverts water into the house and the surrounding building construction is damaged. The only enduring solution to a valley gutter which leaks because its lining is defective is its complete relining with lead sheet, but the existence of a leak may only be a symptom of more serious problems.

The distortion and cracking of the gutter lining may result from the deflection of the supporting *gutter beam*, which is carried on the front and rear walls of the house. An undersize beam is bound to sag, and the settlement of an overloaded central partition which props the gutter beam is also a common cause of deterioration in the lining of the valley gutter. Since the gutter beam carries the ends of the rafters, neglect of a leaking gutter may have caused rot in these members, which leads to the partial collapse of the adjoining roofslopes. Repairs to such defective construction which are not restricted to the renewal of the gutter lining and the affected rafters may include the provision of a new beam spanning the width of the property to give support to the gutter at an intermediate point. Fortunately, the adoption of this irrational and potentially troublesome arrangement of the 'double lean-to' or 'M' profile for the roofs of Victorian houses was the exception rather than the rule, and the more prevalent pitched roof profiles are described below.

ROOF STRUCTURES

In the present day, pitched roofs of houses are generally constructed from 'trussed rafters'.

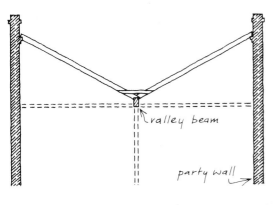

Fig 54

These are light, prefabricated timber trusses, mass-produced to predetermined spans. They are erected on timber wall plates at the head of the external walls of the house and are sited quite close to one another to accept the battens on which the roof covering is laid. However, this practice is very much a modern-day development, and until World War II at least, the pitched roofs of average houses were carried on *purlin* construction, where a longitudinal timber member spanning between gables or party walls supports the normal sloping timbers, or common rafters.

Probably the simplest form of roof structure is the 'lean-to', or 'shed' roof (Fig 55), where the rafters may be simply leaned against a vertical wall, their lower ends resting on a continuous timber wall plate fixed to the top surface of the masonry walling. The roof covering is then applied to this sloping plane. Clearly, this type of construction is suitable only for small spans, because in large spans the load imposed on the head of the supporting wall by the weight of the structure and finish will force the wall outwards and cause the roof to collapse unless this action is restrained.

An almost equally simple construction which suffers the same limitation and which introduces the ubiquitous double-pitched roof shape is the *couple* roof (Fig 56). Here, rafters are simply leaned against each other through a connecting continuous horizontal timber ridge board. Because the timbers are not triangulated (formed into a complete triangle), such construction is very weak structurally and will be found only over small spans not exceeding 3.6m (11ft 10in). This arrangement should not be adopted in new work, no matter how small the span.

Much more common in Victorian houses is the *couple-close* roof, in which the tendency of the rafters to push out the side walls is restrained by horizontal timbers, which act as tension members linking the supported ends of the rafters. Normally, these timbers double as the ceiling joists of the rooms below the roof because they provide a framing to which the plaster ceiling can be applied. This form of roof structure was commonly used over spans of between 4–6m (13–20ft).

A similar structure which was often used in circumstances where greater headroom was

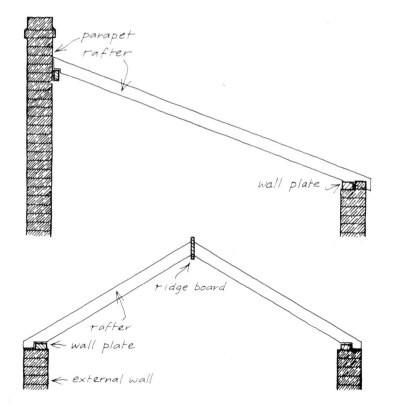

parapet
rafter

wall plate

Fig 55

ridge board

rafter

← wall plate

← external wall

Fig 56

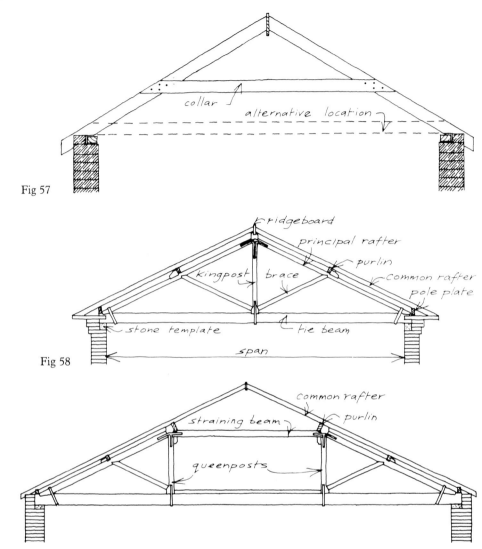

Fig 57

Fig 58

Fig 59

wanted below the ceiling joists was the *collar-beam* roof (Fig 57). In this arrangement, the role of the ceiling joists is performed by shorter beams at a higher level, called collars, which tie the centres of opposite rafters together. As the triangle of structure is smaller than that of the couple-close roof, the form is weaker and is unlikely to be encountered in spans exceeding 5m (16½ft).

More elaborate trusses may be found in large Victorian houses, and they can be categorized as *king-post* or *queen-post* trusses. The king-post truss, or *principal*, splits the simple triangle of the couple-close roof into two identical, but 'mirrored' triangles separated by a central post

which rests on the tie beam or chord (in the same position as the ceiling joist in the couple-close roof) and which terminates at the ridge. Braces or struts link the foot of the king-post with the principal rafters, thus further triangulating and therefore strengthening the structure (Fig 58). Such trusses were commonly used to roof rooms from 6–10m (20–33ft) wide and are therefore likely to be found only in large houses. The trusses would be placed at about 3m (10ft) centres. The purlins and pole plates run from truss to truss, and the common rafters which rest on these longitudinal members are sited at 300mm (12in) intervals. The fairly flat pitches preferred for slated roofs necessitated the use of king-post trusses over wide spans, as internally unbraced constructions would be otherwise susceptible to collapse under the resultant heavy roof loading.

The other main form of 'principal' is the queen-post roof which was used when the void in the roof was wanted for living accommodation. The principle of trussing is the same as the king-post roof, but two vertical queen posts are substituted for the central king post and are sited to either side of the roof centre line (Fig 59). They are joined together at the head by a horizontal straining beam and it can be seen that this arrangement frees the central zone of the roof void from structural members, thereby allowing its use for storage or living space. As a rule, the queen-post roof was used for even larger spans than those appropriate for king-post construction, and in its purest form it was restricted to the largest Victorian houses, in which trusses sited at 3m (10ft) centres spanned up to 12m (40ft).

A variation upon the queen-post truss much used in nineteenth-century dwellings is the *mansard* roof. It is no coincidence that this shape of roof is reminiscent of the skylines of Parisian terraces, for it is named after the seventeenth-century French architect, François Mansart, who designed part of the Louvre. The mansard roof combines the configuration of queen-post construction with the purpose of

keeping down the otherwise excessive height of a steeply pitched roof, by reducing its slope towards the top. Thus a shallow-pitched roof about three-quarters of the width of the complete span sits on top of the more steeply pitched lower roof slopes, which usually terminate at the rear of a parapet capping the external wall (Fig 60). In this way, a large void free from structural obstructions is left at the centre of the truss and it is invariably used for attic rooms. The term 'mansard' was originally used only for roofs which exhibited the characteristic 'twin-pitch' profile on all four sides, but it has come to include all roofs where this is the shape of the cross-section. The simpler 'mansard-section' form is also known as a *gambrel*, or *curb* roof, both terms being of American origin.

In all these types of timber truss construction, the sophisticated carpentry otherwise required to achieve the shapes and joints necessary to guarantee the integrity of the structure was often reduced by adopting iron straps, clamps and wedges which were variously bolted, screwed or driven into the trusses to obtain sound connections. Though they may have obtained a patina of rust since they were first installed, such components are likely to be working equally well today, for cast- and wrought-iron fittings are not so subject to serious deterioration from rusting as is modern

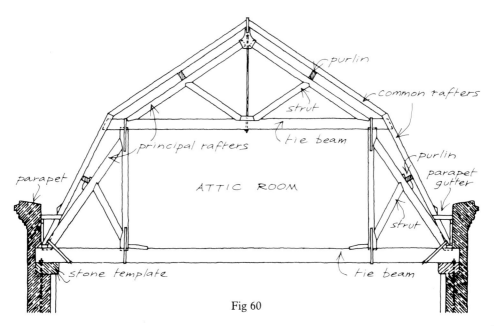

Fig 60

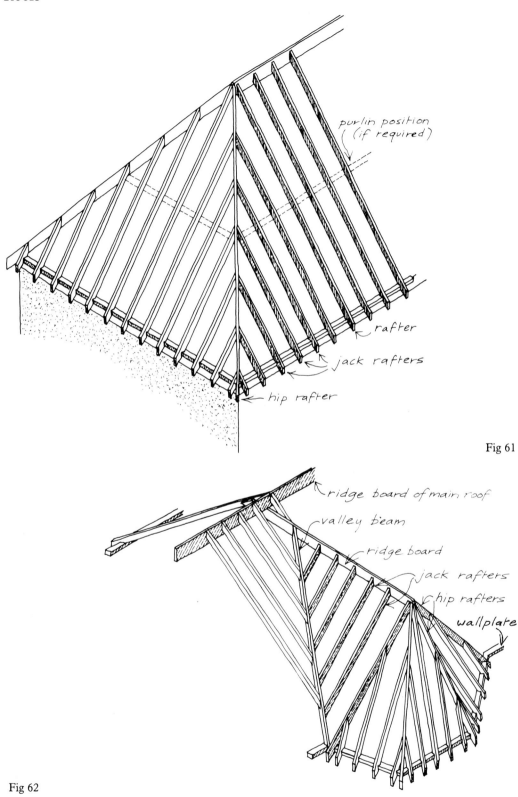

purlin position
(if required)

rafter

jack rafters

hip rafter

Fig 61

ridge board of main roof

valley beam

ridge board

jack rafters

hip rafters

wallplate

Fig 62

ungalvanised steel. Therefore the removal of any straps, bolts or ties or any similar modification of such timber structures should not be attempted before the advice of a structural engineer, architect or building surveyor has been obtained.

Almost as common as the simple gabled form of pitched roof is the *hipped* roof, the purest version of which is a pyramid. In this variant, the essential components of the pitched-roof structure – rafters and ridge board – are supplemented by the pieces which form the hip, namely the *hip rafter*, which joins the corner junction of the wall plates to the end of the ridge board, and the *jack rafters*, so called because they span between the wall plate and the hip rafter and are thus shorter than the common rafters (Fig 61). It would be highly unusual to find a hipped roof sited over a house in an intermediate location in a terrace, but end-of-terrace houses and semi-detached houses commonly display hipped roofs, and they are almost the rule for the roofing of detached houses. However, even in modest terraced houses it is usual for some form of hipped-roof construction to exist, if only as the covering of a projecting square or splayed bay window. Sometimes such a small hipped roof, ancillary to the slope of the main roof and structurally dependent upon it, may reflect a polygonal plan in the bay so that four hip rafters, rather than the two which a square shape would necessitate, are required (Fig 62).

This form of construction also gives rise to a feature which is dealt with in detail under the later section on Roof Coverings – the *valley*. Where the hipped roof of a bay meets the slope of the main roof, an internal angle of roof planes called a valley is formed. It will be appreciated that a valley results wherever two pitched roofs meet at an internal angle.

In addition to these main types of simple pitched roofs, larger Victorian and Edwardian houses often exhibit roofs of special form in the shape of conical, pyramidal, 'ogee' (S-curved in elevation) and domed roofs of turrets, towers or bays. Cones and pyramids, if of sufficient size, can be covered with clay tiles or timber shingles, but the curvature of hemispherical domes or bell-shaped (ogee) roofs generally precludes the use of tile-type coverings, and the sheet metal cladding which is normally applied to these shapes is dealt with in Roof Coverings.

In a conical roof, the rafters are notched over the timber wall plate in the same manner that a couple-close roof is structured, but the mitreing of the upper ends of the rafters at the apex is different. The first four rafters to be erected (at right angles to each other) are simply butted squarely together, but the infilling rafters of each quadrant have shaped ends to ensure that the top surfaces of all the sloping timbers lie in the same cone-shaped plane, in order to accept the battens in preparation for the tiling.

Flat Roofs

Though they are usually associated with twentieth-century buildings, it is clear that the Victorians too made considerable use of flat roofs, particularly where it proved impractical to span an awkwardly shaped or irregular plan with a pitched form. Except where brick vaults enclosing cellars provided support for terrace or garden areas, the type of flat-roof structure adopted by the Victorians was indistinguishable from the most common type of floor construction, namely timber joists spanning on to timber wall plates sited on top of the supporting walls. A weatherproof finish was generally achieved by laying asphalt or sheet metal on top of timber boarding, which was laid as a continuous surface across the timber joists and nailed to them (see Roof Coverings). A roof of up to about 12° pitch (approximately 1 in 4) was defined as a flat roof and anything steeper was generally covered with a tile-type finish which is unsuitable for pitches below 15°. Flat roofs were never finished completely level as some slope was essential for the drainage of rainwater. It is unusual to find any surface exposed to the weather finished to a slope of less than 1 in 60.

ROOF WINDOWS

There are several means of providing natural light in attic or loft spaces contained within pitched roofs, but certainly the most popular device for the Victorians was the *dormer* window, which appeared in a wide variety of types. Dormers project from the roof surface and are framed up when the roof structure is erected.

Regency town houses favoured the *wagon-head dormer* for lighting top-storey rooms contained in a mansard roof behind a parapet.

Fig 63

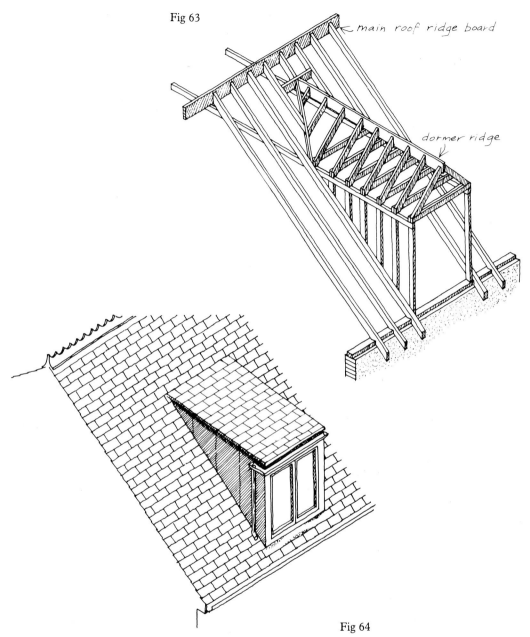

main roof ridge board

dormer ridge

Fig 64

The structure of a dormer is akin to the main roof structure. The common rafters of the main roof are 'trimmed' above the opening, which accommodates the dormer construction with timbers, generally at least 13mm (½in) thicker than the common rafters. Timber uprights or studs are then erected at 300–450mm (12–18in) centres on the floor joists to form the structure of the flanks or *cheeks* of the dormer, and in the case of the wagon-head dormer, these studs are extended up in the shape of a semi-circular arch to form the window's roof structure. The whole construction is finally clad with boarding and cloaked in sheet metal to exclude rainwater.

Much more common than the wagon-head dormer in later Victorian houses were dormer windows with small pitched or flat roofs. Dormers commonly display pitched roofs terminating in miniature gables, and they are constructed in exactly the same way as the main roofs – with ceiling joists and rafters (Fig 63). In steeply pitched main roofs, dormers were sometimes roofed with a structure consisting of common rafters sloped at a lesser angle than those of the main roof, which terminated on a horizontal timber plate sited over the window (Fig 64). This simplified the dormer construction and eliminated potentially troublesome valleys at the junction of the dormer roof with the main roof. It is worth noting that in rural houses where mansard roof construction was hardly ever adopted, dormer windows were sometimes used to increase the headroom of parts of an upper storey, the external walls of which extended only slightly above the attic floor level. Thus only the upper parts of the dormers projected above the main house eaves. Desirable attic rooms were often obtained by this device, and the appearance of the roof mass was made more pleasing because the eaves' line was broken and the roof plane was visually fragmented.

It is obvious that the hip, which is a way of finishing a main roof, is an equally suitable treatment for a dormer roof, and there are many examples of attractive hipped, pitched and tiled dormer roofs, particularly on country buildings. Where a dormer was capped by a flat roof, this was generally finished with sheet metal (lead, copper or zinc) laid to a minimal fall. Though the sheet metal could be used as the cladding for the cheeks as well, these triangular areas were as commonly waterproofed with slate-hanging or tile-hanging, and in some situations they were glazed to admit further daylight into the attic rooms.

Lantern lights, which are almost always sited on flat roofs, are another 'family' of roof windows. The simplest type of lantern light consists of a lower timber 'ladder frame' infilled with glass which extends around all sides of the roof opening. This glazed curb is surmounted by a slightly sloping glazed panel, part or all of which may be hinged and opened to ventilate the room below, or to grant access to the roof surface. The construction of the top surface of this type of lantern light is the same as that of the traditional skylight which is described later. An equally common type of lantern light is shaped like a conventional double-pitched roof, and like that roof it can be terminated either with gables or with hips. Although it may be framed up with timber in precisely the same

way as a dwelling's main roof, this is apt to limit severely the area available for glazing when all the rafters, braces and purlins have been installed. Even in the nineteenth century it was common to resort to the use of decorative iron or steel-angle trusses for the lantern-light structure, the strong but slender sections of the iron or steelwork freeing wide spaces for the glazing. The glass cladding could also be installed in two distinct ways. The traditional arrangement of narrow panes supported by 'T' section wooden glazing bars suffered the general limitation of wood construction that long spans necessitate the use of broad and deep timbers. These bulky glazing bars thus obscured a significant part of the glazed area. This loss of transparency became particularly plain when a hipped lantern light was spanned by wooden glazing bars, as the timber sections had to be sufficiently thick to admit joints of the 'standard' glazing bars with the hip members. Not only was the construction clumsy, it was complicated too.

To simplify and improve the method of obtaining sloping surfaces in glass, the Victorians invented *patent glazing*. One of the earliest systems available, the 'Pennycook' method, provided 'T'-section iron bars incorporating lead 'wings' to either side of the upright of the 'T'. The glass was laid on putty on each flange of the 'T'-section and the lead wings folded down on top to form a narrow flashing from the metal on to the glass. Special components were available to achieve hipped shapes. Thus, the means of obtaining sloping glazing for verandah roofs and lantern lights was greatly simplified, and the thin iron sections which replaced the stout timbers granted a larger area for the glazing. Modern, patent-glazing systems offer metal glazing bars which are more slender still, because aluminium has been almost universally adopted as the constituent metal. The sections used are also more sophisticated in that the bars now incorporate channels designed to collect and drain away the condensation which can form on the underside of the glass. Similarly, 'Neoprene' gaskets or beads have replaced the linseed oil putty formerly used for bedding and securing the glass. However, the individual panes are still likely to be flashed with narrow lead wings, and the sheets may be secured by sprung metal clips or a continuous metal capping of each

Plate 12 A modern hipped-roof lantern light. In this case, reflective glass obscures the views of the interior which would be seen through clear patent glazing (*Author*)

glazing bar. If restoration of a Victorian lantern light with aluminium sections is contemplated, a further advantage of the modern material is the option of obtaining the sections already colour-coated in black, white or a range of standard colours to match existing painted woodwork. This durable 'Syntha-Pulvin' coating requires no maintenance and convincingly approximates to the appearance of the traditional painted timber. Where hips and ridges are formed in the system, it is normal to achieve watertight hip and ridge junctions with sheet lead flashings in the traditional way (Plate 12).

Where a simpler means than the dormer or lantern light was required for illuminating attic rooms, the Victorians incorporated *skylights* or *rooflights* parallel to the plane of the roof slope. A void was formed in the structure by terminating a series of rafters on trimmers sited at the top and bottom of the required opening. On top of the horizontal trimmers and the rafters, or additional raking trimmers forming the sides of the opening, a continuous timber curb was constructed to carry the sash of the skylight above – though normally parallel to – the general roof plane. This sash was framed in the same way as a normal window sash, though made of thicker timber sections, and it was sited so as to overlap the curb, to which it was fixed with a tenoned joint, on all four sides. The top rail was thicker than the sill rail, so that the skylight glass could be grooved or rebated into it. The glass was allowed to run over the sill rail to ensure quick drainage of rainwater, and at the sides it was rebated into the stiles and any intermediate glazing bars (Fig 65). The most durable finish for such a skylight was the provision of a continuous lead sheet covering to the sash frame surface. Ideally, on the top and side rails, this covering was dressed over the putty on to the glass, so that any water running from the lead would not affect the putty joint. A groove was worked into the underside of the sash head section above the junction with the curb, so that any water finding its way past the lead drip might not run into the skylight void via the tenoned joint of the timber members.

Condensation invariably forms on the underside of the glass of any single-glazed rooflight,

74

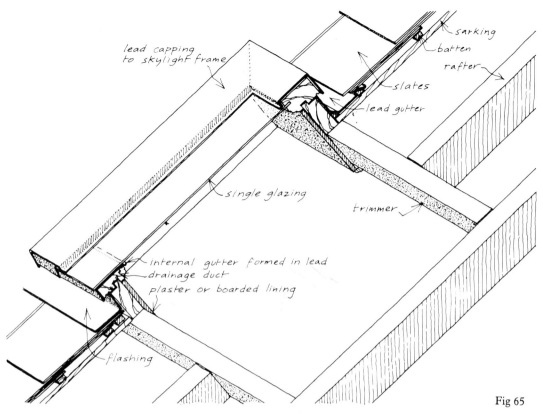

lead capping
to skylight frame

sarking

batten

rafter

slates

lead gutter

single glazing

trimmer

internal gutter formed in lead
drainage duct
plaster or boarded lining

flashing

Fig 65

and to prevent it dripping into the room or roof space below, a channel was often formed in the lead covering the sill rail. The moisture then runs down the underside of the glass and into this channel, from which it is conveyed away on to the roof below via holes or grooves in the lower rail. The lead forming a protection to the curb at the sill lapped the slated surface below as a flashing to keep out the water. Above the head of the skylight, a small triangular fillet eased the joint of the roof boarding with the curb so that the lead sheet at this point could be dressed to form a gutter, enabling water running over the edge of the slates above the skylight to find its way down the sides of the window and thence down the slope of the roof. The slating over the skylight terminated on a tilting fillet in the same way that it would at the eaves of the roof. Opening skylights were constructed in a very similar way, the opening mechanism normally being as simple as a pair of strong, non-ferrous hinges fixed to the sash head and the curb below it.

When it is necessary to renew such skylights completely or to install new windows in an existing roof, the simplest policy is to purchase proprietary prefabricated roof windows of equivalent or approximately equal size through the agency of a local builder's merchant, and to fit them into the pre-existing voids. The range of makes generally available is supplied with flashings matching the metal cladding of the sash surfaces and these flashings are available in differing profiles compatible with slates, tiles or pantiles. The windows are normally supplied with sealed double-glazing already fitted. This prevents condensation. Designed to open fully, they usually incorporate a vent in the window head which can remain open in a rainstorm yet not admit water. The metal cladding is a dark, colour-coated aluminium which blends well with slated roofs. Much effort and expense is spared by fitting a suitably sized prefabricated unit in substitution for outworn Victorian joinery, and the shape and detailing of such a small roof window is not disruptive of the period character of the original roof.

ROOF COVERINGS

Pitched Roofs

SLATING

Natural slates are quarried from a type of sedimentary rock which is not divisible along its planes of bedding, but instead along 'planes of cleavage' which may be at any angle to the bedding.

For building purposes, British slates fall into two main categories. In the first are those slates which have a relatively smooth face, obtained chiefly from North Wales and traditionally known as Bangor or Portmadoc slates. Such slates are habitually dressed to regular sizes and are as thin as possible. In colour they are blue, purple or greenish-grey. In the second category are slates which have a granular cleavage and are obtained from Cumbria (or Cumberland, Westmorland and North Lancashire as the district was formerly known). They are invariably dressed to random sizes and are thicker than the typical Welsh slate. In colour they are green or dark blue. In the nineteenth century, slates which originated from Cornwall or South Wales were much used in the south-west. Dressed like Westmorland slates to random sizes, they are intermediate in character between Portmadoc and Lakeland slates. In colour they are greenish-grey to rusty brown.

Extreme 'mechanical' neatness is associated with roofs covered with North Wales slates, and many architects practising in the late-nineteenth century and Edwardian period thought this to be unattractive. Welsh slate roofs are therefore most common on 'mass-produced' speculative houses with which architects were hardly involved. Westmorland slate roofing was preferred by architects, and it was executed in diminishing courses, the varying sizes of slate being sorted by the slaters. It is worth noting that a neat and orderly exterior is no guarantee of a waterproof roof, for it is found in practice that the rougher texture and thicker edges of Westmorland slates exclude the weather better than smoother and thinner slates which lie close together. This is partly due to the fact that the air contained between the uneven surfaces of the slates reduces capillary attraction, and partly due to the tendency of the thick edges to deflect the wind, thus preventing water from being blown over the lap. Delabole (Cornwall) and Prescelly (South Wales) slates were laid in a similar manner to Westmorland slating and they share many of its advantages, though their textures are less granular than that of the Cumbrian material.

As slates may justly be termed *the* Victorian roofing material, the defects most often found in pitched-roof coverings are dealt with in this section.

Laying Slates

The chief principle of slating is that the head of any course (except the course adjoining the roof ridge) should be covered by the tail of the course next-but-one above it (there are three thicknesses of slate at this point and a minimum of two thicknesses anywhere on the roof). The depth by which the head of the course is covered by the tails of the slates two courses above is called the lap. This varies according to the pitch of the roof on which the slates are laid. For a low-pitched roof (say 25°) the lap will be longer than that which applies on a steeply pitched roof (say 50°). This is so because rainwater running down the roof and entering the joints between adjacent slates will tend to 'fan out' below the slates on top of the under-slating course, and on a very low-pitched roof the water will drop into the joints of this lower course too. If the lap of the slates is not sufficiently deep to provide a further layer of slate below these joints at the point of drainage, the rainwater will enter the roof (Fig 66). Water penetration will also result if the locations of the fixing nails fall within these wet areas. Clearly, on more steeply pitched roofs the spread of water over each slate is less, as gravity assists the rain to run off more quickly, and the lap of the slates can be shorter. The *margin* is the length at the tail of each slate exposed to view, and corresponds to the *gauge* or spacing of the courses and their fixing battens.

Also critical for ensuring weathertightness is the *bond* of the slates. Even if they are laid with an adequate lap, the use of narrow slates will pose the problem of water penetration which results from an insufficient lap. The risk of water penetration is most pronounced at the eaves of a long roof slope where the pitch of the roof is slightly flattened by a 'sprocket-eaves' profile, and where the volume of water passing over the roof is at its greatest. With regularly sized slates, an even bond is reliable, but with

Fig 66

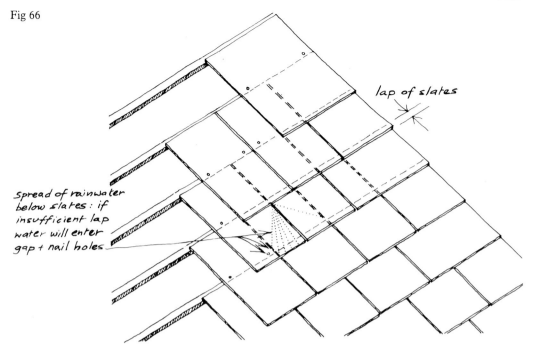

lap of slates

Spread of rainwater below slates: if insufficient lap water will enter gap + nail holes

the random sizes which occur in Westmorland slates, the skill and judgement of the slater determines the weathertightness of the roof.

The fixing of slates is achieved by nails driven through two holes punched either 25mm (1in) below the head of each slate, or a distance above the tail equal to gauge and lap plus 13mm (½in) clearance. In either case, the nail holes are about 32mm (1¼in) from the long sides of the slates. The former technique is called 'head nailing' and the latter 'centre nailing'.

Head-nailed slates always have two thicknesses of the material over each nail hole, and the actual lap is 25mm (1in) greater than the nominal lap, which is measured from the nail holes. Head nailing requires more slates than centre nailing and is therefore more expensive. Apart from its economical use of slates, centre nailing has the second advantage that it reduces the leverage which the wind may impose upon the slates and consequently reduces the risk of the roof being stripped in a gale. Until the middle of the nineteenth century, head nailing was almost universally used, but centre nailing afterwards superseded it as the favoured technique.

Copper or aluminium alloy nails provide the only enduring fixing for natural or asbestos-cement slates (see Restoring pitched roofs with new materials on page 94). Steel nails will quite quickly corrode and are unlikely to last twenty years, whilst natural slate will easily last eighty years or more.

There are two favoured methods for providing a fixing surface for slates on the rafter surfaces of a conventional pitched roof. The simplest and cheapest is the fixing of rough-sawn, rot-proofed timber battens 25mm × 50mm (1in × 2in) to the rafters at the appropriate gauge, a bituminous underslating felt having first been loosely fixed over the rafters. In this way, any water penetrating the slates is allowed to run away into the eaves gutter on top of the felt and below the slates. Much superior to this construction and also much more expensive, is a totally boarded covering of the rafters. The felt is tacked to this continuous wooden surface before counter-battens running up the slope at about 600mm (23½in) intervals are applied, followed by the slate-fixing battens themselves (Fig 67). The omission of the counter-battens is a false economy, for without them, water penetrating defective slates and running down the felt will lodge on the battens and find its way into the batten fixings, causing the eventual rotting of the 'sarking', or roof boarding. The Victorians were fond of yet another form of construction, which may in the

Fig 67

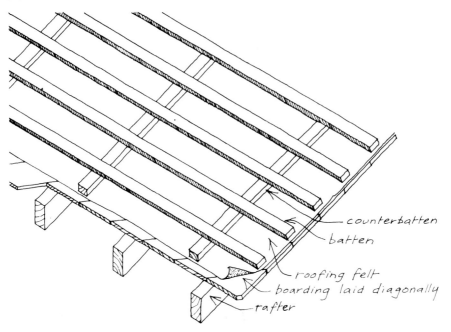

counterbatten
batten
roofing felt
boarding laid diagonally
rafter

long term provide the problems posed by the omission of counter-battens. They sometimes fixed slates directly to the sarking, employing no battens. Where the roof surface is weather-tight, the boarded substrate is protected, but a small chink in the slating caused by a cracked or broken slate will invite water into the narrow cavity below the slates and on to the boarding, threatening the timber with wet rot from the outside or an attack of dry rot from within, encouraged by poor ventilation of the roof space.

Slates eventually decay because of their reaction with weak acids, which are formed from sulphur and similar pollutants dissolved in rainwater. The slates 'exfoliate' and begin to absorb moisture with the efficiency of blotting paper. Slated city roofs are likely to have reached this state after about eighty years' exposure to the polluted atmosphere. Clearly, the 'grip' of a slate on its fixing nails is not assisted by this change in the material, and the dislodged slates often seen on old roof slopes may have slipped because decay has affected those parts of each slate closest to the fixing holes. A much more usual reason for slipped slates is the rusting of the original iron fixing nails. The weight of a slate will eventually sever the corroded shanks of iron nails and high winds encourage dislodged slates to slip further out of place – sometimes on to surrounding

ground or buildings, causing damage to people and property alike (Plate 13).

Slipped slates are resited by extracting the remains of the corroded fixings from beneath the overlapping course with a slater's ripper. The head of a strip of lead, zinc or copper which will form a clip or 'tingle' is then fixed to the sliver of batten accessible through the joint exposed by the displaced slate, and the slate is slid back into place over this strip and secured by folding the free end of the metal over the lower edge of the slate (Plate 14). This clip fixing of slipped slates is merely an expedient which cannot forever put off the day when the permanent refixing or renewal of the entire roof covering is necessary. Roof slopes which display a forest of slowly unfolding metal clips clearly indicate that they are due for renewal (Plate 15).

Sizes of Slates
Though Westmorland slates are supplied in random sizes and require to be sorted by the slater to obtain consistent courses, Welsh slates are supplied in a range of precise sizes which boast attractive titles. 'Doubles' are commonly 300mm × 200mm (12in × 8in), 'Ladies' 350mm × 300mm (14in × 12in), 'Viscountess' slates 450mm × 250mm (18in × 10in), 'Countesses' 500mm × 250mm (20in × 10in), 'Marchioness' slates 550mm × 300mm (21½in ×

Plate 13 The shanks of the iron nails which were formerly used to fix slates eventually rust away. High winds then dislodge the slates, and in due course they slide off the roof (*Redland Roof Tiles*)

Plate 14 The site of a slipped slate which was refixed on a zinc clip clearly illustrates the conventional method of repairing an aged slate roof (*Redland Roof Tiles*)

Plate 15 A distorted chimney flashing and a host of dislodged and delaminating slates on metal clips are signs of an outworn roof surface (*Redland Roof Tiles*)

12in) and 'Duchesses' 600mm × 300mm (24in × 12in). Though they are less common, even larger sizes are termed 'Princesses', 'Empresses', 'Queens' and 'Rags'. Perhaps the most common size of slate used for roofing Victorian houses is the 'Countess', traditionally described in its imperial size 20in × 10in.

Slate Roof Details

Ridge In the simplest form of double-pitched roof clad with slate, the most vulnerable area is the apex of the roof, or ridge. The usual method for shielding the ridge from rain was the installation of a continuous row of fireclay ridge tiles. These tiles, either 'half-round' (semi-circular) or preformed to an inverted 'v' matching the junction of the roof slopes, are bedded on mortar and lap the two top slate courses

adjoining the ridge board. Apart from the ubiquitous 'half round' profile, the 'weaving shed' double-pitched ridge tile is the plainest type. Almost equally common is a tile which incorporates a raised rim at one end so that it overlaps its neighbour. More decorative varieties of ridge tiles incorporating elaborate crests and finials are familiar to keen observers of Victorian buildings. Though most readily available in the reddish colour natural to most earthenware, ridge tiles can also be obtained in the blue colour resulting from the firing of Staffordshire clay, and this finish is more harmonious with the hue of a Welsh slate roof than the orange tones of standard earthenware, which the Victorians usually reserved for chimney pots.

The time-honoured method of fixing half-round or double-pitched ridge tiles is to bed them on mortar. The lime mortar used by the Victorians is eventually eroded by rainwater and a high wind easily dislodges a loose ridge tile overhanging a gable. After it has fallen, the rain has a clear route into the apex of the roof structure.

Slate ridge tiles were sometimes used instead of the fireclay type. Two pieces of thick slate were hinged together with a fragile slate dowel to form a double-pitched 'tile'. High winds or clumsy maintenance fracture this dowel, and when the bedding mortar has been completely washed away, the pieces fall apart, leaving the top of the roof timbers exposed to the weather (Plate 16).

Where slipped fireclay ridge tiles are being refixed, it is essential that the work is carefully carried out, each tile being laid on a thick and continuous mortar bed. Several concrete tile manufacturers now offer a 'dry ridge' system in which moulded plastic ridge tiles are nailed or clipped to the ridge board and the bedding mortar is obviated. These systems are very new and have yet to prove their long-term durability.

Hips If carefully installed, clay ridge tiles can be used to waterproof an otherwise open joint between slates at the hip of a pyramidal roof. However, this treatment can look clumsy where the thick tiles have to be cut to meet at the junction of the hips and the ridge. This criticism applies particularly clearly to the poor finish often seen at this junction in the complex hipped roofs of projecting polygonal bays. A neater, if more expensive detail is the *hip roll*, where a 'broom handle' section of timber is run down the top of the hip rafter and is clad in lead, copper or zinc, with 'wings' of the metal extending out from this capped batten to mask the joint of the slates and thus exclude the rain. This treatment can be equally well applied to the ridge, so that all the external junctions of the slated surfaces are protected by a continuous strip of sheet metal (similar to the shingle ridge, Fig 75).

A third way of protecting the hip junction from the weather, which is a particularly suitable detail for the thicker slates of Cornwall or Cumbria, is the *mitred hip*. Here the slates are shaped to meet close at the hip, and weather exclusion is effected by incorporating sheet-metal soakers below each course at the corner, thus achieving an 'invisible' protection against water incursion (Fig 68).

Plate 16 A dislodged section of slate ridge capping has exposed the ridgeboard of this roof to the weather (*Redland Roof Tiles*)

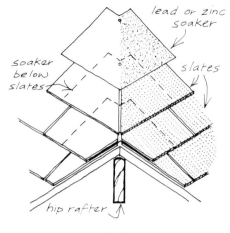

Fig 68

Hips are more susceptible to early decay than the ridge because heavy ridge tiles are more easily dislodged from the slope of a hip than from a level ridge. Where the hip is 'secretly' waterproofed with zinc soakers, corrosion of the metal by the weak acids contained in city atmospheres is a common cause of leaks. In the first instance, a range of ridge tiles sited on a hip must always be restrained against slipping by fixing a hip iron at the foot of the slope (see Fig 72) and where decayed zinc soakers are to be renewed, a long-term repair is achieved only by replacing the zinc with lead.

Valleys In roofs clad with thick slates, valleys may be treated in the same way as hips – the slates being close-mitred at the junction with sheet-metal soakers interleaved between the courses. Less attractive as a detail is the open valley in which a wide wooden valley board at, or below, the level of the slate-fixing battens, is clad in sheet metal lapped by the slates to either side (Fig 69). This detail produces an ugly discontinuity in the roof plane and is better reserved for valleys in thicker tile-type materials such as concrete tiles or pantiles, where its use may be unavoidable. The third and most satisfactory device, though it is a detail requiring great skill from the slater, is the swept valley similar to that often adopted for Cotswold stone slating which is described in the following section. 'Skew' and 'bottom' slates are run alternately up the 215m (8½in) wide valley board, preserving the continuous line of each slating course across the valley. In the best practice, bituminous felt is laid below the valley board which is sited in the plane of the slate-fixing battens.

The internal junction of the roof slopes is probably the area most prone to rainwater penetration, because it acts as a channel for rainwater draining from two roof slopes. The 'swept' valley, which extends the treatment of the rest of the roof to this zone, provides the

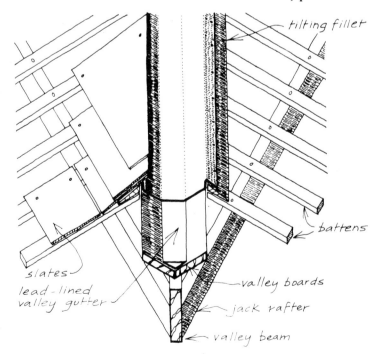

Fig 69

most secure valley cladding. Close mitreing of the slates over zinc soakers is a construction as susceptible to early decay as the equivalent treatment of the hip, whilst where over-long lead sheets have been used to clad an open valley gutter, the metal becomes corrugated and develops fractures which draw in the rain. This common defect is quite independent of the normal deterioration of a metal valley gutter, which is brought about by atmospheric pollution (Plate 17). Where the roof is to be recovered with a tiling system which does not include purpose-made valley tiles (such as asbestos-cement slates), the neatest restoration is achieved by re-forming the valley with close-mitred slates which conceal lead soakers.

Verges The junction of a slated roof with a gable is most simply achieved by carrying the slates across the full width of the wall and terminating them on top of a wooden barge-board, the top surface of which lies in the plane of the fixing battens. Thus, the bargeboard

Plate 17 A multitude of slipped slates adjoining a decayed valley gutter lining is evidence that decay is often worst at the exposed internal angles of a roof covering (*Redland Roof Tiles*)

supports the edge of the slates, protects the end grain of the battens from rot and gives a decorative treatment to the top of the gable. Indeed, the bargeboards of even quite modest Victorian houses were often pierced or formed into intricate profiles by the addition of elaborate mouldings (Plate 18).

A humbler treatment of the verge called for a mortar fillet to be applied to the underside of the slates where they oversailed the gable surface, and the resulting simple appearance is common in country buildings. The most satisfactory means of constructing this detail was to bed an underslating course of slates in mortar on top of the gable masonry and below the battens. The gap between these slates and the roof covering would then be pointed up

Plate 18 An elegant carved and moulded bargeboard attractively complements the decorative ridge tiles which crown the steeply pitched roofs of this mid-Victorian villa (*Redland Roof Tiles*)

with mortar as the slated verge was completed (Fig 70). Where the gable (or party-wall parapet in a city terrace) is carried above the roof slope as a raking parapet, the best water-proofing detail is the inclusion of a stepped metal flashing built into the brick or stone joints of the parapet and masking the junction of the slates with the flanking wall surface. Smaller areas of abutting brickwork, such as chimney stacks, are treated in exactly the same way. The junction of slating with the cheeks of dormer windows was most often achieved with a sheet-metal 'secret gutter', which is partly obscured by the lap of the slates and is constructed in the same way as an open valley gutter, the metal lining of the channel being continuous with the metal cladding of the dormer cheek in this case.

If the cheek of the dormer is slate-hung, the metal gutter is continuous with the vertical flashing concealed by the cut slates. A cheaper and less satisfactory detail for such parapet verges relies upon lead or zinc soakers inter-leaved between the slating courses being turned up against the flanking masonry and capped with a continuous mortar fillet. The risk of a split in the mortar, inviting water penetration of the roof via the joint between the soakers and the neighbouring brickwork, is the main short-coming of this method. In some circumstances, the soakers were omitted and even a small defect in a mortar or tile-and-mortar fillet gives a clear route for water to enter the roof. Such

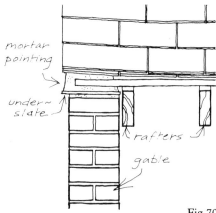

Fig 70

84

outworn features should always be replaced with carefully installed lead flashings (Plate 19).
Eaves As the slates at the verge conventionally end on the bargeboard, so the eaves slates normally terminate over a continuous wooden fascia, itself closed off at its ends by the gable bargeboards. The edge of the slates should project about 25mm (1in) in front of the fascia to ensure that dripping rainwater drains into the gutter fitted underneath; a lesser projection may allow the rainwater to be blown back below the slates and run down the fascia behind the gutter which will have a detrimental effect on fascia and walling alike. The underslating felt should always be run into the gutter below the projection of the slates. Roofs lacking an eaves gutter should project well in front of the wall surface they are shielding, so that wind-blown rain cannot easily be driven back on to the elevation.

A sprocket eaves is common in older, carefully built houses. In this treatment, the pitch of the roof is slightly flattened close to the eaves by projecting short rafters at a shallower slope than the main timbers from positions adjacent

to them. This construction pleasantly 'softens' the outline of the roof and slows the flow of water off its surface, at the point where it is crucial that the accumulated run-off should drain into the eaves gutter. Unfortunately, this slight flattening of the roof pitch renders an already vulnerable area more liable to water penetration, and though the point was made earlier, it cannot be stressed too strongly that great care should be taken to ensure that the slates used are sufficiently wide to prevent water creeping in between the courses. It is clear from the surviving hybrid roof coverings of tiles which give way to slates in the eaves courses that this problem was recognised by the old rural builders. Restorers of any form of tiled or slated roof of a Victorian house should remember that the lowest course always shows an edge of two thicknesses of slate at the eaves; the omission of the under-eaves slate – a little

Plate 19 An outworn tile-and-mortar fillet at the junction of a roof slope and a party wall parapet. It should be replaced with a stepped lead flashing (*Redland Roof Tiles*)

more than half the length of the first full course – will invite rainwater or melted snow into the roof space at its junction with the top of the external wall.

STONE SLATES

Stone slates or tiles are obtained from beds of stone which have the property of laminating in thin slabs along the original planes of bedding. *Yorkshire slates* are taken from sandstone deposits and are traditionally the largest slabs which can be obtained in England. Similarly large sizes were found in the so-called *Horsham slabs* of Sussex. Blocks of stone quarried in the normal manner were cleft with hammer and chisel or wedges to produce these slates. Northamptonshire also had celebrated quarries supplying stone slates, the best known being *Collyweston*. These slates are thinner and lighter than the Yorkshire slabs, but are more regular than the Cotswold stone slates formerly obtained from the Eyford, Stonesfield and Guiting quarries (these are the smallest and roughest indigenous stone slates). For the first time in many years, Cotswold slates are again available owing to the re-opening of a local quarry. Though their use declined with the increasing availability of Welsh slate, expensive Victorian houses sited in rural or suburban areas were sometimes roofed with stone slates, as the material gives a very picturesque appearance and it is reasonably durable. However, because of the very heavy load imposed by this material, stronger roof timbers than those used for any other type of pitched-roof covering are required.

Stone slating is carried out under the same principles of lap and bond applicable to any random-sized slating. The slates are hung with oak or deal pegs which are driven by the slaters tightly into holes near the head of each slate. The slates normally outlast such pegs and in the late nineteenth century brass screws were sometimes substituted for them, two screws being used to fix each slate through holes drilled for the purpose. An alternative to the old technique of bedding the slates in moss and afterwards plastering the underside with haired mortar to the level of the battens, was the Victorian method of laying the slates on a level mortar bed on sheet lathing flush with the battens, each slate being bedded and pointed in mortar as it was laid, though fixed with a nail at the head.

Suitable pitches for stone-slate roofs vary according to the size of slate commonly obtainable in the district. In Yorkshire and Lancashire and in old Sussex roofs the large slates make roofs water-tight at as low an angle as 24°. Because of their immense weight, a pitch steeper than 45° is uncommon. The small Cotswold slates were almost always laid to a pitch of 55°, whilst Northamptonshire stone-slate roofs of middle-sized slates are built at a compromise pitch of 45° or 50°.

Stone-slate roofs are commonly finished at the top by a sawn stone ridge tile. Hips are almost unknown in stone-slate roofs, because of the difficulty of obtaining a neat appearance in such coarse-grained material, but the slates can be mitred in the same way as Westmorland slates (see Slating). Each district had its own method of forming valleys. The typical Cotswold valley was 'swept' by using tapered slates in twos and threes in alternate courses (Fig 71). Two tapered slates in one course are known as 'skews', the three in the alternate course being known as a 'bottomer' and two 'lie bys'. An inverted length of ridge tile was used to form a cross gutter above the meeting of the valleys to keep the rain out of the junction. Roof eaves were commonly projected 150–200mm (6–8in), the eaves 'doubling' course resting on a course of large slates bedded on the wall, projecting outwards and slightly upwards to form an eaves soffit. An open verge can be formed in the same way, but a better and more traditional treatment was to end the roof against a gable extended up slightly above the roof plane and finished with a coping, as this allowed the slates to tuck in against the gable and below the coping, the gap beneath the coping and the top of the slates being closed with a mortar fillet. In some Yorkshire roofs the slates cover the gable wall and the coping is laid on them, bond stones being provided at intervals to tie it in and so prevent slipping.

TILING

Clay tiles are almost as common a roofing material as slate for Victorian houses, and they certainly have a longer history. A fireclay product, like brick, clay tiles have been in use in some areas of Britain for more than four hundred years. Despite the low cost and wide availability of quarried slate from Wales, in some areas such as East Anglia in the nine-

Fig 71

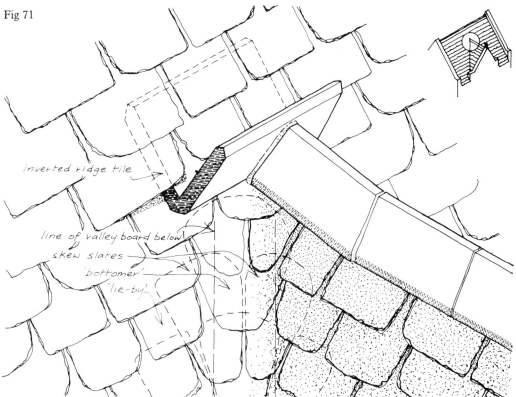

inverted ridge tile

line of valley board below

skew slates

'bottomer'

'lie-by'

teenth century it was still cheaper to use local clay tiles. As a result, many terraced houses in Norwich differ from otherwise identical contemporary buildings in London and the North only in the colour and texture of their roof surfaces.

Plain tiles are relatively thin plates of brick earth of a standard size between 250mm × 150mm (10in × 6in) and 280mm × 175mm (11in × 7in) with a thickness of 13–24mm (½–1in). Each tile is formed with two nail holes in one end during manufacture and it has normally two or more nibs or lugs on the upper edge or head in addition. Slates are naturally flat, but as they are dressed to shape they can be cut into any irregular form almost as readily as the normal rectangular unit. Tiles, in contrast, are an artificial product manufactured in a plastic condition and can be moulded to any simple shape during manufacture. Once fired, they should be cut as little as possible, as the burnt clay cannot be precisely shaped with much success unless a special tool such as a disc cutter is to hand. However, it is a simple matter for the makers to manufacture tiles for special situations, and a smooth appearance in a clay-

tiled roof of complicated shape is always attributable to varieties of special tile being used in conjunction with the plain type. The moulding of the clay during manufacture also allows a camber to be incorporated in the plain tile, which causes the tiles to lie close on the roof whilst preserving an air space underneath, thus protecting the fixing battens from rotting. In almost every district where tile roofing predominated there was a local tile works, although even in Victorian times there were certain regions from which tiles were distributed to other parts of Britain. Notable tile-making districts included the Broseley area of Shropshire, Staffordshire, Berkshire, Bridgwater in Somerset and Loughborough in Leicestershire. Machine-made tiles were produced by some of these tileries, but hand-moulded tiles were universally produced. Such tiles were often called 'sand-faced' because the mould was sanded to prevent adhesion of the clay and to give a granular face to the tile. They tend to be tougher, if more absorbent than the machine-made type, and are less liable than the mass-produced product to delaminate when attacked by frost.

Roofs

The principles of setting out lap and bond in plain tiling are exactly the same as those already described for slating. However, the smaller size of roofing tiles makes them unsuitable for roof pitches of less than 40°. At this pitch it is necessary to nail only every fifth course, but the heavy weight of clay tiling makes it essential to nail every course of tiles on roofs pitched steeper than 60°. At verges, hips and other exposed locations on roofs of shallower slope, courses should in any case be nailed at closer intervals.

In overhauling older roofs, tiles made without nibs and hung with wooden pins driven into the nail holes or lodging on battens may be encountered. Such tiles were commonly bedded at the head, not always in mortar, but sometimes in hay, moss, reeds or other material available in the district. A roof covering liable to penetration by driving rain or powdery snow resulted, and rotting of the battens and fixing pins occurred because sub-surface ventilation was inadequate. This type of tiled covering does not lend itself to piecemeal replacement and complete reroofing with conventional clay tiles should be contemplated.

As it is less liable than slating to conduct heat or cold, the fixing of tiling to an open batten roof (in which battens are laid directly on to the rafters and the boarding is omitted) is a suitable form of construction, though sarking felt must first be laid over the rafters to provide a 'second line of defence' against water penetration should a tile fracture.

Laying Tiles

Ridges The half-round tile for the roof ridge is practically universal and no other type looks as attractive. Special under-ridge tiles 215mm (8½in) long are used to form a course below the ridge and to preserve the gauge, the fixing battens normally being spaced at 100mm (4in) centres. Though special finials or stop-end ridge tiles were sometimes used to terminate a tiled ridge above hips or gables, an ordinary ridge tile with the open end filled in with mortar and pieces of tile or a black bottle-end was as common.

Hips The half-round ridge tile is sometimes continued down the hips but the use of half cone-shaped or 'bonnet' hip tiles grants the smoothest hip finish to a tiled roof. The bonnet hip readily fits the range of roof pitches which

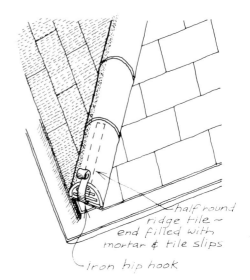

Fig 72

are appropriate for plain tiles. Where half-round tiles are used on the hips, it is essential to secure the lowest hip tile with a shaped metal hip hook to prevent it from sliding off if it becomes loose (Fig 72).

Valleys A sheet metal valley gutter in a tiled roof is an unattractive feature and is not normally necessary, since most tile manufacturers have traditionally made valley tiles to course and bond with plain tiling. However, the rounded valley tile is less satisfactory than the bonnet hip, because the concentration of water resulting from a narrow valley and the fact that the awkwardly shaped valley tiles are often less well burnt than the plain tiles (to restrict warping) together cause the valley to weather darker than the rest of the roof.

The traditional *swept* or *laced valley* avoids this defect by achieving a broader surface and employing plain tiles. It is installed in the following way (Fig 73). A board about 220mm (8¾in) wide is laid up the valley with its top surface roughly corresponding to the top surfaces of the tiling battens. On to this valley board the tiling courses from the two intersecting slopes are turned, each rising up its own roof slope and increasing its tilt until opposite courses interlace along the centre of the valley. Alternately, the courses from each slope are taken over and under each other, the last tile of each course (of which only the corner shows) being a 'tile and a half'. The real difficulty of forming such valleys is the starting and

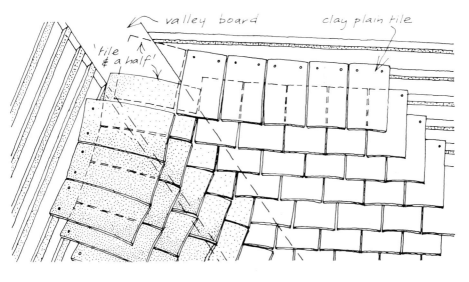

valley board   clay plain tile

'tile & a half'

Fig 73

finishing where some cutting and packing is entailed. Also, the swept valley cannot be properly formed where two ridges intersect at the same level; one must be subsidiary, otherwise the ridge lines must either rise in a point, or one must be humped over the other.

Verges A close verge in tiling usually projects 50–75mm (2–3in) beyond the gable and should be given a slight tilt inwards to throw water away from the edge. This detail is often achieved by bedding a course of tiles on the wall against the end rafter and projecting it to the same extent as the verge, thereby tilting up the battens which terminate about 75mm (3in) from the verge. The ends of the battens are covered by the pointing between this undercloak and the roof tiling. Besides holding the pointing, this arrangement gives a thick verge which is characteristic of old buildings. The inward tilt of the tiles naturally results in a tilt of the ridge tile which gives a 'finished' appearance (similar to slate detail, Fig 70).

For the purpose of preserving bond at the verge, and preventing the use of half tiles which would be difficult to fix, special 'tile-and-a-half' tiles are made. A sophisticated job by a skilled tiler will omit these specials (which tend to weather differently from the plain tiles). Instead, some tiles of each course will be cut to achieve a properly bonded arrangement of apparently standard tiles.

Tiling at the verge may also be terminated over a bargeboard in the same manner as a slated verge.

Eaves The doubling eaves course in a tiled roof consists of specially made under-eaves tiles 175mm (7in) long. Though the other tiles are unbedded, it is customary to bed the eaves course on a mortar joint on top of the wall to ensure a secure fixing.

PANTILES

Dutch or English pantiles and the various related forms of tile are moulded and laid according to a principle which is different from that applying to other types of tile roof covering. They are laid to a single lap and the majority of the roof surface is covered with only a single thickness of tile. There is no bond, the principle being that the tiles form a series of channels from ridge to eaves when laid, confining the water to a straight course and preventing spreading.

The ordinary pantile is of wave section and is 220–250mm (8¾–10in) from side to side. From head to tail it is about 350mm (14in) long. In manufacture it is moulded flat and bent to shape before firing. The thickness is usually about 19mm (¾in), but owing to the single-lap method of installation, a square of pantiling weighs only about half as much as the equivalent area of clay plain tiling. Perhaps for this reason, pantiles were a common finish for outhouses and agricultural buildings with cheap and lightly structured roofs. Over the old houses of Norfolk, Lincolnshire and north Nottinghamshire they are a particularly prevalent roof finish. The tiles are always hung on

Roofs

stout timber battens by the single nib integral to each unit. Particularly where pitches are steeper than 45° they are additionally secured with 50mm (2in) copper nails. It is worth noting that as the water is quickly discharged from a pantiled roof via the corrugations, a very steep pitch may cause the rainwater to overshoot the gutter. In some old roofs, this was acknowledged by covering the lower slopes with plain tiles or slates to allow the water to spread. However, pantiles may safely be laid to a pitch as low as 30°. The headlap of pantiling is from 75–87mm (3–3½in), the sidelap being 50mm (2in). To resist the penetration of wind-blown rain, the side lap of each tile must always be pointed up with mortar.

To those contemplating reroofing an existing structure with pantiles, it should be stressed that the method is really suitable only for use on simple roofs, owing to its relatively bold scale and rigid lines. It does not lend itself to a roof cut up by numerous projections, necessitating valleys which are awkward to form. Hips are not easily formed and pantiling is most compatible with gables terminating in parapets. The conventional half-round ridge is a shape which perfectly complements pantiles. Because of the wavy line of the tiles, the ridge tiles rest only on the rolls, leaving a hollow at each furrow which has to be filled up. This is traditionally achieved by bedding graded strips of plain tile in mortar, more of which is used to seal each hollow completely (Fig 74).

No eaves doubling course is required in a pantiled roof, and because of the bold profile of the tiles, flashings of the roof covering against parapets or chimney stacks are better formed with mortar fillets – supplemented if necessary

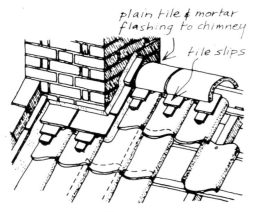
plain tile & mortar flashing to chimney
tile slips

Fig 74

with plain tiles and pieces of waste tile – than sheet metal.

SHINGLES

Wooden shingles have been used to some extent for roofing in the British Isles, particularly for the cladding of small spires, turrets and the roofs of garden buildings. They are widely used as a roof covering in Canada and the USA. Shingles are made by sawing and splitting wood, cleft shingles being preferable to sawn shingles, as the operation of splitting ensures continuous fibres throughout the length of the shingle and this results in maximum durability. In Britain, shingles were traditionally of oak and this material gives a fairly watertight covering. In America, red cedar, white cedar, cypress and white pine are woods which convert well into shingles. Red cedar shingles are increasingly used in the UK.

Ordinarily, shingles are 400–450mm (15¾–18in) or 600–675mm (23½–26½in) long, and range in width from 75–175–250mm (3–7–10in). Thin shingles measure 10mm (½in) thick at the bottom and reduce to 2mm (1/16in) at the upper end. English oak shingles are 300–400mm (12–15¾in) long and 100–200mm (4–8in) wide. It is not uncommon to find a consistent treble thickness of shingles on roofs in exposed locations, the lap being the distance the shingle extends over the third one below it. Where a thickness of two shingles only is adopted, as is general in Britain, the gauge is obtained in the same way as that in plain tiling, being half the difference between the lap and the length of a shingle.

Shingles may be laid above the two types of pitched-roof construction most suitable for slates; battens nailed through bituminous felt into the rafters, or battens fixed to counter-battens which are nailed through the felt into boarding laid on the rafters. It is not advisable to omit the battens or the counter-battens in the second system of construction, as some circulation of air below the shingles is essential if premature rotting is to be avoided. Where shingles are laid on battens without boarding, one to three roof boards should be laid along the eaves and valleys to receive a few of the first courses of shingles. The purpose of these boards is to protect the shingles if it is necessary to walk along the eaves to make repairs. The eaves course of the shingles should be doubled

90

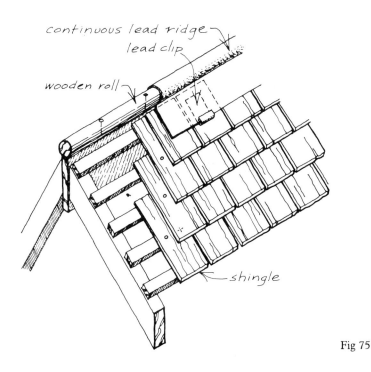

continuous lead ridge

lead clip

wooden roll

shingle

Fig 75

and they should overlap the gutter by about 40mm (1½in). Each shingle is fastened with two non-ferrous nails at a point about 50mm (2in) above the upper line of exposure. In this way, the heads of the nails are protected by the laps, and the shingles are further secured by the nails of each succeeding course passing through the heads of the previous course (Fig 75). Steel nails, even if galvanised, should never be used for fixing oak shingles, as the wood contains an acid which will readily attack the iron and its zinc coating.

The durability of shingles is greatly increased by setting them from 5–12mm (⅕–½in) apart. This permits the water to drain off quickly, secures quick drying of the roof, allows for expansion and prevents buckling. Wide shingles demand the use of a wide joint, while the joints may be made as narrow as 3mm (⅛in) if small units are employed.

Conventional double-pitched roofs clad in shingles usually include two further features which require special treatment.

Ridge Probably the most durable ridge detail is obtained by using a wooden roll covered in metal in the same way as the lead-clad ridge roll which appears at the apex of some slated roofs. In this case, the ridge board is carried up slightly above the shingles, and a wooden roll is

well spiked to the ridge. After the shingles are laid, the roll is covered with lead extending about 150mm (6in) down the shingles on each side. To prevent the metal being lifted by the wind, clips are formed from slips of lead about 150mm (6in) long and 65mm (2½in) wide which are nailed at 600mm (23½in) intervals along the roof under the flashing, and then turned up and dressed about 25mm (1in) over the 'free' edge (Fig 75).

Hips and Valleys In the construction of hips, a metal-covered roll similar to a ridge roll may be used, and a sheet metal valley gutter suitable for other tile-type roof coverings can be used in valleys. However, the use of sheet metal soakers below carefully mitred shingles on hips and valleys, if carried out in the way already described under Slating, will provide a weather-tight detail. In the USA tin is favoured for this purpose and for the finish of ridge and hip rolls. Where oak shingles are used in restoration work, zinc should on no account be used for soakers because it will react adversely with the timber.

THATCH

Though the principle is not at first apparent, the countless straws or reeds of a thatched roof exclude the weather by exactly the same method of the overlap of small units as do roofs of slates, stone slates, tiles and shingles.

Thatch acts as excellent thermal insulation, ensuring warmth in winter and coolness in summer, but it is subject to damage from birds and represents a considerable fire risk, as thatched-house dwellers will know from their insurance premiums! Thus it is confined to rural areas and although it is very rarely used to roof modern houses, because of its picturesque properties it was sometimes employed as the roof finish of nineteenth-century country dwellings.

A roof is prepared to receive thatching by nailing to the rafters wooden battens at 200mm (8in) centres. The thatching is commenced at the eaves and is laid in courses or 'lanes' from eaves to ridge, each lane being about 750mm (29½in) wide. Bundles of straw or reed about 80–100mm (3–4in) thick are laid on the battens and are secured to them with tarred rope yarn drawn by a thatcher's needle. The yarn is tied around the battens or hung on to them with thatching hooks which are tied to the head of each bundle. Starting at eaves level at the right-hand gable, the bundles are laid to the full thickness of 300–375mm (12–15in) until the lane reaches the ridge. After two or three lanes have been put on, they are interlaced with 'withes' or reeds forced diagonally through the bundles of thatch in a 'criss-cross' pattern. The ends of the withes are bound together and nailed to the rafters or tied to the battens with yarn. After a 3m (10ft) width of thatch has been laid, hazel rods are run through the thatch at 600mm (23½in) centres on lines parallel to the eaves. These rods or 'runners' are secured by looping the withes over them and nailing their ends to the rafters with iron pegs. Where old thatch is to be renewed, all the loose and rotten straw and moss is combed out, and if the decay is restricted to small areas of the roof these can be repaired by patching the surface with new straw. A generally poor surface has to be completely covered with fresh material secured with hazel runners and pegs. To limit the damage which can be caused by sparrows, a complete covering of galvanized 'chicken wire' netting is sometimes pinned to the finished surface.

Thatch is unsuitable as a covering for roofs of less than 45° pitch. Dormers cannot be satisfactorily formed in the material except at the main roof verge, where the characteristic 'eyebrow' profile of thatch sweeping over a dormer naturally results. The verge cannot project far and the straw must be raked to project diagonally outwards from the roof slope. After trimming, the straw at the verge needs to be well secured with rods or twine, since thatched roofs are particularly prone to stripping in high winds and the verges are the most exposed features. If well laid and carefully maintained, moisture rarely penetrates thatch, though the collection of the rainwater which drains from the top layers of straw can be difficult to achieve as the great thickness of straw at the eaves and the deep eaves projection of the material (450–600mm [18–23½in] should be achieved) rules out the fitting of a conventional 'half-round' gutter. For this reason, gutters, if used, tend to be continuous, deep, V-shaped hardwood troughs, though it is common to omit the gutter, drainage on the line where the rainwater drops on to the ground below being achieved via a 75mm (3in) or 100mm (4in) diameter land drain with open joints, embedded in a trench filled with broken brick or clean coarse gravel, and surfaced with garden earth.

RESTORING PITCHED ROOFS WITH NEW MATERIALS
A good deal has been said about the restoration of roofs with traditional materials. There are additionally some modern materials which can provide durable roof surfaces of reasonably 'period' appearance.

Asbestos cement slates
Asbestos cement slates have been used for roofing since Edwardian times, though the earliest application of the material (which produced a pink, diagonally gridded roof plane susceptible to disfiguration from algae growth) seems to have been as a roof covering for sports pavilions and similar 'temporary' buildings of lightweight construction. In recent years, asbestos cement slates have been used increasingly as a material for replacing roof surfaces of decaying natural slate. The arrangement of bond, lap and nail fixing for these slates is exactly the same as that for natural slates, but because the asbestos cement sheets are much lighter in weight than the quarried material, the tail of each slate has to be restrained against stripping by the wind. This is usually achieved by locating a disc-headed

copper rivet in the narrow joint between the slates of the course below and hooking the lug of this rivet through the top slate via a hole provided for this purpose. An alternative system for securing the tails of the slates which has recently become available relies on a bent metal clip, which 'ties' the underside of each slate to the fixing batten below. A similar system has long been in use in Europe as a means of fixing quarried slate, but the host of shiny metal clips which consequently appear on the newly slated roof may contrast strongly with the roofing material, contradicting the aim of obtaining a uniform appearance.

All the ridge and hip details suited to natural slate may be used with the synthetic substitute, and the half-round or tapering semi-cone-shaped ridge and hip tiles which are available in matching asbestos cement are specifically designed for use in these locations. However, mitred cutting of the slates is difficult because asbestos cement is a brittle material, and though it will snap cleanly on a line at right angles to the edge of the slate if the surface has been scored with a sharp knife first, the forming of irregular shapes is successfully achieved only by sawing, and the practical objection to this is the health hazard posed by inhalation of the resulting dust. Even if they can be successfully formed in this way, it may be difficult to obtain secure fixings for the resulting irregularly shaped slates where they are applied to a hip.

Though the natural colour of asbestos cement is grey, a blue-black coating is applied to most of the commercially available slates so that a reasonable approximation to the colour of Welsh slate is achieved. This shiny coating distinguishes the material from the matt surface of natural slate. However, following a few years' exposure to the polluted atmosphere of cities, the surface begins to resemble that of natural slate.

Asbestos cement slates are readily available in the two sizes most common in natural slate used on houses: the 'Countess', of 250mm × 500mm (10in × 19½in), and the 'Duchess', of 300mm × 600mm (12in × 23½in). They are normally guaranteed to last for thirty years, which is the minimum life of a clay plain-tiled roof.

Concrete Tiles

The familiar profiles of clay plain tiles, pantiles and indeed large natural slates, are reproduced in a modern roofing material which predominates today – plain and interlocking concrete tiles.

With the exception of stone slates, concrete tiles are the heaviest generally available pitched-roof covering. The slate-like product was the first of the interlocking types to be introduced, and it can be laid to a roof pitch as low as 17½°. The flat top surface of these tiles, or 'interlocking slates', has a matt finish similar to that of natural slate, but the machine-made appearance of each unit and its inevitably fat profile where its full thickness is exposed at an oversailing verge, detracts from a close resemblance to the favourite Victorian roofing material. Being a concrete or 'reconstructed stone' product, the tile will remain in place by its own weight on a roof of low pitch, and nailing may not be needed. Thus such tiles are quick and simple to lay. The bolder, corrugated or 'pantile' profiles which are also available are only suitable for more steeply pitched roofs, and a proportion of these tiles will need to be nailed, rather than simply located on the battens. It is certain that the pantile-profile tiles more closely resemble the clay products on which their design is based than does the flat variety the slated surface it aims to reproduce, but the ribbed or corrugated types have to be accepted as a frankly modern system of roofing, as they bear only a slight resemblance to the clay plain tiling to which their colour relates. A reasonably convincing copy of Cotswold stone slate or North Country roofing is also achievable through the medium of 'reconstructed stone' concrete tiles, which have been moulded to give a markedly 'rustic' shape and surface texture. Concrete tiles which reproduce the appearance of clay plain tiles are the same size as the clay product (267mm × 165mm [10½in × 6½in]) and are fixed in exactly the same way.

Because of the enormous weight of the concrete covering, a careful assessment of the capability of an existing roof structure to accept the increased load must be made. In the mid-1970s one inner London borough was experiencing annually some twenty roof collapses in houses where the original slates had been replaced by concrete tiles, and no attempt had been made to strengthen the roof structures. If such a change of roof covering is planned for any older house, it is advisable firstly to obtain the opinion of an architect, structural engineer or building surveyor on the suitability of the existing structure to accept the increased load.

Most manufacturers of concrete tiles offer the standard tile as part of a complete roofing system, so that special verge and valley tiles as well as ridge and hip tiles compatible with the standard product are readily available.

Bituminous Felt

The underslating felt which should always be installed below the battens or counter-battens of any pitched roof clad in tiles is a less durable version of the bituminous felt, which is sometimes used to finish small areas of flat roof and the pitched roofs of ancillary buildings such as garden sheds. This stouter variety of felt usually has a granular surface, which may be green or red if it is not the blue-black natural colour. To be reasonably durable it should be consistently three layers thick, with flashings into any adjoining masonry and saddle-section ridge cappings being formed in additional thicknesses of the same material. It suffers the limitation of all continuous sheet materials in that it is likely to be badly affected by climatic extremes; contraction or expansion of the felt or the boarding on which it is laid eventually causes blisters or fractures in the felt, which will open up and admit rainwater or melted snow to the roof boarding below. For this reason, felt should only be regarded as a means of covering house roofs temporarily, pending the application of more permanent materials. The increasingly unattractive appearance of ageing felt roofs supports this recommendation.

Bituminous Wash

Slated roof surfaces which appear to have been coated with grey or matt-black paint are a common sight in areas of Victorian housing. They result from the adoption of an expedient which attempts to defer the 'evil day' of reroofing – the application of bitumen-based paint to the surface of the slates with the intention of rendering a decaying roof surface weathertight. It will be appreciated that an advantage of any tiled roof covering is its capacity to tolerate thermal movement in the structure, because the roofing units are able to slide backwards and forwards over each other. Once covered with a continuous skin of paint which does not match its flexibility, this

property of the slating is negated and the extremes of temperature experienced in Britain over a year will open up hair cracks in the paint surface, drawing water by capillary action on to the increasingly porous surface of the slates. The rainwater will collect at particular points from which it was formerly able to drain away, and if these spots coincide with decaying and delaminating slates, it will penetrate the roof. Therefore the application of bituminous paint to slating may actually accelerate the decay of the roof covering and its use cannot be recommended if a long-term repair is sought.

Corrugated Sheet Materials

Although it is usually associated with industrial buildings, corrugated asbestos sheeting provides a cheap and watertight roof covering. Like its predecessor, corrugated iron (against the use of which the Victorian artist, craftsman and poet, William Morris, was in constant complaint), corrugated asbestos bears no resemblance to traditional materials, and it may make a particularly unpleasant impact on a rural landscape. Less objectionable in this respect is clear corrugated pvc, which is easily obtainable through most DIY stores; it is easy to cut and fix (though it becomes brittle when continuously exposed to sunlight) and is much used for the roofing of outhouses. It cannot be recommended for the recovering of large areas of house roofs in exposed locations, because it is a lightweight material prone to stripping in high winds. Since it is brittle, like corrugated asbestos it will not tolerate access for maintenance unless roof ladders are used to spread the weight of workmen and materials across the supporting structure. Plainly, its suitability for weatherproofing Victorian structures permanently is very limited.

Sheet Metal Roof Coverings

Apart from thatch and the tile-type roof coverings (slates, stone slates, tiles, shingles and pantiles), the third main roofing technique practised in the nineteenth century and still in use today is the cladding of structures with malleable metal sheeting. In Victorian times, lead and copper were the materials commonly employed, but zinc grew in popularity with the arrival of the twentieth century, not least because it was cheaper than the other metals. However, it weathers to a rusty colour which is

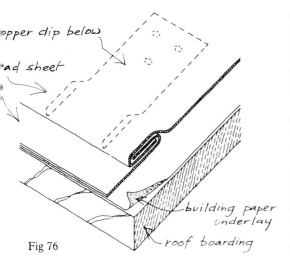

opper clip below

ad sheet

building paper
underlay

roof boarding

Fig 76

sheets of metal together). A secure fixing of the metal to its substratum is guaranteed by folding into each welt at 600mm (23½in) intervals copper clips about 120mm (4¾in) long and 50mm (2in) wide, which are nailed to the roof boarding (Fig 76).

The remainder of the details familiar in the sheet-metal cladding of cupolas, domes and turrets are also used in the flat roof installations and are described in the following section.

Flat Roofs
SHEET METAL COVERINGS

It is an advantage of sheet metal roof coverings that they can be laid to the very low pitches (12° and below) classified by the Victorians as 'flat' roofs.

Where copper is used on flat roofs, roll joints are generally adopted. Copper clips about 190mm (7½in) long and 40mm (1½in) wide are nailed to the roof boarding at 900mm (35in) intervals below the line of a timber roll of tapering section, the roll being about 32mm (1¼in) wide at the top, 40mm (1½in) high and 40mm (1½in) wide at its base. The edges of the copper sheets are then turned up against the roll on each side, and the clips are bent down and turned over these edges. The roll joint is completed by the addition of a continuous copper cap which has stopped ends where the roll is not terminated against a vertical surface. Alternatively, the sheets flanking the tapering sides of this 'batten roll' can be flanged over at the top parallel to the roof surface (Fig 77). A prepared capping strip is then folded and slipped over these two flanges, and the whole assembly is dressed down the sides of the roll. The joints of sheets which lie in the path of

not nearly so attractive as the whitish patina which forms on lead, or the brilliant blue-green of oxidising copper.

Sheet metal is most conspicuous as the roof covering of those cupolas and turrets of Victorian houses and commercial buildings which are either too small or too awkwardly shaped to take a tiled or shingled finish. Copper is marginally better than lead as a covering for steeply pitched roofs and domes as it remains static in such locations, whilst lead will tend to creep under its own weight and the expansion and contraction induced by exposure to widely varying temperatures (sheet copper is about one-sixth of the weight of sheet lead of equivalent durability). Where copper is laid on pitched roofs of any shape, allowance for expansion and contraction of the metal is made by joining the sheets with flattened welts (joints formed by folding the edges of neighbouring

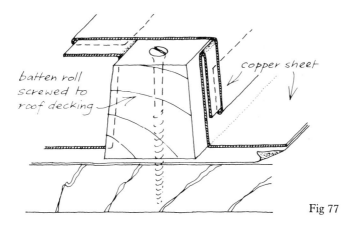

batten roll
screwed to
roof decking

copper sheet

Fig 77

draining rainwater are made with a double-lock cross welt. Where the sheets meet brickwork at their upper ends, they are turned up the wall surface below a copper flashing built into the wall surface. The junctions of rolls with the wall are capped by purpose-made copper saddle pieces.

Copper may also be laid on flat roofs with its joints formed as flattened welts or standing seams. It is difficult to guarantee the water-tightness of flattened welts where they run counter to the slope of the roof, and standing seams (similar to flattened welts, but allowed to project up from the general roof surface) cannot be used on flat roofs where much maintenance traffic is expected, because they are easily damaged. When renewing copper roofs it is important to obtain a perfectly level surface of the substratum as any projecting nail heads in the boarding may eventually punch through the copper sheet. Above the boarding a continuous layer of brown flax felt or building paper should be laid to lessen the possibility of 'wearing' in the sheet metal on top, as it expands and contracts.

The same care in the preparation of the sub-surface is essential in the renewal of *lead* flat roofs. This material is probably the metal most widely used for covering small roofs over bays and dormer windows and at the junction of pitched roofs, as well as for flashing pitched roof surfaces to adjacent parapets, dormers and chimney stacks.

Lead sheet is available in two forms, cast lead and milled lead. Though cast lead is difficult to obtain today, it was a familiar roofing material in the nineteenth century and it is more durable than the milled variety. As it is cast in sheets from the molten metal, it is not a consistent thickness. It may contain flaws and sand holes which make it unsuitable as a covering for steeply pitched roofs.

Lead is still specified by its weight in pounds per square foot, although '5lb' lead may be termed 'Code 5' lead and so on. The weight of lead sheet commonly used for flashings, soakers and roof coverings varies between 4lb and 8lb per square foot, the heavier weights naturally being more durable. As lead sheet expands or contracts considerably with changes of temperature, the length of any one piece used for a gutter lining or flat roof covering should not exceed 2.7m (9ft) and the fall of a gutter or flat

should not be less than 25mm (1in) in 2.7m (9ft). If the pitch of a 'flat' roof exceeds 75mm (3in) in 3m (10ft), there is a danger that the lead will 'creep' down the slope, and if there is a rise in temperature, a lead sheet covering a pitched roof will expand, but will not contract to its former length when the temperature drops; this permanent stretching will eventually produce cracks in the surface.

As milled lead sheet is normally only available in rolls 600mm (23½in) wide and the maximum recommended length of sheets between joints is 2.7m (9ft), there are very few lead roofs which can be renewed without forming joints between adjacent sheets. The joints fall into two categories: those sited across the flow of water (lap and drip joints) and those parallel with the flow of water (rolls, hollow rolls, seams or welts). Like copper, lead sheets may be joined with flat welts or seams. These are made by fixing lead or copper clips at about 600mm (23½in) intervals at the junctions of the sheets. One sheet is bent up against the clip which is hooked over it, and the adjoining sheet is bent over both as an 'overcloak'. This profile is then folded flat on to the lead roof surface. On flat roofs such welts are not as good as rolls.

Wooden rolls for lead coverings are made round or 'loaf shaped' in section, in contrast to the tapering profile of copper rolls. Usually

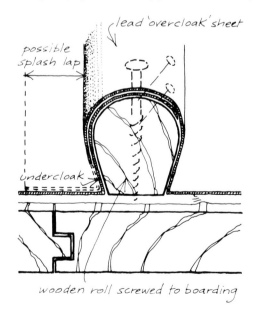

Fig 78

they are about 50mm (2in) in diameter, and are best installed at the joint of sheets by screw fixings into the roof decking (invariably rough boarding in Victorian construction). The sheet lead is then dressed around the roll and tucked well into the angles to obtain a firm grip. This lower sheet or undercloak is dressed to half the height of the roll, and tapered off with a rasp to a fine edge. The sheet is then nailed to the roll along this edge, and the upper sheet or overcloak is dressed completely over the roll and its partial lead covering to finish on a line on the flat, about 38mm (1½in) on the opposite side of the roll (Fig 78). However, this narrow extension of the lead on to the roof surface is sometimes omitted, for if snow is likely to lie for long upon the roof, it is possible that the water will be drawn up over the roll between overcloak and undercloak by capillary action. To avoid this circumstance, the overcloak may be dressed over only about three-quarters of the roll. In either case, the free edge of lead should be on that side of the roll which is *not* exposed to the prevailing wind (south-west in England).

Rolls without a wooden core – hollow rolls – have been extensively used for centuries on steeply pitched roofs of churches, and they may be encountered on porch roofs of nineteenth-century houses. They are made by fixing to the boarding with two brass screws a lead or copper clip every 600mm (23½in). The edges of each lead sheet are turned up the clip in exactly the same way that a seam or welt is formed, but the greater depth of material allows the combined thicknesses of lead to be formed into a hollow cylinder. Although this produces a watertight detail, obtaining a consistent thickness in the completed rolls may be a result achieveable only by a highly skilled plumber! Because they are fragile, hollow rolls are unsuitable for use on flat roofs where even infrequent foot traffic is anticipated. Rolls of both types are usually sited at about 500mm (19½in) intervals, a spacing determined by the standard width of mass-produced milled lead sheet.

Lap joints should not be found on flat roofs, for good practice restricts them to horizontal joints on the inclined surfaces of lead-covered pitched roofs. Where a steep pitch is lead covered and a small lap of sheets (say 100mm [4in]) is sufficient to keep the surface watertight, lead clips fixed to the boarding and sited at 600mm (23½in) intervals are used to restrain the edge of the lap, because high winds put sheet roof coverings at risk. Shallower roof pitches call for correspondingly deeper laps to resist water penetration by capillarity and an uneconomical use of lead naturally results. The

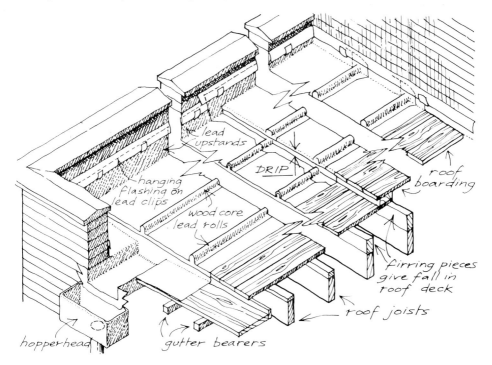

lead upstands

DRIP

roof boarding

hanging flashing on lead clips

wood core lead rolls

firring pieces give fall in roof deck

roof joists

hopperhead

gutter bearers

Fig 79

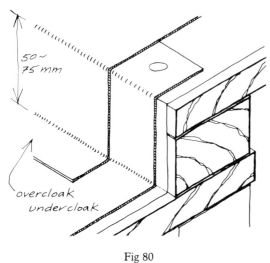

50 ~
75 mm

overcloak
undercloak

Fig 80

problem of joining adjacent lengths of lead sheets in long gutters and large flat roofs is overcome by treating the area as a number of plane surfaces, slightly inclined and raised a little one above the other, forming a number of low steps called drips which should not be at a greater distance than 2.2m (7ft) apart (Fig 79). Drips are commonly 50mm (2in) high, though 75mm (3in) is better to resist thoroughly water penetration by capillarity. Thus a drip joint is simply a lap joint with a step built into it (Fig 80). Where the step in the roof decking is less than 50mm (2in), a groove should be formed in the vertical surface before the lead is dressed over. If this anti-capillarity groove is omitted from a shallow drip, water will be drawn between the lap, leading to rotting of the woodwork.

Where flat roofs terminate above vertical surfaces, the lead covering may be formed in a

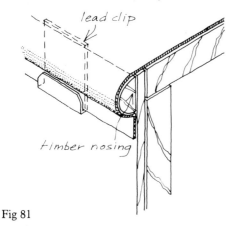

lead clip

timber nosing

Fig 81

nosing, which allows the metal to shrink or expand freely. This can be achieved by nailing a half-round timber moulding on to the vertical surface. The horizontal leadwork is then dressed around the moulding, and the flange forming its underside is secured against the wind with lead clips (Fig 81). Alternatively, a welt may be formed as the nosing at the top of the vertical surface. In this case, lead or copper clips must be folded into the welt and must be fixed to the edge of the roof decking to anchor the joint of the sheets. Where the lead flat roof abuts a wall surface, the roofing sheets are turned up against the masonry and masked by a flashing installed in a horizontal brickwork joint with lead wedges. In exposed locations it is also necessary to secure the underside of this cover flashing with lead clips at regular intervals. It is now possible to obtain from most DIY stores thin lead sheet in a roll which is bonded to a bitumen adhesive. This material has done much to simplify the installation of flashings and gutter repairs, but it will *not* endure for the sixty to eighty years normal for the pure metal where it is correctly installed.

The third sheet metal covering which achieved some popularity even in the nineteenth century is *zinc*. It is lighter and cheaper than either copper or lead, but will not last so long. In polluted industrial areas it may be good for only twenty years, though forty years is its usual lifespan under average conditions. An important, if rather comical fact, is that it is quickly corroded by cat's urine, so that zinc-covered flat roofs should be inaccessible for these pets! Zinc sheet is less liable to expand than lead, but it moves more than copper, and this property is acknowledged in its detailing. No 14 gauge zinc is the minimum grade used for roofing, and joints between sheets on flat roofs are formed in the roll-cap system (similar to the batten-roll method of laying copper roofs) or with standing seams. This latter method is much more popular in Europe than the UK, and it is more sensible for pitched roofs than flats because of the risk of damage to the seams from maintenance traffic. In the treatment of roll ends and corners, the most important difference between zinc and lead is that zinc can be bent but not 'bossed' (formed to a domed shape) or dressed into corners. When the work is done by the plumber, the angles are usually cut and soldered. 'Soldered shields' are used to

Fig 82

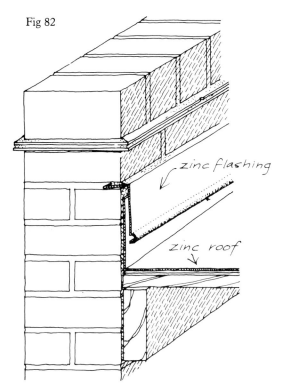

zinc flashing

zinc roof

foot traffic. For this reason, asphalt was adopted as a finish for the flat roofs of many city buildings and it also provides the roof surface of many bays, porches and other small, flat-roofed extensions of older houses.

Rock asphalt consists of rock impregnated with a natural pitch called bitumen. The asphalt used for roofing is mastic asphalt and it may consist of a mixture of rock asphalt imported from Europe and bitumen-rich Trinidad lake asphalt from the Caribbean. Asphalt is laid hot in at least two layers to a total thickness of 20mm (¾in) or 25mm (1in). If it is carefully installed, it forms a sound and substantial covering for flat roofs. It can also be used on vertical or sloping surfaces, and it is conventional to form skirtings to an asphalt flat in the material itself. Where the asphalt is turned up against an abutting wall surface, its thickness must be increased to three coats, in order to guard against splitting. The particular risk posed by a right-angled junction with a flank wall is nowadays avoided by installing a

clad the roll ends, and saddle pieces similar to those employed with copper sheet are used where walls abut vertical surfaces. Elsewhere, soldering should be avoided as it may restrict the capacity of the zinc to move without fracturing. As zinc sheet can be obtained up to 900mm (35in) wide, the rolls on which it is joined may be spaced further apart than those used with lead. Drips can be spaced as much as 2.8m (9ft) apart, and hanging flashings of the roof covering against perimeter walls, which are also carried out in zinc, differ only from lead detail in that the underside of the metal is turned into a 'bead' to stiffen the edge (Fig 82). Because zinc sheet is quite thin, and retains precisely any shape to which it is formed, it is often used for soakers below hips of slate roofs and under mortar flashings masking the joint of slating with parapets and chimney stacks. Its susceptibility to early deterioration in city atmospheres suggests that outworn zinc soakers should be replaced by sheet-lead flashings.

ASPHALT

Even in Victorian times, it was appreciated that sheet-metal coverings were unsuitable for flat roofs over which there was likely to be much

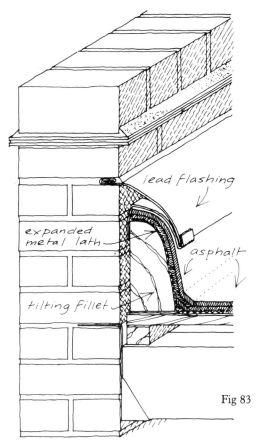

lead flashing

expanded metal lath

asphalt

tilting fillet

Fig 83

triangular bitumen fillet against a timber curb clad with expanded metal, over which the asphalt is carried to terminate in a 'sliding' joint below a continuous lead flashing built into the adjacent wall (Fig 83). The problem posed by laying asphalt on deep vertical surfaces or sloping planes is the tendency of the material to creep under its self-weight – a characteristic which is heightened by its exposure to sunlight. Such movement will eventually result in splits in the surface which will admit water. On flat surfaces this problem is minimised by laying light-reflective white limestone chippings across the asphalted area, but this solution cannot be adopted on sloping sections or on roofs which regularly carry foot traffic. A special solar-reflective paint is sometimes applied to these panels and it undoubtedly increases the lifespan of the material.

One great advantage of asphalt over other forms of 'sheet' roof covering is its tolerance to being 'patched' *in situ*. Small repairs may be made to a damaged surface by flooding the affected area with molten asphalt after the defective section has been cut out. The eventual physical breakdown of the material is delayed by careful preparation of the substratum, and it has always been safer to lay asphalt on roofs of solid construction (such as concrete or stone slabs) than on boarding. Where an asphalt roof on boarding is to be renewed, the level boarded surface *must* be covered with bituminous felt before the asphalt is applied. The felt acts as a membrane which isolates movement in the boards from the asphalt, the natural elasticity of which may not be sufficient to absorb such movement. Where the asphalt meets vent pipes or other features which project above the roof surface, it is dressed around the projection in the manner of an asphalt skirting, but the top of the asphalt must be shielded, and this is done by fixing a metal collar to the projection which masks the joint of the different materials.

BITUMINOUS FELT

Bituminous felt is often used to provide the finish for new flat roofs, or the new surface of old roofs. The limitations of the material have been discussed in the earlier section on 'Restoring Pitched Roofs with New Materials' (p92), but it is only fair to state that the tendency of felt fixed to a flat roof surface to stretch, deform and puncture with continuous exposure to the weather is much less marked than where it is applied to a pitched roof, because the essential precaution of covering the felt on a flat with light- and heat-reflective stone chippings minimises thermal movement. To stabilise further the condition of the finish, it is advisable also to ventilate the substratum on which it is laid, so that a fairly consistent temperature and moisture content is maintained within the decking. This accounts for the colony of small, plastic, mushroom-shaped ventilators which are sometimes seen 'sprouting' from felted flat roofs. A good specification and careful workmanship are the best guarantees of durability, particularly in the case of three-layer felt flat roofs.

Flat roofs finished in sheet metal or asphalt, which are materials tolerant of thermal movement, are also prone to the internal deterioration which sometimes befalls felted flat roofs. The incorrect positioning of the impervious vapour barrier, or worse still, its omission, may cause an increase in the moisture content of the timber decking, which creates conditions conducive to dry rot with disastrous consequences for the entire building construction. Opinions differ on the best position for the vapour barrier, but it would seem safest to locate it on the warm side of the roof insulation. Where an existing flat roof construction is being relined internally, a vapour barrier is very simply installed by utilising aluminium-foil-backed plasterboard for the new ceiling.

5
Internal Floors

The damp-proofing of cellar walls and floors was a subject which engaged the interest of the Victorians, as much as it preoccupies today's owners of nineteenth-century houses. A favourite method for excluding damp involved laying 75–100mm (3–4in) of broken brick or stone over the newly excavated ground. The whole area was then covered with a 75mm (3in) thick layer of concrete. When the concrete was dry, it was covered with a 13mm (½in) layer of asphalt which was carried through the enclosing walls, then up the outside of the wall against the earth and back through the wall to form a damp-proof course above the ground level. (Fig 84).

Clearly, this is quite a sophisticated form of construction, and most Victorian domestic basements relied only on the concrete or an equally thin layer of stone slabs as a protection against dampness from the ground. It was hoped that external walls one-and-a-half bricks thick (327mm [13in]) would resist water incursion around the sides. Without the asphalt there can be no guarantee of watertight construction.

GROUND FLOORS

The difficulty of damp-proofing floors next to the ground was acknowledged in nineteenth-century construction by the almost universal adoption of timber for the floor structure, positioned over a layer of concrete (intended to keep the damp out) with an airspace in between. This ground layer was normally 150mm (6in) thick, and the underside of the ground-floor joists was generally at least 300mm (12in) above its top surface. This applied because of the location of the damp-proof course; to ensure that ground water or rainwater splashing up around the building's perimeter did not penetrate the outer walls, the

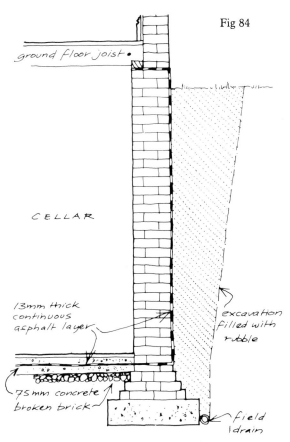

Fig 84

ground floor joist.

CELLAR

13mm thick continuous asphalt layer

excavation filled with rubble

75mm concrete
broken brick

field drain

damp-proof course was ideally sited at least 150mm (6in) above the external ground level. As the airspace between the floor joists and the ground level must be ventilated to prevent damp and a stagnant atmosphere congenial to dry rot, the ventilation ducts installed in the external walls were located above the damp-proof course and below the timber wall plate supporting the ends of the floor joists (Fig 85). A high void or crawl space underneath the suspended floor resulted.

The wall plate was commonly sited on a ledge

101

Internal Floors

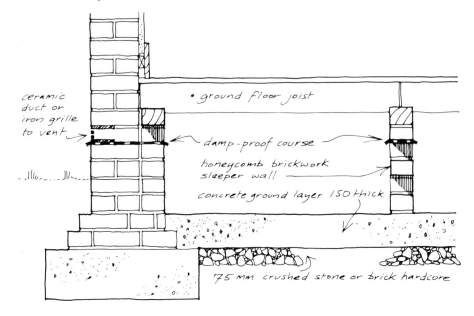

ceramic duct or iron grille to vent

ground floor joist

damp-proof course

honeycomb brickwork sleeper wall

concrete ground layer 150 thick

75 mm crushed stone or brick hardcore

Fig 85

on the inner surface of the external wall, because the wall construction at this low level was 112mm (4½in) (half-a-brick) thicker than the remainder of the wall. Below floors of large rooms it was often necessary to install intermediate supports for the joists at, say, 3m (10ft) intervals, and these were provided by sleeper walls of single-skin 'honeycomb' brickwork capped with timber wall plates. Gaps were left between the individual bricks of a sleeper wall, giving a honeycomb appearance, to allow air movement through the whole of the underfloor void. In cheaply constructed houses, it is often found that the concrete ground-layer has been omitted from the sub-floor construction, and the sleeper walls turn out to be founded on brick rubble. Providing the wooden floor is raised sufficiently over generally dry ground, the omission of the concrete should not cause problems.

The suspended timber ground floor invites difficulties other than the possible establishment of dry rot encouraged by poor ventilation. The airspace below the boards is a favourite nesting place and route for rodents invading the premises from the garden or neighbouring properties. The airspace is also a source of draughts because a stratum of cold air is continuously present below heated rooms, and the cold air is exchanged for the warm air through gaps between the floorboards and skirtings. In a thorough renovation of a Victorian house, it is

worth contemplating insulating a draughty, suspended-floor construction by taking up all the boards and stapling plasticised wire garden netting into the sides of the floor joists so that a comprehensive mesh layer is obtained below the floor level. A continuous glass-fibre quilt is then laid between the joists on top of this netting and the floor boards are relaid on top of the joists. As this procedure often involves the removal and refixing of skirtings, it is worth wedging a foam plastic sealing strip between the boards and the internal wall surface beneath the skirting to discourage draughts further (Fig 86). If dry rot or woodworm has ravaged the floor timbers it is logical to consider the complete replacement of the wooden construction with concrete laid on a continuous polythene damp-proof membrane which must connect with the damp-proof course in the external walls.

Around the turn of the century, it had become clear to some designers of modest houses that there was little merit in complicated suspended ground-floor construction when a solid floor of concrete which obviates draughts could be laid directly on to the ground, its top surface being water-proofed with asphalt before a floor finish of timber boards or a sand/cement screed was applied. In kitchen and hall areas, solid slate slabs or ceramic tiles provided surfaces more impervious to spillages than boarding. By the inter-war period, this type of

102

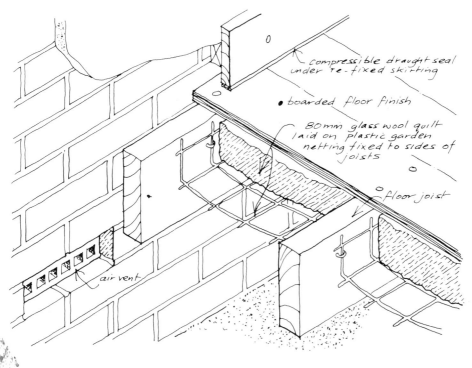

compressible draught seal
under re-fixed skirting

boarded floor finish

80 mm glass wool quilt
laid on plastic garden
netting fixed to sides of
joists

Floor joist

air vent

Fig 86

solid construction had effectively superseded the suspended ground floor in small houses without basements. The air bricks or gratings necessitated by the ventilation of voids below suspended floors which are familiar features of the external walls of Victorian houses were thereby omitted, though they remained a common component of the larder walls in 1930s semi-detached houses.

UPPER FLOORS

Wooden floors are composed of floor boards supported by joists, and in addition to the floor load, they usually carry on their undersides ceilings of plaster and wood. According to the size of the room the upper floor was required to span, it might be *single joisted* or *double joisted*. In the single-joisted floor, the members span the entire distance between the bearing walls and their ends either rest on wall plates bracketed off the walls, or are built into the supporting masonry. In the double-joisted floor, the joists rest on wooden beams or 'binders' which are supported at their ends by the bearing walls.

The joists of a single-joisted floor are usually spaced 350–450mm (14–18in) from centre to centre and generally vary in size from 75mm × 50mm (3in × 2in) to 280mm × 75mm (11in × 3in), though because 'machined' (precisely squared) timber was not generally available until the late nineteenth century, early Victorian houses often incorporated irregularly shaped floor and roof timbers.

Where the joist ends are built into the external wall, a detail common in the best work involved supporting the members on stone templates which are less liable to be crushed or displaced by the loaded joists than common brickwork. However, the danger of damp entering the joist ends through the thin remaining section of external wall is not reduced by this detail. In Chapter 3, *External Walls*, it is stated that outside walls were often reduced in thickness at the top of each storey to provide ledges for the continuous timber wall plates to which the upper floor joists were fixed. Alternatively, wall plates could be bracketed off a wall surface on a continuous brick corbel (an inverted 'stepping out' of brickwork from the wall) or iron angles built into the masonry. Each of these methods more securely insulates the joist ends from damp penetration than 'building-in' and the projecting construction

103

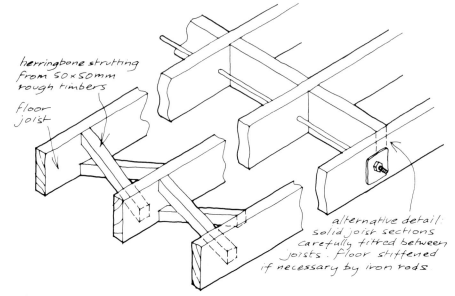

herringbone strutting
from 50×50mm
rough timbers

floor
joist

alternative detail:
solid joist sections
carefully fitted between
joists. floor stiffened
if necessary by iron rods

Fig 87

could be concealed behind the curve of the cornice of the room below the floor being supported.

Floor joists often terminate on internal as well as external brick walls. In this circumstance, a wall plate granting simple timber-to-timber fixings was sited on top of such an internal wall. To 'level up' joists sited on an uneven surface, thin slivers of slate were generally used to 'pack up' low timbers. Wood packings were less satisfactory as they are subject to crushing.

Even if built into the walls, the joists will tend to topple over or curl out of position unless some side restraint is provided and traditionally this was achieved by installing *herringbone strutting* – short struts of timber in section 38mm × 63mm (1½in × 2½in), fixed diagonally between the joists, to which they were nailed (Fig 87). Scrap wood was often used for this detail, but a quicker method which required accuracy from the carpenter was to fix short lengths of joist tightly between the main spans. In either case, the strutting would be installed at about 1500–1800mm (59–71in) intervals along the joists. In small houses, where the floor spans are short (perhaps 3m [10ft]), there may be no strutting to stiffen the joists, but its omission from below small areas of floor will not cause problems. Where floors were required to carry large loads, iron tension rods were sometimes passed through the joists at right angles to them and alongside the solid struts. Tightening up the nuts at the ends of these rods compressed the struts and the floor was thereby stiffened.

A complication in timber floor construction which arises in almost every upper-storey room is the accommodation of the fireplace hearth and its flammable contents in a non-fire-resisting structure. The reconciliation of these apparently incompatible qualities was achieved by forming a zone of floor, clear of all timbers, in front and to the side of the fireplace. This was done by terminating three or four joists on a line about 600mm (23½in) in front of the chimney breast with their ends attached to a trimmer or cross-joist, transferring the load from that area of floor to flanking trimming joists built into brickwork to either side of the chimney breast. These three timbers, framing the void in which the hearth was constructed, were conventionally up to 25mm (1in) thicker than the regular floor joists (Fig 88).

What form of construction then fills the hole between the joists and provides a fireproof hearth? Brickwork was commonly used as the substructure of the hearth in the form of a trimmer arch which spanned between the body of the brickwork of the chimney breast below, through a section of segmental arch, on to a splayed block nailed to the side of the trimmer (Fig 89). On top of this semi-arch some other non-combustible material such as tiles or cement provided a finish level with the floor boards, extending out at least 450mm (18in) in

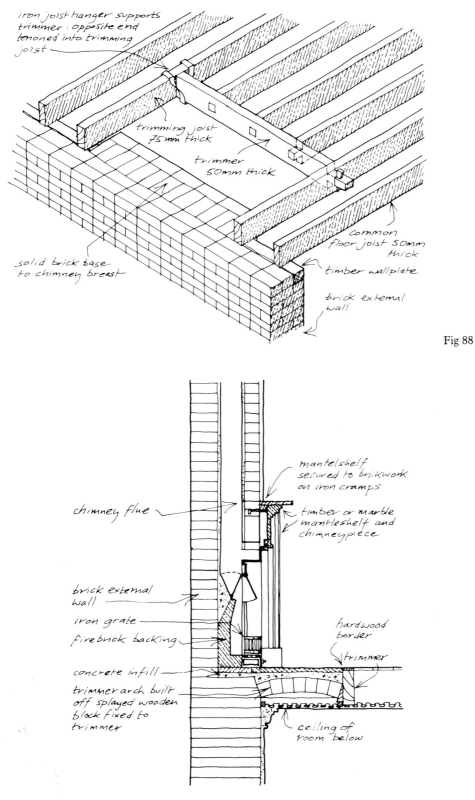

iron joist hanger supports
trimmer: opposite end
tenoned into trimming
joist

trimming joist
75 mm thick

trimmer
50mm thick

solid brick base
to chimney breast

common
floor joist 50mm
thick

timber wallplate

brick external
wall

Fig 88

mantelshelf
secured to brickwork
on iron cramps

chimney flue

timber or marble
mantleshelf and
chimneypiece

brick external
wall

iron grate

firebrick backing

hardwood
border

trimmer

concrete infill

trimmer arch built
off splayed wooden
block fixed to
trimmer

ceiling of
room below

Fig 89

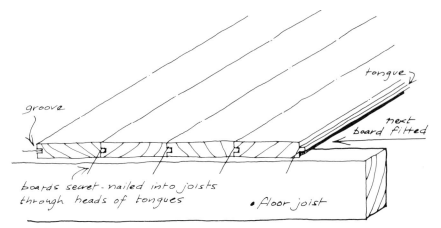

groove

tongue

next
board fitted

boards secret-nailed into joists
through heads of tongues

• floor joist

Fig 90

front of the grate and 150mm (6in) to either side of the fireplace opening. In good-quality construction, a hardwood border was fixed around the hearth to give a neat finish between it and the boards.

The floorboards themselves were of two distinct qualities. A plain, or square-joint floor consists of 'second-quality' boards nailed directly to the joists, each board being 150–250mm (6–10in) wide with a plain, butt joint edge-to-edge with its neighbour. A tongued-and-grooved or matched floor consists of selected material, the joining edges of which have been machine-moulded with a tongue-and-groove profile so that the boards interlock. Such 'T & G' flooring is often 22–29mm (⅞–1⅛in) thick and was always secret-nailed in the original installation. The nails were driven into the upper angle of the tongue (Fig 90), and in hardwood boards they would be punched in so that their heads were well below the surface of the wood. The grooved edge of the next board then covered the tongue, hiding the fixings. Thus only one line of fixings was necessary and fixings through a board's top surface were confined to the 'first and last' boards abutting the walls.

Though 'matched' flooring appealed to the Victorians as a device for excluding draughts, its advantages are much less obvious in the modern home. Because the boards are fixed through their tongues, it is virtually impossible to remove them without damaging these mouldings, and even if the boards are removed intact, their successful reinstatement may be difficult because the tongues tend to deform or splinter as the boards are taken up. Jobs such as

rewiring, or the installation of central heating, which often necessitate the temporary removal of individual boards turn a T & G floor into more of a liability than an asset. On reinstating a previously raised board over a pipe run or cable route, it is advisable firstly to remove the tongue so that the board can function as an easily removed access trap for the future maintenance or replacement of services.

An even more frustrating form of floor decking which may be encountered in the grander Victorian houses is the *double floor* in which a surface of tongue-and-groove boards is laid on top of a plain-boarded substratum. The advantage of such extravagant construction for the builder lay in the opportunity of completing the coarse work such as plastering and the first coats of painting over the plain-boarded sub-floor, which granted easy access to all areas, yet could tolerate damage from this heavy work. The better quality T & G boards would then be laid on top of this sub-floor when the joinery work was in progress. To prevent the shrinkage of the sub-floor from causing open joints in the finished floor, the lower layer of boards was commonly laid diagonally across the joists so that the top layer, laid at right angles to the joists, and nailed to them, was also aligned diagonally to the sub-floor. In this way, shrinkage of the lower boards tended to pull the upper boards together more tightly. In reinstating the top layer of such construction, it is essential to fix the boards through to the joists, not just to the sub-floor boarding, as otherwise future shrinkage of the sub-floor will cause the top layer of boards to buckle and split.

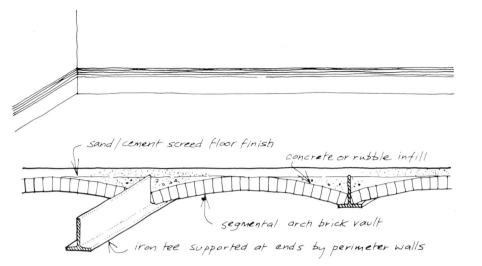

sand/cement screed floor finish

concrete or rubble infill

segmental arch brick vault

iron tee supported at ends by perimeter walls

Fig 91

Brick Jack Arches

Although it is a form of construction more common in commercial buildings than in houses, ground floors spanning basements were sometimes formed from brick vaults or 'jack arches'. The system is similar to the pavement vault construction described in Chapter 2, *Basements*, but the segmental brick vaults were often of smaller span than those used to roof a pavement vault, and they were built side-by-side in a continuous range in order to obtain a soffit as close to a flat plane as possible. This was achieved by arching the brickwork between inverted, cast-iron 'T' sections which spanned between the side walls (Fig 91). The top ground-floor surface was then made level by infilling the spaces over the springing of the arches with rubble and forming a level floor finish in concrete or a sand-and-cement screed.

FLOOR FINISHES

Although in modern construction, solid concrete floors are generally covered with a level sand-and-cement screed 50mm or 75mm (2in or 3in) thick, and it is left to the occupier to provide his own floor finish in the form of a carpet, this was not a practice followed by the Victorians. A wealth of floor finishes was available to them; sometimes the finish was also the floor construction which was intended to keep out rising damp; this applied particularly to stone and slate ground floors. Slabs of stone or slate from 32–63mm (1¼–2½in) thick were simply laid on a roughly level surface with no

damp-proof membrane between the floor finish and the earth. According to the normal condition of the ground, such surfaces may not be affected by dampness, though slate slabs will prove more impervious to rising damp than other types of natural stone. A superior arrangement, incorporating slate as the floor finish, which was adopted in the halls and kitchens of some late Victorian architect-designed houses, placed thick slate slabs on a mortar bedding on continuous 100mm (4in) thick concrete.

Tiles

More popular than natural stones as a floor covering were the many varieties of tiles. The proliferation of small Victorian tileries produced a bewildering variety of tile patterns which it may be difficult, if not impossible, to match with modern products. However, Victorian tiled-floor finishes can be categorized into four main types.

QUARRY TILES

In spite of their title, quarry tiles are *not* quarried from the ground. Like bricks and roofing tiles, they are a fired clay product and the name is probably a corruption of the French word *carré*, meaning 'square'. Like many clay components, they were chiefly manufactured in Staffordshire, though a famous brand of 'Heather Brown' quarries originated at Ruabon in North Wales, where they are still made today. Staffordshire quarries have traditionally been available in red, blue and buff, and they

107

were a favourite floor covering for kitchens, larders and downstairs lavatories. A superior grade of quarry tile which was more carefully shaped and finished than the Staffordshire 'standard' was also used by the Victorians, but contemporary quarries have eroded the former distinction between differing qualities of the material by adhering much more closely to certain standard sizes and thicknesses.

Quarry tiles are normally unglazed, the vitrification caused by the firing process granting them the silky surface finish they normally display. Victorian Staffordshire quarries were commonly 300mm (12in) square and 38mm (1½in) thick, or 215mm (8½in) square, although the 150mm (6in) square size is nowadays the most familiar tile, and in the nineteenth century these were 25mm (1in) thick. Contemporary tiles of this face size are 19mm (¾in) thick. Plain geometrical floor tiles of quarry-tile type came in smaller sizes too: 115mm (4½in) square, 75mm (3in) square, etc, in diagonal halves of these sizes, and in octagons, hexagons and diamond shapes. Rectangular tiles were also made to be used in border strips. Such 'geometrical' tiles were normally 13mm (½in) thick.

From this great variety of types it was possible to form tessellated paving in an almost unlimited range of designs, and patterns unique to individual rooms will be found in expensive Victorian houses.

Modern quarry tiles are laid on a 10mm (⅜in) thick bed of sand and cement mortar on a recently laid 20mm (¾in) thick floor screed of the same mix, on concrete. Alternatively, they can be laid directly on to a firm surface (preferably concrete) with a stiff mortar mix about 16mm (⅝in) thick. A thicker mortar bed will reduce the likelihood of obtaining a level surface in the finished work. Where new tiles are used to replace or extend the area of antique tiles in an existing surface, the width of joint in the old work must be followed, but in entirely new quarry-tiled floors it is advisable to adopt an 8–10mm (⁵⁄₁₆–⅜in) wide joint to conceal small irregularities in the tile shapes. If it is difficult to incorporate a damp-proof membrane below a newly quarry-tiled, ground-floor finish, this is unlikely to invite problems from rising damp, because the tiles are as impervious to ground water as they are to cleaning water. In a modern, centrally heated environment, quarry-tile floors will expand and contract appreciably, so that an expansion joint, filled with cork strip and pointed with polysulphide mastic, at the junction of the tiling with the surrounding walls, reduces the risk of fractures which will trap dirt and draw in moisture.

Quarry tiles were sometimes used as a paving for garden paths and external terraces. Fractured tiles in such locations are as likely to result from severe winter weather as from impact damage from a garden roller, because quarries are not immune from frost attack. Therefore it is wise to restrict the thinner modern tiles to sheltered locations if they are to be used externally. As they are extremely hard and dense, quarries are notoriously difficult to cut. Rather than adopting the laborious technique of 'nibbling' away the excess area of a tile with a hammer and chisel, where many tiles must be cut neatly (as at the edge of a newly laid floor) it is well worth hiring a special tile cutter from a local tool hire service for the purpose.

ENCAUSTIC TILES

This type of tile represented an improvement over quarry tiles for the decoration-conscious Victorians, as it not only contributed to the overall tiling pattern, but also incorporated its own motif. Encaustic tiles were produced by in-laying a pattern of coloured clay in the surface of a tile body of different colour when it was in the clay state. The pattern was then burnt in as part of the tile itself. The surface of the tile thus produced was level and the pattern was generally complete on a single tile, though it could extend over a series; in this way it was possible to achieve a large number of varied designs for differing floor surfaces. *Incised tiling* is a version of the encaustic tile. This variant was made with sunken lines or patterns, which, like the joints between the tiles, were often filled with cement after the tiling was laid.

Encaustic tiles are not now produced in the massive numbers which made them stock items at every Victorian builder's merchant's yard. Though they can be obtained, they are available

Plate 20 In 1976 the main floors of the Smithsonian Institution, Washington, DC, were restored by installing new encaustic tiles which faithfully reproduce the colours and patterning of the original Victorian floor surface (*H. & R. Johnson*)

Internal Floors

only to order. The recent restoration of some spectacular tiled floors in important Victorian public buildings has prompted the small-scale reproduction of replacement patterned tiles, and at least one Midlands manufacturer will produce tiles to match your Victorian originals, though the cost will far exceed that of modern patterned ceramic tiles! (Plate 20).

CERAMIC MOSAIC

Mosaic paving in which the small elements, or *tesserae*, composing the design are made of clay is distinguished from marble mosaic and vitreous mosaic (where the paving material is glass) by the title *ceramic mosaic.*

'Roman' ceramic mosaic comprised 13mm (½in) tile cubes which were laid in succession, or in a series of concentric arcs. This was accomplished either by placing the tesserae one by one in position on a prepared bed of cement and afterwards levelling the pavement before the cement set, or by a clever technique of the manufacturer, whereby the pieces were fixed with glue, face downwards on a full-size drawing of the design. The complete pattern was then divided into manageable sections and these fragments were taken to their intended positions in the house where the mosaic pieces with the paper upwards were placed on a prepared bed of cement and carefully levelled. The paper pattern was afterwards removed by soaking it in water. The restoration of such a complex surface is best left to an expert paviour!

MARBLE TILES

Marble in small slabs was widely used for paving halls and corridors where it provided a very durable surface. Almost endemic to the material was the familiar pattern of black and white tiles 300mm (12in) square or 450mm (18in) square, laid parallel, or diagonal to, the flanking walls. Also popular, and rather more elegant, was a combination of white octagonal tiles with smaller square black tiles set diagonal to them (Fig 92). Old tiles may be 19–25mm (¾–1in) thick, but their modern replacements may be as thin as 10mm (⅜in) for 150mm (6in) square slabs. Normally they are laid on a thin bed of cement and sand on a level concrete sub-floor, but some varieties of marble are stained by Portland cement and so should be bedded on, and pointed with, a special cement called *Keenes* or *Parian.*

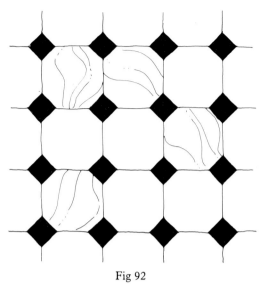

Fig 92

Varnished Boards and Wood Blocks

Boarded surfaces of joisted upper floors have already been described. Though they were commonly covered with sheet materials – carpet, oilcloth or linoleum – expensive timber boards were sometimes left exposed to be varnished or polished. This treatment applied in particular to beech-, pine- and maple-boarded floors, as these timbers exhibit distinctive patterns of grain. Often such boards were quite wide, giving an opulent effect, in contrast with the standard, deal plain-edge boards found in meaner Victorian houses. The Victorians were also fond of wood-block floors which are both durable and quiet in use.

Because of their small size, blocks (sometimes known as *parquet*) cannot do the structural job of boards which span between the joists, thus stiffening a suspended timber floor. Therefore they were generally laid on a solid sub-floor of concrete or brick vaults levelled with a sand-and-cement screed. Individual blocks were 75mm (3in) wide, from 215–375mm (8½–15in) long and 25mm (1in) thick. Connections between the blocks were made with dowelled or tongue-and-groove joints, complete interlocking of the units normally being achieved by adopting herringbone or basket-weave patterns in the blocks (Fig 93). The blocks were often secured to the sub-floor and protected against rising damp in ground floors by bedding them in a thin coating of hot bitumen. Unfortunately, this pitch bedding

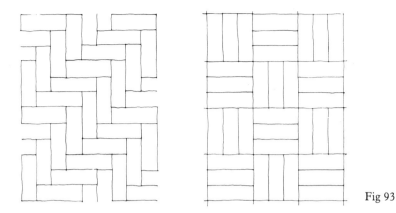

Fig 93

becomes brittle with age and the consequent loss of adhesion will lead to loose or hollow-sounding areas, which it may be possible to replace or secure only by taking up and relaying a large area of floor. However, modern epoxy adhesives provide a more secure fixing for the blocks than the adhesion achieved by the original laying technique. A wide variety of timbers was employed for such wood-block floors, including mahogany (light, red-brown), teak and oak (light, yellow-brown when unstained). Mahogany is liable to indent slightly in use. Among softwoods, pine and fir were also used in wood-block floors.

Sheet Coverings
Fitted carpets are an innovation of recent times. Carpets and rugs in Victorian homes rarely extended to the perimeter walls of rooms. Carpets generally appeared like large rugs, bordered by an exposed rim of boards, tiles or wood blocks. In the same way, stair carpets never extended to the full width of a stair flight but were bordered by the exposed treads to either side, the carpet being secured at the junctions of treads and risers with stair rods of wood or brass.

The most common 'overall' surface for cheap boarded floors was *linoleum*. This is made from powdered cork mixed with mineral fillers and oxidised linseed oil and resins on a jute canvas backing; pigments were added to this compound to achieve the desired colours, which in Victorian 'lino' were often many and varied. Similarly, it was possible to inlay a pattern through the whole thickness of the material or print it on the surface. *Oilcloth* is an inferior form of linoleum, being simply canvas coated with an oil which sets hard, though the two titles seem to be interchangeable in common parlance.

It may be possible to find stocks of old material in small traditional carpet shops, but most of the elaborate patterns of former times (often imitating wood-block or marble flooring) have been discontinued by the manufacturers in favour of simple geometry and plain colours.

Granolithic Paving
Most of the floor finishes already described were used in the grandest rooms of Victorian houses, but cellars and service rooms (laundries, coal houses, etc) often did not merit even a stone-slab floor, and various types of 'composition' floor covering were employed instead. *Granolithic* was a popular type of jointless floor covering. Although in the present day it is always laid on a concrete sub-floor, a firm and roughly level surface sufficed for the Victorians. The material consists of Portland cement and fine hard stone chippings in definite grades and proportions, and produces a hard, grey surface which is inclined to dust if it is not sealed. Because it is jointless the surface can be turned up surrounding wall surfaces to give a matching skirting.

The laying of granolithic is a skilled job. The top surface is levelled and steel trowelled, and is then allowed to cure over seven days under a covering of wet sand or sawdust. Small repairs to cracked granolithic can be made by the handyman with sand-and-cement mortar; in view of the patching effect this produces and the material's tendency to dust, coating the surface with a 'concrete floorpaint' is recommended.

6
Internal Walls

Victorian houses are almost universally of *mass* construction; that is, they rely on load-bearing brickwork or masonry to support the intermediate floors and roof. Except in the tiniest houses, the unbraced 'box' of the external walls alone was insufficiently strong to guarantee the stability in all conditions of two- or three-storey construction. Thus certain internal walls were also carried out in brick-work. These brick partitions acted as supports for timber floor joists and the trimmers of staircase openings too, where these members could not be arranged to span between outside walls.

TIMBER-FRAMED PARTITIONS

Other internal walls which simply subdivided the internal space could afford to be of lighter construction. They were normally assembled in the same way as balloon-frame external walls, with timber stud uprights 100mm × 50mm (4in × 2in) in section sited at 300–400mm (12–15¾in) intervals, housed in continuous wooden sole plates at floor level and continuous head members which were fixed to the under-side of the ceiling joists, with intermediate horizontals and cross-bracing to give rigidity.

The presence of timber-framed partitions does not guarantee that they play no part in supporting the structure. Timber-framed walls were often used to support the ends of floor joists, and where the plan allowed it, such partitions were often carried up through two or three storeys, the top members of each wall panel supporting the joists of the intermediate floors. Therefore it is essential that the con-struction at the head of any existing timber partition is fully investigated before any attempt is made to adapt or remove it. It may be holding up a floor, part of the roof, or both!

The fact that the floor joists run parallel to a timber-framed partition does not mean that the wall is not helping to support the floor. The ceiling plate of the partition may be supporting short blocking pieces which span between the joists (Fig 94).

Even more confusing for new owners of Victorian houses may be the discovery that some apparently 'solid' brick walls turn out to be timber-framed partitions whose voids have been filled with brickwork. This 'brick nogging' may be restricted to square panels between horizontal and vertical timbers, or, in the absence of wooden uprights, it will extend to the full length of the wall, horizontal 'bonding timbers' being found at approximately 450mm (18in) intervals vertically. These forms of construction seem to have been attempts to build rigidity into the structure and yet avoid the laborious task of bonding partition brick-work into the external wall construction. For some reason, brick-built internal walls of older properties are rarely bonded into the external brickwork; they simply butt up against an adjoining surface, producing a continuous joint and consequent cracking of the plaster internal wall finish. Timber-framing or bonding timbers introduced a type of continuous construction which was intended to 'tie in' the parts, and the wooden members were also useful as grounds for fixing joinery (eg doorframes at openings in the wall).

The brick nogging of a fully framed partition is clearly a simple infill which can usually be removed without adverse effects upon the struc-tural stability of the wall (although its removal will reduce the partition's sound-deadening properties), but continuous brickwork layered between bonding timbers obviously supports these members and large sections of it cannot be extracted without endangering the stability of the wall.

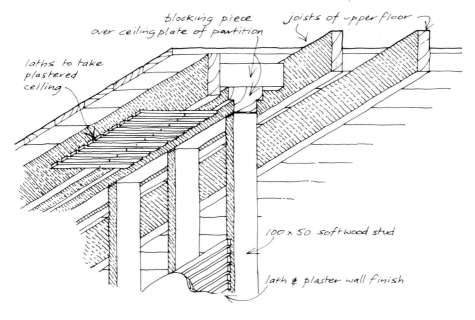

blocking piece over ceiling plate of partition

joists of upper floor

laths to take plastered ceiling

100 × 50 softwood stud

lath & plaster wall finish

Fig 94

Door Openings

A door opening in any internal wall naturally introduces a structural weakness. In a conventional, half-brick-thick partition, door openings were usually spanned by timber lintels, the brick panel above the door opening being built off the top surface of the timber. In the present day, such wooden lintels have been replaced by narrow precast concrete members or lightweight pressed and galvanised steel lintels which are stocked by every builder's merchant. In a timber partition, it was a simple matter to span a horizontal brace between the studs flanking a door opening to form a lintel. Where the partition was load-bearing, double studs would be incorporated at each jamb in order that the internal pair could support the lintel and gain stiffness from the outside posts to which they were nailed, extending up to the full height of the partition. The oversize gap opened up between the studs by the door opening might necessitate trussed construction above the timber lintel in order to transfer load down to the double studs framing the opening (Fig 95). Clearly, such an opening cannot be enlarged without expert advice first being obtained from a structural engineer. The internal pair of such double studs was sometimes used to terminate lathing and to provide a ground for fixing architraves (the wooden 'trim' to a door opening), but it was more normal to fit

a 'false jamb' into a prepared opening in a timber-framed partition. This deeper section of joinery work granted the opportunity to correct dimensional inaccuracies in the carpentry, as well as providing a surface against which to terminate the lath and plaster. Such a secondary frame fitted within the carpentry opening performs this latter function usefully in the modern plasterboard-clad partition. But remember to account for the thickness of this internal frame when forming the door opening in the stud partition!

WALL CLADDINGS

Lath and Plaster

Where airspace rather than brickwork formed the 'infill' between the members of a lightweight timber partition, no substratum was available for the conventional plaster wall finish, so the backing for the plaster had to be added to the face of the timbers. Long before the advent of plasterboard, this was achieved by nailing horizontal wooden laths at very close intervals across the surface of the timber framing. The laths were generally thin strips of softwood 25mm (1in) wide, 6mm (¼in) thick and about 1200mm (47in) long, and a gap of 6–10mm (¼–½in) was left between successive laths. The plaster was then applied to this horizontally slatted surface, and it adhered to

Internal Walls

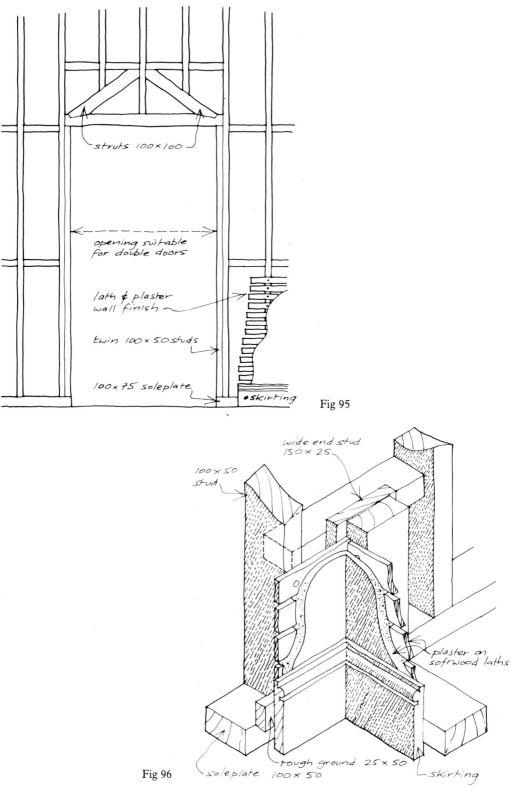

struts 100×100

opening suitable
for double doors

lath & plaster
wall finish

twin 100×50 studs

100×75 soleplate

skirting

Fig 95

wide end stud
150×25

100×50
stud

plaster on
softwood laths

Fig 96

soleplate
100×50

rough ground 25×50

skirting

the lathing because some of the material squeezed through the gaps, so 'gripping' the lathing on setting.

At a right-angle junction of two framed partitions there is a potential lack of fixing surfaces for the lathing. This problem was avoided by inserting a wider stud than the standard uprights into the thickness of the main partition and against the end stud of the abutting partition (Fig 96), thus providing a narrow timber surface for fixing the ends of the laths. This detail is equally useful today as a means of providing end fixings for the sheets of plasterboard which have replaced lath and plaster.

Nineteenth-century plaster always contained lime and sand, and very often horsehair or ox hair was included in the mix to ensure cohesion of the material. Do not be surprised if you discover tufts of thick black hair in plaster you have hacked off an old partition! As will become apparent on demolishing the lath and plaster finish of a wall or ceiling, the material is surprisingly heavy, even at its conventional thickness of 25mm (1in).

A hollow-sounding surface on the inside of an external wall may betray lathing behind the plaster; in some circumstances plaster was applied to a wooden grillage on vertical battens fixed to the structure, rather than directly to the masonry itself.

Where the laths remain behind a small hole in lime plaster, they will provide sufficient support for a 'patch' of new gypsum plaster. If they are damaged, an additional key must be provided. If the hole is not more than 75mm (3in) wide, the key is obtained by inserting into the hole a piece of jute sacking (or scrim) soaked in plaster of Paris before the new surface is formed with gypsum plaster. The repair of larger holes calls for the use of panels of plasterboard or sheets of expanded metal lathing which must be nailed to the studs to provide a flat substratum for the new *in situ* plaster finish.

Plasterboard and Plastering

Expanded metal lathing came into use during the nineteenth century, and it is a modern substitute for split pine laths. Much more convenient than metal lathing and *in situ* plaster if the complete re-cladding of an old partition is contemplated is *plasterboard*, which is a pre-fabricated paper-faced sheet of gypsum plaster either 1.2m × 2.4m (3ft 11in × 7ft 10½in) or 0.9m × 1.8m (2ft 11½in × 5ft 11in) in area, and approximately 9mm or 12mm (⅜in or ½in) thick. It is fixed to timber with short, galvanised, clout-headed nails, and variations upon the standard product include sheets which are laminated with expanded polystyrene insulation. Plainly, this variety of plasterboard can be used to renovate old walls whilst increasing their insulating properties.

Where small areas of defective plaster need to be replaced, modern gypsum plasters ('Carlite', 'Sirapite', etc) will adhere well to the old lathing and are compatible with the retained lime plaster. Similarly, curved or complex shapes or small surfaces in new work (for instance, the underside of an arch) are best formed from timber framing clad in expanded metal which is itself coated to the required profile with new *in situ* gypsum plaster. Unlike the erection of plasterboard sheets to create large flat areas, plain or decorative plastering is a skill which cannot be quickly learned, and there is much to be said for employing an expert tradesman to carry out this job.

Although many elaborate mouldings in *fibrous plaster* (plaster profiles cast in the mould at the factory and erected at the site as pre-fabricated features) became available from the middle of the eighteenth century, internal cornices at the head of walls were often 'run' in *in situ* plaster in precisely the same way as the external rendered ornament described earlier (see Chapter 3 *External Walls*). For householders undertaking an ambitious restoration of a grand Victorian interior, there is a very wide choice of patterns of fibrous plaster rosettes and medallions produced by several manufacturers. Copies of 'prototype' mouldings found in the existing building can also be made by fibrous plaster specialists, but be prepared to pay a special price!

Skirtings

At the foot of a conventional plastered wall, whether it was of timber-framed or solid construction, a wooden skirting was installed. In Victorian houses there are almost limitless design variations upon the traditional moulded wooden skirting, and it may be very difficult to match exactly an elaborate existing profile with a pattern of skirting generally available today.

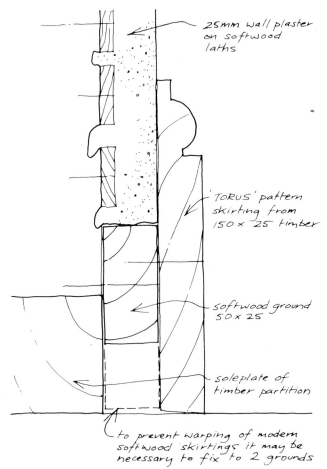

25mm wall plaster
on softwood
laths

'TORUS' pattern
skirting from
150 × 25 timber

softwood ground
50 × 25

soleplate of
timber partition

to prevent warping of modern
softwood skirtings it may be
necessary to fix to 2 grounds

Fig 97

However, profiles similar to the simpler mouldings used by the Victorians are readily available, and one such is the 'Torus' pattern which is supplied in a range of heights (Fig 97). Perfectionists may wish to consider commissioning precise copies of existing mouldings to obtain complete authenticity; most joinery works are able to reproduce surviving profiles in new material, but a small order will generate a disproportionately high cost for the service. Nor is the economical use of material likely to distinguish the original detailing; wooden skirtings of Victorian drawing rooms could be as much as 350mm (14in) high.

Like other joinery items (such as deep architraves around door and window openings and picture rails) skirtings were fixed to the walls through wooden grounds. In a timber partition, these grounds were thicker than the laths by the thickness of the plaster finish, so

that they would act not only as a fixing for the timber 'trim' but also as an edge against which to finish the plaster (Fig 97). On brick walls, the grounds were fixed into wooden plugs built into the vertical joints of the brickwork. Fixing a continuous horizontal ground to the studs of a timber partition was a simpler operation. If a timber partition is being constructed with contemporary materials, timber grounds may be equally necessary. Skirtings cannot be screwed securely into plasterboard!

Wainscoting

There was a clear hierarchy of wall finishes for the Victorians. Superior to painted brickwork, yet cheapest and least admired of the plaster treatments was painted plaster, which was favoured for utilitarian rooms like kitchens. Wallpapered plaster was better regarded and was certainly the most common wall covering, though superior to this were the forms of wooden wall cladding. Painted panelling was second-best to a surface of polished hardwood, which was seen as the most sumptuous and durable finish achievable in wooden cladding.

The shallow moulded skirting at the foot of a wall is the most minimal form of panelling, but wainscoting was a 'half-way house' often adopted by the Victorians to provide a partially panelled wall finish in halls, on staircases and in other areas of large houses which were subjected to heavy use. A chair rail was installed in front of a wooden ground fixed about 900mm (35in) above the floor to prevent chairbacks damaging the plastered surface. Between this rail and the skirting, continuous wooden panelling was inserted by the joiner. The resulting wainscot or dado might be painted or waxed and polished (if of hardwood), or even grained in imitation of more expensive timber if it was of softwood.

Cheaper than a fully panelled dado was a surface of tongue-and-groove matchboarding of a similar type to that used in flooring, but incorporating a bead moulding in the joints in this circumstance. Although the construction of panelled wainscotings may differ according to their complexity, the basic principle of their assembly was the prefabrication of a framework of uprights and cross-members carefully jointed into each other, which was infilled with panels of thin sheet timber, housed in grooves in the framing members and able to shrink and swell independently of the framework (Fig 98). This arrangement is essentially that of panelled door construction, but on a larger scale. The frame and its infilling panels were assembled on the joiner's bench where the tenoned joints were clamped and glued together. The ground which finished the plaster on a horizontal line at the rear of the chair rail (like the skirting, applied as a separate moulding on top of the dado) was used as a top fixing for the wainscot, and the ground at the foot which secured the skirting board also accepted the underside of the panelling. An intermediate ground was usually provided to secure the wainscot along its horizontal centre line, and in a long run of panelling, vertical grounds were also installed to provide further fixings at 2.5–3m (8ft 2½in–10ft) intervals.

Providing replacement timber comparable in quality to the original material can be obtained (thus minimising the risk of non-uniform movement in the restored, and therefore hybrid construction), the repair of panelled dados with modern wood glues and the ingenious timber fixings now available can be very successfully carried out if care is exercised by the skilful handyman.

Ceramic Dados

Where resistance to rough treatment was the first quality demanded of a wall surface in an entrance hall, staircase or corridor, the Victorians sometimes adopted a tiled or glazed brick finish which required no maintenance other than the occasional wipe with a damp

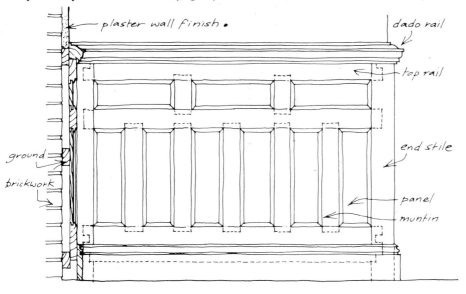

Fig 98

117

cloth. *Faience* was a popular material for this application. In composition it is identical to terracotta (see Chapter 3) but it owes its distinctive glossy surface to a second firing of the material which was carried out after a coloured glaze was applied. Green was probably the most popular colour for faience tiling employed in interiors, although ochre and peacock blue can be found amongst other distinctive shades. It was common for the tiles to carry patterns, either incised into the material or built up in relief. This effect was achieved by applying patterned metal dies to the clay when it was in its plastic state.

Even in the present day, faience tiling has institutional associations for many people – it is remembered as a wall finish in municipal slipper baths and similarly 'sanitary' buildings. For this reason, restorers of Victorian houses may find that the original shiny surface of their tiled dado has been carefully concealed by a previous owner behind boarding or sprayed and textured paintwork. However, less easy to conceal than the flat surface of the tiles is the horizontal, moulded waist rail of matching material which always trimmed the top of such a glazed panel.

Panelling

A really sumptuous effect could be obtained in grand rooms by extending the panelled treatment of a dado to the whole wall surface thus creating a completely panelled interior. In this instance, the techniques adopted for the assembly of wainscoting were simply extended to the entire wall area.

By the late nineteenth century, the Victorians had recognised that full-height panelling was apt to make a room rather gloomy, and from the 1870s it became conventional to terminate the panelling at some intermediate level, the remainder of the wall extending to the ceiling being treated as a plastered and painted frieze. This frieze might be painted the pale plain colour of the ceiling, or, in a more 'artistic' interior, it could carry elaborate stencilled decoration in multi-coloured paintwork on a pale-painted background. Ending painted or exposed hardwood panelling on a horizontal line at some intermediate level along the walls was the favoured treatment for the low-ceilinged drawing- and dining-rooms which proliferated in houses erected during the 'Arts

and Crafts' phase of Victorian and Edwardian architecture, because the illumination of these rooms with their small windows benefitted from the light reflected from the pale ceiling and frieze surfaces. Any form of varnished or painted panelling is a rarity in all but the best 'bespoke' Victorian houses. Restorers of commonplace Victorian houses which were built as a speculation will be more preoccupied with stripping apparently innumerable layers of decaying 'Anaglypta' wallpaper than contemplating the repair of elaborate wall panelling!

Doors

The plain surface 'flush' door of modern times was not widely adopted in housebuilding until after World War II, and it was unknown in the nineteenth century. Two main types of door are found in Victorian houses: *ledged* doors and *panelled* doors.

Although they were sometimes used in internal partitions of the late nineteenth-century 'cottage' houses, ledged doors were most often used as back entrance doors. The simplest ledged door is formed from tongue-and-groove boarding nailed to three horizontal ledges or back bars, extending across the width of the door. This is a weak type of construction, and with use, such simple doors will 'drop' away from the hinged edge because they incorporate no cross bracing. The *ledged and braced* door avoided this difficulty. Diagonal braces were introduced between the ledges to stiffen the construction, and if the door was hung on the side from which the braces rose to reach the 'leading' edge, it was prevented from 'dropping' (Fig 99). Making a new ledged and braced door from 'v' jointed tongue-and-groove boards and standard timber sections is a simple project for the average handyman.

A more sophisticated form of ledged door which was often fitted in kitchens and sculleries at the external entrance is the *framed and ledged* door, which, as its name suggests, framed its boarded surface with solid timber members which were tenoned into each other. The stiles (vertical framing members) and rails (horizontal members) of this door type are as thick as the boarded cladding and the conventional ledge of a standard ledged door added together, but the intermediate lock rail passes behind the boards so that an uninterrupted boarded surface

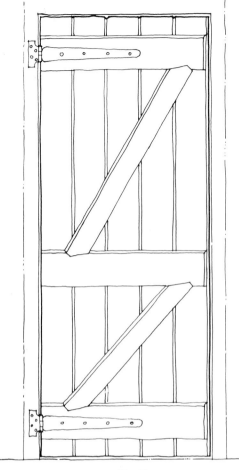

Fig 99

stile, the conventional mid-rail was sometimes replaced by the intermediate rails framing an additional central panel. This left the outer stile solid so that a mortice lock could be inserted without weakening the door construction. In cheap houses this difficulty was avoided by using a type of lock which was applied to the door face, thus obviating surgery on the door stile. Some enrichment of the junctions between the panels and the framing member was almost always included in the panelled door. The simplest treatment was a moulding formed on the inner edges of the stiles and rails to 'soften' the joint between framing and panels. More elaborate – and more expensive – was the adoption of 'planted' mouldings, masking or enriching these junctions (Fig 101). This enrichment could be carried further by incorporating mouldings in the infilling panels themselves. The familiar 'bulging' or projecting

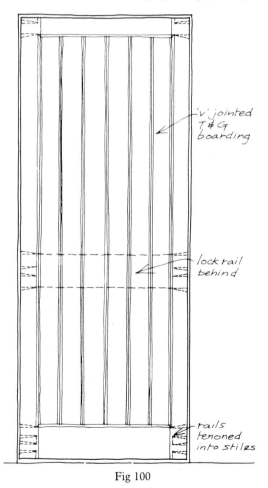

Fig 100

appears externally (Fig 100). Even more robust than this substantial form of door was the *framed ledged and braced* door which added diagonal braces to the framing.

Panelled doors were almost invariably the original internal doors of Victorian houses, and those fitted to the cheapest houses represent the simplest type of panelled joinery which will be found in Victorian domestic architecture. The door frame is formed from solid stiles and rails tenoned into each other. These members are grooved on their inside faces to accept the infilling panels which, in the nineteenth century, were slabs of solid timber as little as 8mm ($\frac{5}{16}$in) thick (plywood is a more recent invention). Locks or latches were sometimes mortised into the leading edge of the outer stile of the door, but as the insertion of a lock could destroy the tenon joining the mid-rail to the

Internal Walls

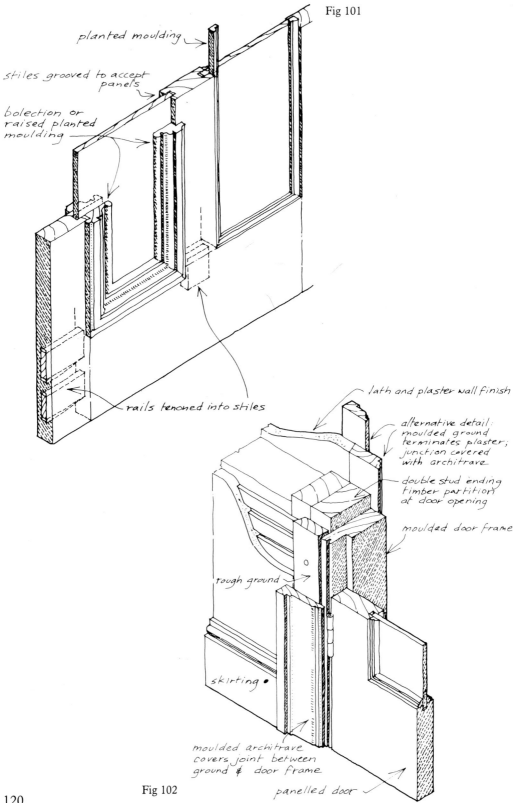

planted moulding

Fig 101

stiles grooved to accept panels

bolection or raised planted moulding

rails tenoned into stiles

lath and plaster wall finish

alternative detail: moulded ground terminates plaster; junction covered with architrave

double stud ending timber partition at door opening

moulded door frame

rough ground

skirting

moulded architrave covers joint between ground & door frame

panelled door

Fig 102

panels of monumental internal doors (as encountered in the dining-room of a Victorian town mansion) are known as raised and mitred or fielded panels.

Internal hinged doors of all types – single, double or folding – were hung in wooden frames inserted in the rough framing of a timber partition or a masonry opening spanned by a wooden lintel. The wide joint of this 'finished' frame with the wall finish applied to the brick or timber structure was concealed by a continuous moulded wooden architrave, which also terminated the skirting at floor level (Fig 102). Like skirtings, architraves could be machined from one section of timber, or if a more elaborate appearance was wanted they would be assembled from two or more separate mouldings. Such a bewildering range of moulded profiles was produced by the numerous local joinery works operating in the nineteenth century that it may be impossible to match surviving Victorian mouldings with modern products, though 'ogee' profiles similar to those used in the late nineteenth century continue to be made, and at least one major joinery retailer in the south-east has recently expanded his range of 'period' mouldings to include patterns which are Victorian in spirit. In the last resort, seekers of complete authenticity can arrange to have surviving mouldings copied, identical profiles being machined out of solid timber sections of a stock size slightly larger than the desired form. Expect the cost to far exceed that of standard mouldings!

Glazed panels were almost as common an infill between the stiles and rails of panelled door construction as the timber panels already described. Internal doors, as well as panelled front entrance doors sometimes incorporated colourful panels of stained and painted glass above mid-rail height.

The glazed door treatment was also extended into internal wall construction where glazed partitions or screens were used to subdivide rooms or enclose 'service stairs', thus separating the servants' area from the employer's territory, yet 'borrowing' precious daylight from this better illuminated accommodation.

WALL FINISHES

Wallpapers

The use of wallpaper as a decorative wall finish was established in Britain in the sixteenth century, but the mechanised printing of wallpapers which emerged in the nineteenth century brought about an enormous expansion of the range of papers available and the number of firms producing them. An important innovation of Victorian times was 'Anaglypta', a dense paper into which the pattern was embossed during manufacture by the use of metal dies. When painted or varnished after being applied to a wall, the pattern remained prominent, giving a richer effect than that of simple printed papers. 'Flock' wallpapers which incorporate a shallow velvet pile produce a similar effect, but, unlike 'Anaglypta' or its rival 'Lincrusta', they cannot be successfully over-painted when the original surface has dis-coloured.

The handful of national wallpaper manufacturers in existence at the present time are the direct descendants of the myriad firms which produced many thousands of elaborate wallpaper patterns in the nineteenth century, yet changing fashions have dictated that very few Victorian designs are currently available. Those patterns which can be obtained are likely to be expensive, to the designs of the Victorian artists still famous today (such as William Morris and C. F. A. Voysey) and may not be printed in the original colours. However, balancing the scarcity of genuine Victorian patterns and colours is a wide range of contemporary papers which are generally Victorian or Edwardian in appearance. Be prepared to pay more for them than the standard 'washable vinyl' wallcovering suitable for your kitchen.

Some of the wallpaper patterns developed by noted Victorian designers also appeared on fabrics which were hung as curtains or used to upholster furniture. This arose because no clear distinction was made between cladding a wall in a printed paper and cladding it in pleated, printed fabric. Among late nineteenth-century designers, William Morris in particular regarded the cladding of internal walls with shallow-pleated fabrics hung from brass hooks secured to the picture rails as a finish more durable and attractive than a papered wall surface.

Internal Walls

Paint

The range of paints available to the Victorians was much narrower than the materials on offer today.

Limewash was a solution of powdered lime and water which was applied to external brick walls of yards and areas in cheap houses to increase reflected daylight in these otherwise gloomy enclosures. For the same reason, it was applied to cellar walls, and in the meanest construction, to internal ceilings too. A slightly superior material was *whitening* which was a solution of finely powdered chalk, size and water. This was more generally used as a ceiling paint. It suffered the limitation of all *distempers* in that the pigment or colour (in this case the white chalk) was not dissolved but merely suspended in the solution, and relied upon the size to fix it to the surface after the water had evaporated. Dilution of the mixture simply reduced the effectiveness of the size, rendering the colour unstable and likely to drop off the surface as a powder. This accounts for the patchiness and dusty texture of the unmaintained distempered ceilings and friezes which surmount the picture rails on the internal walls of unmodernised Victorian houses. White was the pigment most generally used in distemper, but other pastel colours were employed. Contemporary *emulsion paints* containing plastic compounds have enormously improved the performance of water-based paints, completely superseding the old distempers.

Superior to water-based paints for the Victorians were oil-based paints. Modern gloss paint may owe its viscosity to a petroleum by-product, but Victorian oil paint was generally based on linseed oil which is produced by the compression of flax seed. It was the oil most used for house painting and could only be used where white lead gave pigment to the paint. *Boiled linseed oil* was used in combination with all powdered or dry colours. An important shortcoming of the old oil-based paint which contrasts with the properties of today's gloss paint was its slowness in drying. It was also prone to discoloration after drying, light tones becoming progressively yellower. Despite these disadvantages, the Victorians preferred it to water-based paints as an internal wall finish.

Ideally, fresh plaster was coated with four separate applications of oil paint, the first two coats – which would be largely absorbed by the plaster – being kept thinner than the finishing coat. On large surfaces, this final coat was often applied in such a way that a matt appearance resulted. The special composition of the paint used in such 'flatting' caused it to dry very rapidly so that two, four or even six workmen might have been employed at one time in decorating a large wall surface in this way. Doors too were sometimes finished in 'flatted' paintwork, but as it was appreciated that improved durability was achieved with a glossy surface, the general intention was to lay on the oil paint so that a gloss finish resulted. The high gloss of today's mass-produced paint could only be achieved by applying a varnish over the surface of the dried oil paint.

As common a treatment of woodwork in Victorian interiors as oil paint in simple colours was *graining*. Through this process, essentially cheap timber was made to look like more expensive wood by applying patterns to its surface in imitation of the rarer timber's grain. Water-based paints were used for graining in the imitation of soft woods (such as pine and fir). The grainer began his work only after the painter had given the new wood three or four coats of plain paint. His first job was to lay on the graining ground, which differed in composition according to the wood to be imitated. On top of this ground, a further coat of paint matched to the tone of the desired timber was applied, and the grain of the wood was reproduced by drawing steel combs of different sizes across the still-wet surface. When the desired effect had been achieved, and the grained surface had dried, the finish was sponged down with a mixture of beer and whitening before overgraining with a thin coat of complementary colour, and the finishing varnish coats were applied. Clearly, the skill of the grainer determined the ease with which a convincing copy of the natural wood was obtained, and competent graining was rated much more highly than good plain painting. Many of the older generation of interior decorators still retain this skill for which there is now a much reduced demand.

A variant of graining which is a still rarer skill is *marbling*. As its name suggests, it is the finishing of painted surfaces in imitation of marble. Though rare in run-of-the-mill Victorian houses, it is found as a finish for imitation 'marble' columns and wainscotings in the entrance halls and staircase lobbies of grand town houses. A convincing result in this technique is only achieved through a greater knowledge of the original material and a higher level of skill than that called for by graining.

This has been a necessarily brief account of Victorian painting techniques. The range of materials described is now entirely obsolete, though the fanatical perfectionist may wish to return to using the traditional ingredients to produce an authentic Victorian drab or ochre! However, a word of warning is relevant here. Victorian paints almost invariably relied upon lead compounds to provide the colour or accelerate the drying of the paint. Although the adhesion of these old, lead-based paints to external woodwork compares very favourably with the performance of modern paints (as householders who have laboured to strip these ancient coatings from original window-frames will testify) lead compounds can be injurious to health, and it is for this reason that they have been excluded from modern paints. On no account allow young children to come into contact with old flaking paintwork on the original features of your Victorian house, for fingers contaminated with a banned paint ingredient can lead to fatal lead poisoning.

Despite their poorer adhesion as a result of the omission of lead compounds, in defence of today's paints it must be said that they are much easier to apply than the Victorian product. In an age when labour was cheap, time could be lavished on the careful preparation and laborious application of purpose-mixed paints. The use of factory-prepared, mass-produced paints spares the average handyman an irksome sequence of tedious and very time-consuming procedures.

7
Staircases

STONE STEPS

A hard stone step was often used as a threshold to a main entrance door, and in London and the south of England, Portland stone was favoured for this application. The step's top surface was slightly sloped from front to back by about 3mm (⅛in) to throw water off and the front edge was often moulded with a nosing. Only the ends of the step were supported, as a central support could make the stone wobble when stepped on and differential settlement could cause cracking. Where a short flight of stone steps connected the pavement with the ground-floor level, each stone was made to overlap the one below by at least 38mm (1½in), and quite commonly the stones were rebated into each other (Fig 103). Some risers below front entrance steps, though they appear to be stone, are actually formed from a type of 'artificial stone', namely concrete with a stone-dust

surface. Where this form of construction was adopted, the risers of the staircase are often very thin (perhaps 19–25mm [¾–1in]) and continuous exposure to the weather and heavy use may badly damage the material, leaving large gaps in the risers. This defect does not threaten the stability of the steps and cosmetic repairs to such construction can be easily carried out with sand and cement mortar, but the surfaces will always lack the durability of solid stone.

Natural stone was sometimes used in a similar way for the complete construction of external stairs. Treads of York stone, 63mm (2½in) or 75mm (3in) thick with risers 50mm (2in) thick, were erected to give an external profile identical to solid stone steps but without their durability. To be stable, such stairs must be built into walls at both sides. Where the stair flight was narrow (as in the case of an access stair to a cellar) slab treads might be installed without risers.

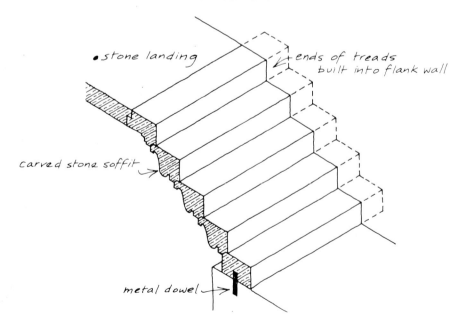

Fig 103

124

Stone steps were also used internally. Hanging steps, where the flights of stone stairs cantilever (project out) from an internal wall, are a familiar feature of older buildings, including large Victorian houses where the servants' back stair is as likely to be constructed of plain stone steps rebated into each other as the main stair is to display stone steps finished with an elaborately carved soffit (Fig 103). In both cases, the end of each step was left square in cross-section so that it could be easily built into the flanking support wall. Sometimes this end bearing was as little as 150mm (6in), though 215mm (8½in) was more common. In current structural design, in which precast concrete steps have replaced stonework in order to satisfy the structural codes, a much longer bearing would be required for each tread. Cohesion of the stonework in a flight of hanging steps was achieved by rebating the top landing into the tread of the topmost step and bearing the toe of each step on the tread of the step below. To resist the outward thrust resulting from this arrangement, the bottom step was firmly held in place by a metal dowel set into the floor.

TIMBER STAIRS

Wood is the material most commonly used for stair building in dwellings. The type of staircase invariably used in those countless urban terrace houses where the kitchens, bathrooms and ancillary bedrooms are located on mezzanine levels at the rear of the structure, was the *dog-leg* stair which omits the central well-hole, causing the handrail of the lower flight to meet the soffit of the upper flight because the outer string of the upper flight is vertically over that of the lower one.

A more generous arrangement which admitted a continuous handrail was the *open-newel* stair. More sophisticated still was the *geometrical* stair in which the *string* or fascia forming the side of the stair flight was continued, unobstructed by newel posts, in a curve around the well-hole. The existence of a string inclined in elevation and curved in plan usually results from the incorporation of *winders* or radiating steps, in the staircase.

There are two distinct types of construction for straight-flight timber stairs, the first of which was generally used only for rough work,

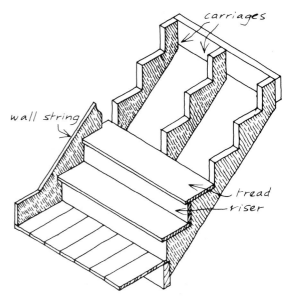

Fig 104

such as cellar stairs or temporary installations. In this version, rough timbers or *carriages*, cut to the sawtooth profile of the underside of the treads and risers were installed between levels, and the wearing surfaces simply fixed on top (Fig 104). To obtain the wall string (or 'sloping skirting') abutting the stair, boards the same thickness as the standard skirting with which it was connected were cut to fit closely over the treads and risers. Obviously it is very difficult to fit the wall strings satisfactorily, and even when a good fit is achieved, shrinking of the timber and jarring of the wooden surfaces with use of the stair is likely to show imperfections.

Much more satisfactory is the form of construction in which the treads and risers are housed or grooved 10–16mm (½–⅝in) into the strings. In this arrangement any carriages sited below the steps at intermediate positions are not cut to the profile of the undersides of the treads and risers, but are simply straight timbers of sufficient strength to help support the stair and its likely load. They serve the double purpose of supporting the middle of the steps and the laths of the sloping plaster soffit below the stair flight. They were often birdsmouthed on to the trimmer which supports the landing at the head of the flight. Rough brackets nailed to the sides of the carriage and fitted tightly under the treads, to which they were secured by angle blocks glued in position, guaranteed a firm

125

Staircases

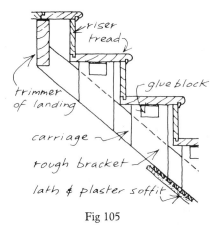

Fig 105

intermediate support for a wide stair (Fig 105). However, 'standard' staircases within speculatively built houses were normally constructed without such centre carriages. The strings in which the treads and risers were housed on both sides of the stair were reckoned to provide adequate support. Although formed from only three basic elements – treads, risers and strings – the manufacture of such a staircase was quite a complicated operation. This fact is clear to anyone who inspects the debris resulting from a demolished staircase of even a cheap Victorian house. The string adjacent to the flank wall, or close string, was first of all marked out with the profile of the

stair by drawing around a triangular template or pitch board placed on its broad surface on a line parallel to the top edge of the string. Templates representing the thickness of the treads and risers but with sloping, rather than flat undersides, were then sited on these lines to give the outline of the housings. To form the housings, holes were bored 10–16mm (½–⅝in) into the string adjacent to the position of the nosing of each tread, and a small amount of adjacent timber was cut away until the rest of the housing could be cut out with a saw and gouge. The treads and risers were then located in the housings, jointed and glued together, and also glued to the strings. A close fit of treads and risers with the strings was ensured by driving hardwood wedges into the tapered parts of the housings remaining below and behind the treads and risers, thus forcing these components tightly against the slots in the strings (Fig 106). The depth of the string adjoining the stair (the top surface of which was normally finished with a moulding) was reconciled with the standard skirting moulding on landings by ramping its top surface at the foot of the stair and incorporating a knee at its head (Fig 107).

Various methods of joining tread and riser were practised. It was most common to house the full thickness of the riser into the underside of the tread behind the nosing, reinforcing the

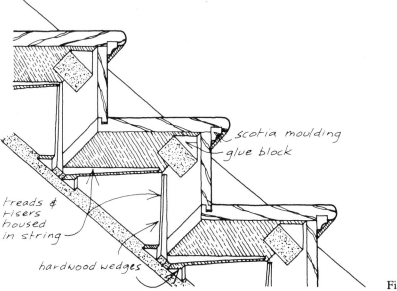

Fig 106

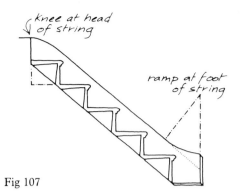

knee at head of string

ramp at foot of string

Fig 107

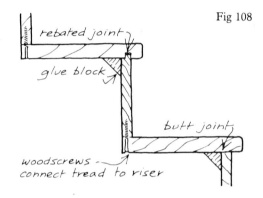

Fig 108

rebated joint

glue block

butt joint

woodscrews - connect tread to riser

joint with angleblocks. More sophisticated than this was a rebated joint of tread and riser. A simple butt joint of each tread with the underside of the superincumbent riser was also adopted, woodscrews joining the tread to the riser at 300mm (12in) intervals to ensure that the two components did not pull apart (Fig 108). Mass-produced timber staircases are produced in the same time-honoured way today, but each unit is not fabricated for each particular location, as applied in the nineteenth century. An improvement in the appearance of the junction between the underside of the tread and the top of the riser which was commonly adopted by the Victorians involved housing a small scotia moulding into the tread's underside to mask the related joint (Fig 106).

Where stairs terminate over a cut string rather than against a close string (ie when the edge of the stair is exposed to view), the ends of the treads and risers were prepared to fit the return nosings and the shape of the string. The risers were mitred at their ends to fit corresponding bevels on the string, while the treads were mitred behind the nosings to intersect with the return nosings. These latter

pieces were machined from the same timber as the tread, and moulded to the same section as the combined nosing and scotia. When planted at the ends of the treads, they give the impression that the nosings are continued across the ends of the steps. The return nosings also serve to conceal the dovetail sockets formed in the ends of the treads to accept the balusters, or wooden uprights, supporting the handrail which flanks the stair (Fig 109).

Balustrades to Timber Stairs
The thin wooden balusters, spaced two per tread, which usually flank a stair flight which shows a cut string, provide insufficient support for the handrail. Even where a proportion of these slender uprights are of metal rather than wood, it is normal for the handrail to have an end fixing into the underside of the stair's upper flight, or into otherwise free-standing posts at changes of direction, called newels. Those placed at the bottom of staircases are called starting newels, and when in this location, the centre of the newel post is normally in line with the face of the first riser. Angle newels at landings are often less elaborate than starting newels, and are invariably smaller. Again, the face of the adjoining riser should be on the centre line of the newel. Similarly, the centre line of the handrail should be that of the newel post and the centre of the string, whilst the centre of the balustrade should correspond with the centre of the string and the handrail.

The balusters themselves may be of many different designs. They not only help to support the handrail, but also they act as an ornamental guard to the side of the stair. The Victorians favoured ornate balusters turned to a 'spindle' profile, though a square base to each baluster gave a better fixing than a round end. Holes were drilled about 25mm (1in) into the underside of the handrail to receive the balusters, whilst a dovetailed fixing into the treads prevented the uprights from pulling out if there was any settlement of the stair flight which did not equally affect the handrail (Fig 109).

Handrails surmounting such balustrades were usually of hardwood. If continuous over 2–3m (6½–10ft), they were often stiffened with an iron core 6–10mm (¼–⅜in) thick and 25–50mm (1–2in) wide, fitted in a groove in the underside of the rail. The balusters were fixed

127

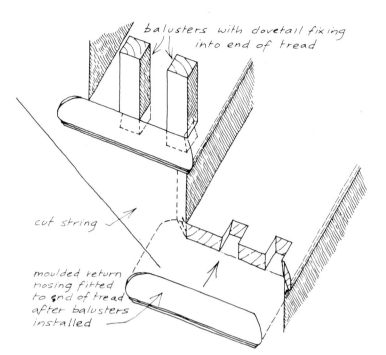

balusters with dovetail fixing into end of tread

cut string

moulded return nosing fitted to end of tread after balusters installed

Fig 109

to this core with screws, and the core was screwed to the handrail. The cheapest form of handrail was the plain deal mopstick, almost circular in section, as its name suggests; a flat plane was formed on its underside to connect with the balusters. An elliptical-section polished hardwood rail grooved in its underside to accept a continuous metal core makes a handsome handrail, but the most sumptuous section regularly employed by the Victorians was the toad's back pattern (Fig 110). Most timber merchants stock a modern version of this section called the frog's back handrail, but it is usually available only in softwood and is of a much slighter section than its Victorian ancestor.

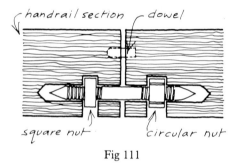

handrail section   dowel

square nut   circular nut

Fig 111

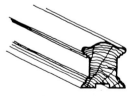

Fig 110

Lengths of handrail were butt-jointed together and secured with handrail bolts which have a square nut at one end and a circular nut at the other. A hole for the bolt was drilled in the ends of adjoining lengths of rail as near the

centre of the section as possible and the nuts were lodged in small mortices in the underside of the rail, the bolt then being screwed into the captive square nut. After this the circular nut was tightened on to the handrail bolt by rotating it with a screwdriver engaging in slots in its surface. In this way abutting lengths of handrail were drawn tightly together, and an inconspicuous joint was made more likely if two or more hardwood dowels and a glued connection were also incorporated at this point (Fig 111). Wall-mounted handrails were normally supported on curving brackets screw-fixed to timber plugs set in the flank wall of the stair. Alternatively, if great strength was sought, the brackets could be built into the masonry while the wall was erected.

Replacing a Timber Staircase

As one of the largest timber constructions in an average town or suburban house, the staircase is particularly susceptible to attack from dry rot or wood-boring beetles. It is in danger from dry rot because most under-stair spaces are poorly ventilated, and warm yet damp, particularly if they provide access to a cellar. If rot exists, it may not be at all apparent until the plastered soffit is stripped away, and the skeins of the fungus are revealed behind the laths. In this circumstance, the entire timber construction must be ripped out and replaced. Where woodworm provides the problem, a small area peppered with the flight holes of beetles does not threaten the structural integrity of the stair, but a timber surface in which shallow channels unite these holes suggests that the internal substance of the wood has been largely eaten away. In the first instance, treatment of the timber with insecticide preservative will arrest the decay; in the second case, replacement of the ravaged wood is necessary.

Although a specialist joinery workshop may be well able to manufacture a timber stair to replace a demolished flight, the cost of commissioning a purpose-made item will be large, and it is well worth considering adapting one of the standard prefabricated straight-flight timber stairs which are produced by the national and regional joinery manufacturers for sale through DIY outlets. Because these staircases are mass produced they are inexpensive, yet their construction and appearance differ in only small details from the Victorian prototype (the one exception to this rule is the 'open-riser' timber stair which is very widely available). The standard widths of these products are 864mm (34in) and 915mm (36in), though stair enclosures marginally wider than these standard dimensions can be reconciled with narrower stairs by adding timber mouldings to the top surfaces of the unmoulded strings. In any case, this is a sensible measure if an authentic 'Victorian' treatment of the string of the stair is desired.

Modern mass-produced staircases are constructed to comply with the requirements of current building regulations with regard to the pitch (slope) of the stair, the width of the treads and the height of the risers. These dimensions may not accord with the arrangement of your existing wooden staircase which was probably erected before the introduction of national building codes. In small houses, the original staircase is likely to be pitched at an 'illegally' steep angle produced by unacceptably high risers and insufficiently deep treads. Your new stair will be pitched lower and will account for a modern storey height almost certainly lower than that adopted in most Victorian houses. Where sufficient headroom can be maintained below any related upper-floor construction, this discrepancy can be absorbed by incorporating a landing at the foot of the stair or at an intermediate level, so that, for instance, fourteen stairs give access to an upper floor where thirteen previously performed the task. Thus the new stair will comply with modern building codes at the price of absorbing a small additional area of floor. Installing a new stair which conforms to the Building Regulations can become important if the local Building Inspector's clearance of alterations is required before payment of an Improvement Grant!

METAL STAIRCASES

Although metal spiral staircases have been installed as prominent internal features of many open-plan houses erected in the last forty years, and certain designs are highly ornate, indicating that they were developed in the nineteenth century, it is unusual to find an iron spiral stair as an original fitting of the interior of a modest Victorian house. Large nineteenth-century houses and public buildings sometimes included spiral stairs as space-saving devices for granting access to basements, attics and library or conservatory walkways, but metal staircases were otherwise restricted to external locations. Access from the street to the front basement areas of town houses may be via iron stairs and landings, though the high cost of even 'mass-produced' prefabricated staircases caused them to be used in this circumstance only where it was impractical to build-in stone steps guarded by a metal handrail.

The cast-iron treads and risers of such stairs were invariably patterned with a grillage of metal in imitation of foliage or other elaborate natural forms. The risers were usually open to prevent stair users from tripping against plain metal surfaces, and sometimes displayed a 'rope' pattern of interlocking circles so that the small area of solid material which contrasted

Staircases

with the voids produced a light appearance. This looked the more daring if solid-stone goings rather than pierced iron treads were used in conjunction with the 'open-work' risers. The spiralling balustrade could be equally decorative, its cast-iron balusters incorporating shapes in imitation of flowers and fruits. The whole construction was erected on a sectional centre column, ingeniously formed by stacking the tubular endpieces of the cast-iron risers (Plate 21).

For economy's sake, modern versions of the metal spiral stair are likely to be of pressed steel and timber rather than cast iron, and they naturally omit the luxurious ornament of their Victorian predecessors. Therefore, the replacement of broken ornamented components from an antique staircase can be difficult. The original manufacturer is unlikely to be still in

business, and few foundries producing cast-iron components operate today. If the broken part has a sister component which can be used as a pattern from which to make a mould for casting the replacement piece, cast aluminium is often a satisfactory substitute material. Most British cities harbour an ironfounder whose speciality is the manufacture of engineering prototypes in cast aluminium, and copying an antique item in a modern metal is a simple matter for these specialists. Similarly, one or two foundries have turned to restoration work as the chief market for their traditional smithing and foundry skills, and they are also geared to the production of 'one-offs' in aluminium or cast iron. When painted to match the appearance of the surviving iron construction, aluminium parts cannot be readily distinguished from the original components.

8
Windows and Glazing

The earlier chapter on External Walls (Chapter 3) deals thoroughly with the treatment of window openings in outside walls, yet the windows sited in these openings are important elements of architectural design and innumerable variations upon the types of windows described below are to be found in Victorian houses.

BAY WINDOWS

The most common type of complex window incorporated in Victorian houses is the bay window. Nineteenth-century architects and builders recognised that the sitting-rooms of the suburban terrace houses they designed and built would seem spacious and distinctive if the windows of the main entrance wall enjoyed several different aspects. Thus the square bay and the splayed bay window made their appearance in countless speculative dwellings. A view up and down the road from such a window was as possible as a view across the street to the identical house opposite. Early morning or evening sunlight could slant into a room which, without a bay window, would merely face a sunlit street. As an external architectural feature, the bay broke up an otherwise sheer front elevation, creating shadows and gradations of tone which a flat surface would lack; it also suggested expensive construction and detailing and so gave a good 'selling point', though the embellishments of the bay and adjoining porch were usually superficial, such elaboration being restricted to the street elevation. Thus the additional expense of incorporating a bay even in cheap houses was thought worthwhile. Neither was its appeal ignored by the speculative builders of the thousands of semi-detached houses erected between the two world wars – though the *segmental bay*, formed from a shallow curve of

rendered brickwork or timber framing, joined the splayed bay as a popular treatment.

Construction of Bays

Bay windows may be multi-storey or single-storey. Single-storey construction is straight-forward. The window structure was conventionally of timber or stone built off a brick or stone dwarf wall erected to the desired plan shape. Individual sashes or casement windows were then inserted within this structure to form the facets of the bay. A timber roof structure was erected on top of the vertical framing and clad with a material matching the finish of the main roof. Multi-storey bays could also be framed up in timber, and a rendered finish may indicate that there is lightweight framing behind the weather-excluding coating (Plate 22). Alternatively, brick panels below the windows of upper-storey rooms dictated corner piers of stone or brickwork to support this heavy construction, so that the window area was restricted to only a proportion of each facet of the bay, and much of the transparency from the addition of a bay was therefore sacrificed (Plate 23).

Roofs of bay windows may be flat or pitched, but in nineteenth-century houses they commonly comprise a wooden structure of 75mm × 50mm (3in × 2in) or 100mm × 50mm (4in × 2in) rafters and 75mm × 50mm (3in × 2in) ceiling joists, giving a flat soffit internally even where a pitched roof was employed. Flat roofs were finished in asphalt or sheet metal if surrounded by a parapet, and clad in metal if overhanging. Pitched roofs display most of the tile and sheet materials used on main roofs, namely slates, clay tiles, pantiles, shingles, zinc, copper and lead. The roof claddings over bay windows are essentially the same as those over dormer windows.

Plate 22 Two-storey timber-framed bay windows lighten the street elevation of these houses at Lynton in North Devon. Note the rendered finish of the infill panels sandwiched between the upper and lower windows (*Author*)

Plate 23 Brick corner piers support the large splayed bays of these substantial semi-detached houses. Consequently the areas left for the windows are smaller than the clear space created by fully timber-framed bays. Note the slate-hanging which has been applied to the gable brickwork as additional weather-proofing (*Author*)

ORIEL WINDOWS

A variant upon the bay which was sometimes used, particularly for small windows lighting bedrooms and staircases, is the oriel window, which differs only from the bay in that it does not extend down to the ground but is cantilevered off the main building structure. Except in the case of small triangular oriels lighting staircases and secondary rooms, it was necessary to reinforce the wooden structure of oriels with timber or metal brackets supporting the underside of the projecting construction (Fig 112 and Plate 24). In the case of upper-storey oriels, a 'full height' window can share the floor construction of the upper storey, the standard floor joists being extended to provide the short cantilever necessitated by the projecting window. However, to obtain a sturdy appearance, brackets were often added for aesthetic, if not for structural reasons, so the right advice must be to retain these 'supports' in every instance!

When renovating or rebuilding an oriel window, never fail to introduce insulation not only into the roof of the construction, but also into its soffit, as this surface will otherwise as efficiently lose heat to the fresh air as the glazing itself.

Plate 24 Timber-framed oriel windows projecting from the upper storey of a Surrey cottage. The rendered finish of the concave surfaces below the window sills conceals the triangular timber brackets which support these features (*Author*)

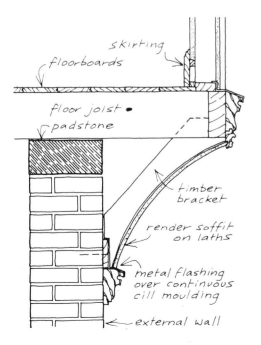

Fig 112

133

Windows and Glazing

CASEMENT WINDOWS

The casement is the simplest form of opening window. It may hang on hinges at the side, top or bottom, or can be fixed on pivots so that it swivels vertically or horizontally. The *French window* or French casement is the grandest type of casement window. In traditional rural buildings, the breadth of the wooden frame surrounding the glass in an outward-opening casement is often surprisingly wide. In small windows, the area of wood can easily equal the area of glass, and many houseowners restoring older dwellings make the mistake of replacing these stout old frames with mass-produced modern joinery of slender cross-section which looks feeble alongside the old woodwork. It was not unusual for the fixed frame of a casement to be machined out of 125mm × 100mm (5in × 4in) softwood, and for the frame of the opening light to be from 75mm × 63mm (3in × 2½in) timber, the wider dimension showing on the outside face. If painted white, as was usual with softwood frames, the surface would appear even wider in its contrast with the darker glazed area. Casements are sometimes paired, closing against one another at meeting stiles and they can be grouped in a range between stone or timber mullions.

Wrought-iron casements were produced throughout the nineteenth century and in the early years of this century. They were favoured by some architects for their freedom from rattling in high winds – a flaw to which wooden windows which shrink and swell with the changing climate were sometimes susceptible. After World War I they were effectively superseded by steel windows, the rusting of which poses a completely different set of problems for owners of inter-war semi-detached houses.

Casement Window Fittings

Wooden casements were almost universally hung on butt hinges similar to those used to hang internal panelled doors, but other, more specialised, ironmongery is required to retain and secure a casement. A *pin-stay* or *peg-stay* attaches the casement to the window frame and allows a graduated opening of the window; the horizontal bar of the stay, which is pivoted off the bottom rail of the window, contains a series of holes which engage on the pin fitted to the

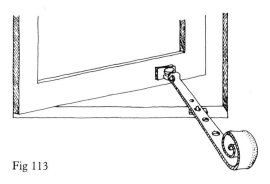

Fig 113

window sill. Peg-stays were made in a wide range of designs and 'black iron' (wrought iron) fittings which end in the traditional metal 'spiral' are still available today if you are prepared to hunt for them (Fig 113). They are much more suitable in a restoration than the contemporary aluminium alloy fittings which seem to monopolize the window ironmongery sections of chain stores and DIY shops. Sliding stays and telescopic stays were more elaborate, and less reliable, types of casement stay which gave a graduated opening. On small and unimportant windows, a simple hook-and-eye stay was used.

The most common form of fastening of casement to frame was the *cockspur* fastener. This device is fixed on the casement and there is a striking plate fixed to the frame. A slot in the striking plate accepts the tongue of the fastener. Like the peg stay, the handle of the cockspur fastener was sometimes ended with a metal spiral, and the sweep of the handle could be used to space it well clear of the glass, thus

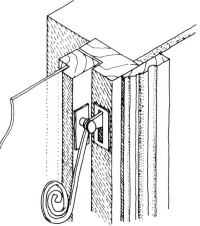

Fig 114

facilitating hand operation of the fitting (Fig 114).

On French windows, further fastenings of the casements to the fixed frame are necessary. A modern answer to this problem is the fitting of securing bolts at the head and sill of the window by recessing special *flush bolts* into the joinery, but such slender items in lightweight alloys were unknown to the Victorians and a much clumsier arrangement which was often adopted involved the fixing of full-height *French* or *Espagnolette* bolts to the inside surface of a door's meeting stile. Both devices incorporate a central lever or handle which causes the full-length bolt to engage in keeps fitted to the fixed frame at the head and the sill of the door opening. In spite of the ornamental appearance aimed at in the designs of these fittings, the multitude of bracket fixings to the wood which are required to keep the bolt in the correct alignment and ensure its efficient operation make it an ugly addition to the door surface, and in the restoration of French windows a much less obtrusive detail results from the inclusion of brass flush bolts.

Fanlights are, of course, a type of casement window if they are arranged to open. They invariably open inwards and are hinged at the bottom (another term for this type of window is a hopper vent). The most usual type of stay for a fanlight is a quadrant stay which consists of a curved metal bar on which slides a small catch attached to the fanlight. *Shad-bolt stays* are thin, flat metal bars fixed to the static frame of the window in which screws or pins in the sides of the fanlight move. This device allows the fanlight to take only two positions, shut and wide open. Simple butt hinges are a suitable means of hanging the window from the sill.

SASH WINDOWS

More sophisticated in construction than casements, and much more common in nineteenth-century town houses were double-hung sash windows. In this type of window, the sashes slide vertically, and are counterbalanced by weights hung on flax cords or chains, or by spring sash balances. Where weights were used to counterbalance a sliding sash, a complicated construction had to be adopted for the window jambs as they were required to conceal the weights as well as to provide wooden surfaces

retaining the sashes. The full thickness of the weight box was often not apparent from the exterior, as part of its thickness was commonly concealed behind a projecting nib of the external brickwork (Fig 115). Against this nib is sited the outside lining of the sash box which is generally of timber about 25mm (1in) thick. This is grooved to accept the pulley stile at right angles to it, which may be 25-32mm (1-1¼in) thick. The internal tongue of this component is, in turn, placed in a groove in the inside lining of the weight box, which again may be 25mm (1in) thick. When covered with a back lining, these three pieces form a box in which the two sash weights hang. Where the weights were large, or the space containing them was small, they were separated with a wooden tongue to prevent them striking together when the sash was raised and lowered. The pulley stile was grooved on its face to receive a parting bead which, with a 13mm or 16mm (½in or ⅝in) projection, retained the upper sash in one plane and provided a vertical channel in which this panel slides. This parting bead was often made of hardwood 13mm × 25mm (½in × 1in) or 16mm × 32mm (⅝in × 1¼in) in section, merely nailed in place so that it could be removed if it was necessary to take out the top sash. The lower sash slides inside the parting bead and is secured in place with a similarly removable stop bead which projects about 16mm (⅝in) in front of the face of the pulley stile.

At the head of the window, the three-sided arrangement of the jamb frames is reproduced, but here there is no necessity to accommodate sash weights and so a top lining is omitted, the window head being simply grooved into the inside and outside linings which match the equivalent components of the window jambs. In the same way that the outside linings of the jambs may be partly obscured by projecting brickwork nibs, so much of the outside lining at the window head was commonly obscured by a segmental arch of brickwork.

At the meeting of the horizontal top and bottom rails of the lower and upper sashes, it was usual to rebate or chamfer the adjoining wooden surfaces so that draughts admitted through the resulting gap were minimised. It was also good practice to slope the underside of the bottom rail of the lower sash and to incorporate a throating, so that wind-blown rain

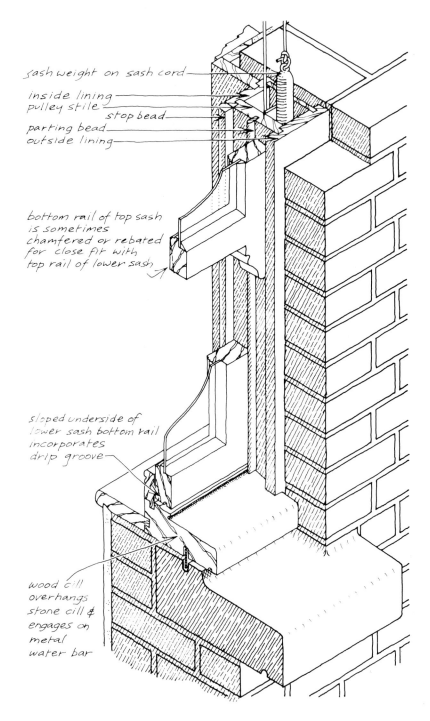

sash weight on sash cord

inside lining

pulley stile

stop bead

parting bead

outside lining

bottom rail of top sash
is sometimes
chamfered or rebated
for close fit with
top rail of lower sash

sloped underside of
lower sash bottom rail
incorporates
drip groove

wood cill
overhangs
stone cill &
engages on
metal
water bar

Fig 115

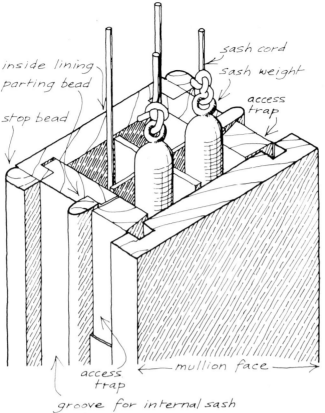

inside lining
parting bead

stop bead

sash cord
sash weight

access trap

access trap

groove for internal sash

mullion face

Fig 116

penetrating this joint would naturally trickle out over the complementary sloping surface of the hardwood sill (Fig 115).

When a double-hung window has been fixed in position, it is necessary on occasions to gain access to the weights contained in the window jambs. This is normally obtained through a flap formed in one side of the pulley stile, which is an opening cut into the stile, closed by means of a bevel-edged board which is simply kept in place by its tight fit against the adjoining surfaces, or is secured with screws.

Where two or more double-hung sash windows were included in a continuous range of windows, neighbouring sashes were separated by mullions which usually accommodated the sash weights for both flanking frames. As each mullion might have to contain four weights, its inside and outside linings had to be wider than those used for the jambs of a single window. The pulley stiles, stop beads and parting beads were detailed in exactly the same way as those in a single frame. In high-quality work, a parting strip was placed between the two sets of weights to prevent them

knocking against one another and jamming in the box, and this refinement necessitated access traps in the pulley stiles on both sides of the mullion (Fig 116), otherwise access to all four weights via a single flap in one side of the mullion could be obtained only with difficulty.

A familiar combination of real and 'fake' sash windows is the *triple window* in which a central, double-hung opening window is complemented by fixed sashes to either side. Although the mullions dividing these three lights may be made wide enough to house the sash weights, the resulting proportions were sometimes thought inelegant and thin parting mullions were installed which necessitated a different arrangement for the sash weights. One solution was the adoption of spring sash balances fitted in shallow mortices in both jambs of the fixed frame. The general unreliability of these spring steel balances often caused the central opening window to be hung on cords or chains which ran over two sets of pulleys to pass horizontally over the fixed side lights. These cords were finally attached to sash weights in the box jambs at the outside edges of the

137

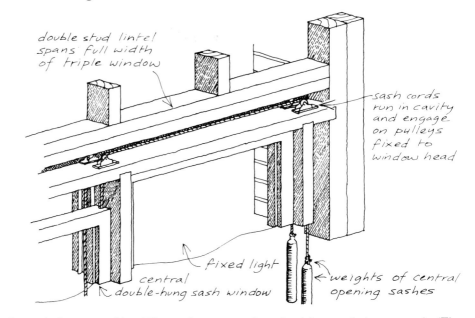

double stud lintel
spans full width
of triple window

sash cords
run in cavity
and engage
on pulleys
fixed to
window head

fixed light

central
double-hung sash window

weights of central
opening sashes

Fig 117

complete three-window assembly. The sash cords had to pass through holes in the window head and a continuous void over this wooden member housed the pulleys and the horizontal run of the cords. This arrangement necessitated a further fixed head frame over this void and below the structural lintel. An external wooden fascia then weatherproofed this void and its internal lining was removable to allow access to the pulleys and cords (Fig 117).

The sizes of the various wooden components forming a sash were fairly standardised. Sash windows in modest houses were 44–63mm (1¾–2½in) in thickness, the bottom rail being 87–102mm (3½–4in) deep, the stiles 50mm (2in) wide and the top rail 50mm (2in) deep. The meeting rails at the centre of the window were 36mm (1⅜in) deep and chamfered or rebated to fit tightly together when the window was closed. Very large sashes glazed with heavy plate glass are likely to be at least 50mm (2in) thick with a bottom rail 100–125mm (4–5in) deep.

The bottom edge of the lower sash of a double-hung window is vulnerable to water penetration by capillary action, and for this reason a groove was usually incorporated in its underside; similarly, the fixed wooden sill often included a groove in its vertical face in the plane of the outside face of the lower sash and a further groove behind the bottom rail of the lower sash, to induce any wind-blown rain

penetrating the joint to drain outwards (Fig 115). These features should be insisted upon in any purpose-made replacement of a decayed installation.

Removing and Re-hanging Sashes

To remove the lower sash of a double-hung window it is necessary first to remove the stop beads which retain the sash at both jambs. The lower sash can then be swung into the room on its cord ends and these cords – which are sometimes nailed into grooves in the edges of the stiles or simply 'knotted' into cavities therein – can be detached from the window, freeing the sash so that careful repair work can be carried out on the workbench. To remove the upper sash it is necessary to take out the parting bead. The top section may then be swung into the room for inspection and repair.

Replacement of broken sash cords is the normal reason for repairs to double-hung windows, but if the sash weight is missing or needs to be replaced it is essential that the combined weight of the replacement weights for an upper sash are at least 0.23kg (½lb) heavier than the window, whilst for the lower sash the weights must be at least 0.23kg (½lb) lighter than its weight. This displacement of weights tends to keep the sashes close together and tight against the window head and sill when closed.

To reunite a top sash with weights which

138

have become detached from the window, the pockets have to be opened by removing the access traps to gain access to the weights. Then the new sash cords are carried over the pulleys by threading fine but strong string, attached to the cord, through the small void between the pulley wheel and its fixing plate. The string is led over the pulley and down the void of the box jamb by a small lead weight called a 'mouse' (though a bent nail is equally good for guiding the thin cord of a small sash). When the sash cord is visible through the open trap at the foot of the lining, the string and mouse are detached from it, and the cord is tied to the top of the sash weight. With the top sash resting level on the window sill, the sash weights are pulled up to the pulleys and the cords are cut off just long enough to permit knots to be tied at the required level. Then the sash is removed from the frame far enough to permit the cords to be pushed down through the grooves in the edges of the stiles and secured by means of the knots which sit in purpose-designed circular voids at the ends of the grooves. The sash is then replaced in the frame and pushed up and down a few times to test its efficiency. After refixing the parting bead, the lower sash is rehung in a similar manner and reassembly of the window is completed by refitting the internal stop bead. Do not forget to secure the access trap tightly to the pocket to prevent it from obstructing the lower sash! Sashes sometimes work inefficiently because the pulley wheels are rusty. The removal, de-rusting and cleaning of the pulleys is called for in this circumstance. Care is needed to avoid damage to a pulley's brass face plate if it is necessary to prise the cast metal case from the lining.

Sash Ironmongery

The sash pulleys used in antique double-hung windows are of two types: *frame* pulleys and *axle* pulleys. A frame pulley is a cast-iron fitting containing a brass wheel which revolves on iron pins projecting from the inside face of each cheek of the case. The pulley fixing plate, which is fitted flush with the inner lining of the weights box, also commonly displays a brass finish though this is often only a thin brass face rivetted on to the cast-iron case. This type of pulley was already in use at the beginning of the nineteenth century.

Axle pulleys were a superior product in which the pulley wheel revolved on an axle which passed through the wheel and cheeks. Continuous use of the window sash was less likely to dislocate the wheel of such a pulley from its case than equivalent treatment of a window fitted with frame pulleys. The axle pulley too was an established building component long before Victoria's reign.

Because of their integral construction and consequent susceptibility to damage from over-vigorous handling of jamming sashes, frame pulleys were generally employed in low-quality work and for light sashes. Heavier windows and careful building construction demanded the use of axle pulleys, which normally combined brass face plates, pulley wheels and axles with cast-iron cases. By the end of the nineteenth century, the smooth operation of heavy sashes was assisted by adopting ball-bearing pulleys, a grease-packed race of ball bearings allowing the concave-section pulley wheel to revolve freely around a hollow circular moulding formed in the pulley case. All patterns of well-made sash pulley were produced with face plates made semi-circular, rather than square, at the ends, so that the plate could be easily fitted flush with the weight box inner lining by occupying a recess formed with a brace-and-bit (Fig 118).

Standard sash pulleys were made in sizes from 44–75mm (1¾–3in) in diameter, increasing in 6mm (¼in) increments. Sash cord was available in a range of thicknesses. 'Samson Spot' cords were available in six thicknesses between 5mm and 10mm (¼in and ⅜in), the thickest cord being suitable to support a load eleven times heavier than the 5mm (¼in) diameter product. Very heavy sashes neces-

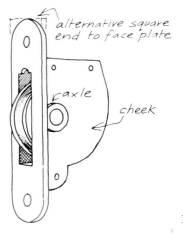

alternative square end to face plate

axle

cheek

Fig 118

139

sitated chain connections with the sash weights. Chains were available in steel, brass and copper in about five sizes. Sash cord can be difficult to obtain today, but traditional ironmongery shops generally have a supply in stock. Sash chains may prove impossible to replace with identical modern material, though various patterns of light-gauge brass chain may be bought by length at most DIY shops.

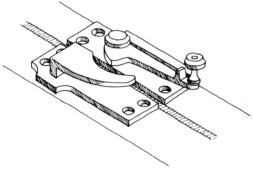

Fig 119

Many different makes of sash fastener were available until recent years, but certain distinct types, all of which remain available, are readily identifiable. One of the most familiar is a latch which operates horizontally, instead of vertically like a door latch. A metal bar swings through a quarter-circle to engage in a keep fitted to the top of the lower sash (Fig 119). The Fitch fastener comprises a helical metal cam which is fastened to the top of the meeting rail of the lower sash and which engages in a hook secured to the bottom of the upper sash. Its chief advantage is that its operation draws two sashes together horizontally and forces them in opposite directions vertically; in this way it holds the sash fast and prevents rattling and

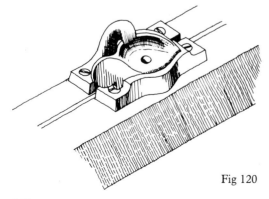

Fig 120

draughts (Fig 120). The screw sash fastener accomplishes the same result as the Fitch fastener, drawing the sashes together by the tightening of a thumb nut on a fine-pitched screw. This circular nut operates against a shaped lug fitted to the lower sash, thus developing great pressure in the desired direction. Though it takes much longer to operate than the other types of fastener, it may be preferred for the greater security which it offers against attempts to force the sashes apart from the outside.

Small double-hung windows can be raised and lowered by pushing against the meeting rails or horizontal glazing bars, but the tendency of the wood to pull away from the glazing which is encouraged by this procedure makes sash lifts essential fittings for large windows. The simplest type is the hook sash lift which was generally supplied in brass (Fig 121). A pair of such projecting fittings is fitted to the inside of the bottom rail of the lower sash to facilitate easy opening of the window. A stronger type of fitting which preserved a plain appearance in the internal frame surface was the flush sash lift, which had to be housed in the wood of the window's bottom rail. Both types of fitting are still obtainable from the small number of brass ironmongery manufacturers which operate today.

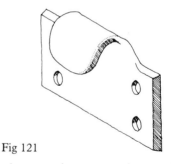

Fig 121

In low-cost houses cast-iron sash weights were standard equipment. Where only a narrow space was available for the weight boxes sited to either side of a double-hung window, or where the use of plate glass resulted in very heavy sashes, lead sash weights were employed, as this material is about 80 per cent heavier than an equivalent mass of cast iron. Lead weights were usually made to special order, in contrast to the mass-produced, cylindrical cast-iron components. The 'bespoke' nature of a lead weight was reflected in its price, which even in the nineteenth century was approximately five times that of an equivalent iron weight. The latter were invariably cast from low-quality waste iron, and each incorporated an eye at its upper end through which the sash cord was knotted. They vary in weight between 12–24kg (26½–53lb) and in length from about 300–800mm (12–31½in). No volume producer of iron sash weights operates today, so it is wise to retain and store carefully any apparently 'redundant' sash weights found in your house for possible future use. Weights replacing those missing from windows scheduled for restoration might have to be purpose-made in lead!

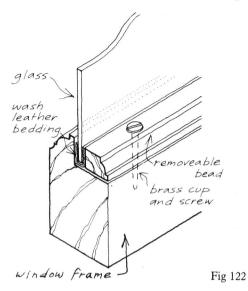

Fig 122

VICTORIAN GLASS AND GLAZING

There was a common principle for glazing all types of inexpensive sheet glass window in the nineteenth century: the glass was bedded in the rebate of the window frame in linseed oil putty and was secured with small metal pins or *sprigs* (copper preferred) before the sprigs were concealed with a sloping profile of putty. Ideally this putty fillet was terminated 1.5mm ($^1/_{16}$in) below the top surface of the internal frame so that slight overpainting of the putty on to the glass surface was not noticed from inside. This method is still perfectly suitable for fixing single glazing today. A very similar technique was used for glazing wrought-iron casements, the difference being that short metal pegs fixed in pre-drilled holes performed the function of the sprigs.

Beaded Glazing

Top-quality construction, in which hardwood was used for the window frames, demanded a better means of securing the glass than simple putty fillets. Separate glazing beads of matching material were fixed to the window frames with fine metal pins or brass screws located in brass cups (Fig 122). In this arrangement, the edges of the glass were first of all bedded in wash leather to remove the risk of fractures posed by direct contact with the rigid timber window frame and to prevent rattling. When replacing such glazing, it is satisfactory to replace the obsolete wash leather with a proprietary glazing tape.

Victorian Glass

Modern sheet glass is widely available in 3mm (⅛in), 4mm (⅙in), 5mm (⅕in) and 6mm (¼in) thicknesses, and it is almost all produced by the semi-secret 'float' glass process in which the molten material is 'floated' over a tank of molten metal, producing large clear sheets of consistent thickness. Very large sheets of polished plate glass are at least 6mm (¼in) thick, but individual lights in even grand houses are unlikely to require glass of this thickness.

Until recent years, glass was sold according to its weight per square foot, 15oz, 21oz, 26oz, 32oz, 36oz and 42oz glass being the readily available weights. Much domestic glazing was carried out in 26oz glass which is less than 3mm (⅛in) thick. The 3mm (⅛in) glass which is its modern equivalent is suitable for glazing small windows where the glass size is not more than 600mm × 400mm (23½in × 15¾in), but larger sizes require 4mm (⅙in) or even 5mm (⅕in) glass. If it was unacceptably thin by current standards, Victorian glass also often contained blemishes which are absent in the modern material. These occurred because old-fashioned sheet glass was produced by blowing the molten material out into a hollow cylinder. The ends of the cylinder were cut off and a straight cut was made longitudinally down the tube, which was then put in an oven and flattened out under the influence of heat. After manufacture, the sheet glass was sorted into classes according to quality, known as 'bests',

Windows and Glazing

'seconds', 'thirds' and 'fourths'. Clearly, much fourth-quality sheet glass was installed in speculative housing, and a wavy or broken appearance in objects seen through the windows of a Victorian house points to the survival of the ancient glass sheet glazing.

Leaded Lights

Plain glass was only one variety of glazing adopted by the Victorians. In an age obsessed with decoration, the patterning of the glass itself was a popular treatment. This was often achieved by installing leaded lights, in which small pieces of glass, or quarries, were carried in channel-section lead strips called cames or calms. This practice dates back to medieval times when glass was expensive and only available in small pieces, but the decorative effect of the technique was its overriding attraction for the Victorians. The cames were made in various versions of the H-shaped channel profile, the width of the lead varying from 5mm (⅕in) to 19mm (¾in) on the face. Each small pane of glass was inserted into the grooves in the encircling cames, bedded in a special cement containing plaster of Paris, linseed oil and lampblack among other ingredients, and the thin lead wings were folded back on to the surface of the glass to secure it. To prevent rattling and rigidify large panels of leaded lights against the potentially destructive effects of high winds, horizontal iron square- or round-section saddle-bars were fixed into the jambs of the window frame across the rear of the glazing. Twin copper wires soldered to the junctions of the lead cames were twisted around these saddle bars, thus strengthening the lead 'grid' which frames the quarries in a typical leaded light. The inclusion of a few special cames incorporating an iron core obviated saddle bars but their consequently thicker section ruled out their use in the cottage-style domestic architecture practised by late nineteenth-century architects. Joints between cames were soldered and a finished light could be fixed in a casement with putty or removable beads.

Used as the glazing of a non-opening window, a leaded light could be fixed directly into a wood frame or stone mullions without the intervention of a casement. This was done by forming a groove in the wood or stone surrounding the opening. The leaded light was worked into this groove by bending back the

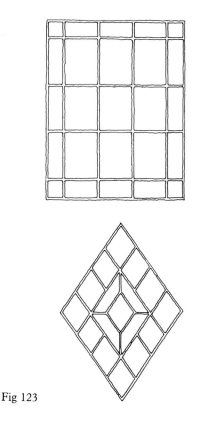

Fig 123

leaves of the perimeter cames, and, once inserted, straightening them out again. If in stonework, the groove was then filled and pointed with cement, and putty was used for securing a fixing into wood. The light was never bent or 'sprung' into position in case the cement in the glazing should be cracked and leaks invited.

Plainly, a limitless range of patterns can be formed in leaded lights. A simple rectangular grid and a diagonal grid of lozenge-shaped (or diamond-shaped) pieces are the most familiar forms (Fig 123), but combined with different colours and varieties of glass (such as 'reeded glass', 'roughcast glass', and obscure glass with a ground surface) straight or sinuous combinations of lead cames can produce numberless variations upon a theme – a property of the material which was not lost on the Victorians.

Coloured Glass

Coloured or stained glass produced in Victorian times was of two types, *pot metal* and *flashed* glass. The colours were obtained by adding metallic oxides to the glass constituents before firing. Pot metal is a glass uniformly coloured all the way through. Flashed glass is ordinary glass with a thin film of coloured glass on one side. It could be patterned by removing the coloured film in the desired geometrical shapes, leaving the plain transparent glass, and this treatment was often adopted to provide decorative semi-transparent panels of coloured glass in front entrance doors. Alternatively, clear glass could be painted. An antique treatment of leaded lights with lozenge-shaped panes was to paint a small geometric pattern in dark red in the middle of each piece of glass. The remainder of the surface was covered with a pattern of conventionalized foliage in a yellow-green tint. Victorian versions of this treatment often included images of flowers, or conventionalized flower forms such as the fleur-de-lis. A durable finish to the painted glass was achieved by firing the glass after its surface had been painted with pigments formed from the mixing of iron oxide and other mineral oxides. Truly luminous colours were obtained only if the glass was fired three times.

Coloured glass is not nearly so readily available today as coloured plastics. Various brands of acrylic sheet are available in a wide range of colours, surface finishes and thicknesses. Though it may quite satisfactorily replace very small pieces of broken coloured glazing, acrylic sheet lacks some of the reflectivity of glass, it is warmer to touch, scratches and marks more easily on contact with fingers and tools and melts at quite low temperatures, giving off toxic fumes. For this reason alone, on no account should it be used for replacing large broken glass panes in attached conservatories, etc; in any case it is unlikely to be approved for this purpose by the local building inspector, who will insist on non-flammable or at least 'self-extinguishing' properties in the reglazing material.

Replacement Leaded Lights

The renovation of leaded lights is specialised work best performed by a skilled craftsman. Many local glaziers continue to offer the services of repair and manufacture of leaded lights and various types of lead cames are still available from the traditional supplier of this material. To increase the appeal of their products, many specialist double-glazing contractors now offer tailor-made double-glazed units patterned with lead cames, which match the surface treatment of the existing glazing of houses where double glazing is contemplated. The size and shape of the individual quarries is measured and the entire pattern is carefully reproduced on the outer and inner faces of the external leaf of glass by applying thin lead strips to the glass surface with adhesive. It is a decorative treatment in contrast to the decorative *and* structural purpose of the old lead cames. Because a single sheet of glass has a pattern applied to it, the rattling of individual quarries which have worked loose from their encircling cames is eliminated. However, it is essential to insist upon the pattern of leads being reproduced on the inside face of the outer leaf of glass, as otherwise the view through the undecorated inside leaf will be of the adhesive which fixes the lead strips to the outside face of the double-glazed unit!

SHUTTERS

In homes heated by coal fires the elimination of draughts induced by the burning fuel easily becomes an obsession, and because they were also mindful of the bleaching effect bright sunlight would have upon fabrics which were not colour-fast, the Victorians generally installed internal shutters in all but the cheapest houses, to minimise draughts and guarantee gloominess. *Folding* or *rolling* shutters were the two main types employed. Inside shutters were normally made of wood in the finish of the joinery of the room which contained them.

Inside folding shutters gave a neat finish to the reveals flanking the inside of the window. They were invariably arranged so that when closed into the shutter box which occupied the window reveal, the exposed leaf of shutter showed a panelled finish to the interior. The leaves of the shutter usually fold into a square jamb, but a grander effect was obtained if they were arranged to fold into a splayed reveal. In this arrangement, the panelling shows up to better advantage and the room benefits from daylight reflected off the splayed surfaces. Where folding shutters were fitted, the space between the window sill and the floor was often covered with a *panelled back* or *breast* which returned below the shutter boxes in the reveals with the same pattern of panelling. The inside

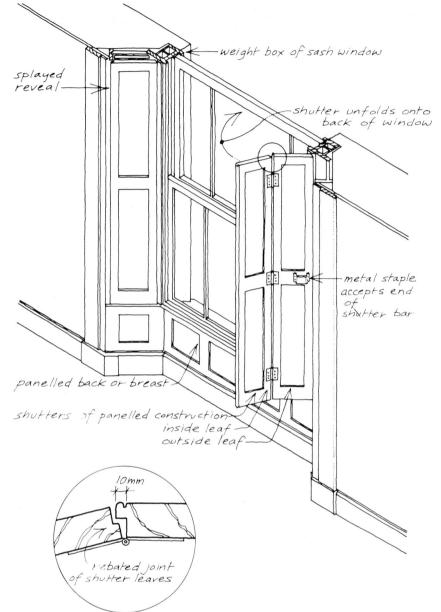

splayed reveal

weight box of sash window

shutter unfolds onto back of window

metal staple accepts end of shutter bar

panelled back or breast

shutters of panelled construction
inside leaf
outside leaf

10mm

rebated joint of shutter leaves

Fig 124

lining of the weight box of the sash window frame normally forms the outside lining of the shutter box, and the inner lining of the latter is generally part of the interior finish in the form of an architrave. The shutter which becomes the window lining when it is retracted (or 'outside' leaf) is hinged both to the inside lining of the weight box and the 'inside' leaf, which swings out of the box to meet the corresponding shutter of the opposite reveal at the centre of the window. This leaf is hinged to the outside leaf in such a way that the knuckle of the hinge is entirely hidden within the edge of the outside leaf's stile. This method of hanging permits the inside leaf to swing back sufficiently from the edge of the stile to secure it from any danger of catching on or against the edge of the architrave when the leaves are retracted into the box. The inside leaf was also made 19mm (¾in) narrower than the outside leaf so that there was no tendency for it to become jammed in the box (Fig 124). The rebated joint between the two leaves is 10mm (⅜in) deep and exists only to ensure a light-tight joint. It is worth noting that shutters fully contained in boxes in splayed jambs (the 'inside' leaves) must be 38–50mm (1½–2in) narrower than the 'outside' shutters if the whole assembly is to fold back into its recess without jamming. When folded across the inside face of the window, such shutters were often secured by slotting a U-shaped flat iron bar into shallow metal staples fixed to the backs of abutting shutter panels, thus rigidifying the entire assembly.

Less common than folding shutters are the rolling shutters which are sometimes encountered in Victorian houses. They operate on precisely the same principles as the double-hung sash window. A pair of framed shutters counter-balanced by lead or cast-iron weights on sash cords is sited internally, behind and below the window sashes. When lowered the shutters are concealed by the panelled back of the box in which they are housed when out of use (Fig 125). The top of this box is both the

internal window sill and a hinged flap which lifts to allow access to the shutters so that they may be raised in the same way as a conventional window sash, in this case to *exclude* daylight. Clearly, the upper shutter has to travel twice as far as either window sash and so the sashcords and weight boxes are proportionately longer than those of the windows. The lower section of each weight box is concealed behind the panelled back which also conceals the retracted shutters. To raise the 'parked' shutters, a recessed brass staple or ring pull is provided in the top rail of each shutter. This fitting allows the hinged flap to close tight to the top of the retracted panels and it is easily pulled out, enabling the operator to roll the shutter upwards. In many houses these fittings have fallen out of use, but if the old paintwork is penetrated and the accumulated dust and dirt sucked out of the cavities between the panels and their carcase with the nozzle of a vacuum cleaner, the good quality of the old timber from which they were made should make it a simple job to recondition the formerly redundant shutters.

External Shutters

Many purely decorative external shutters can be seen on the elevations of modern and 'modernised' houses, but the value of genuine external shutters in excluding rough weather has always been acknowledged by the inhabitants of exposed rural and coastal settlements. When open these shutters lie flat on the external wall surface flanking the windows, an arrangement made possible by fitting them with projecting butt or Parliament hinges, which pivot the shutter leaves out of the window opening. Such shutters are normally hinged from a hanging stile separate from the outside lining of the weight box of a sash window, or the jamb frame of a casement. Sometimes a demountable iron frame from which the shutters were hinged was fitted into the external recess of the window opening, the whole assembly being removed during the mild summer months. External shutters were commonly made from a durable timber such as pine. To admit some light and air even when the shutter was folded across the window, the external frame enclosed a panel of pivoting horizontal louvres. Contemporary 'decorative' shutters reproduce this treatment, but the

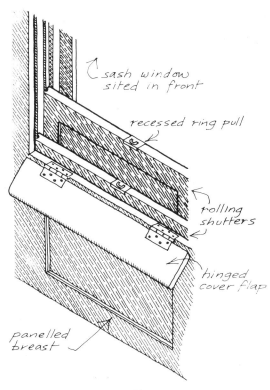

sash window sited in front

recessed ring pull

rolling shutters

hinged cover flap

panelled breast

Fig 125

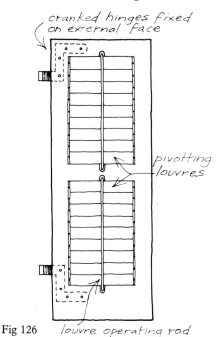

cranked hinges fixed
on external face

pivotting
louvres

Fig 126   louvre operating rod

shutters of large windows can be very heavy, and substantial non-rusting hinges will be needed if it is intended to reinstate fittings which have been dismantled and stored for a period. In shutters shielding high windows, it was unwise to incorporate only a single panel of louvres as this assembly would quickly suffer damage from high winds. Each shutter was split, therefore, into two, three or even four panels of louvres, each activated by its own operating rod and separated from its 'neighbours' by horizontal mid-rails which strengthened the wooden framing (Fig 126).

Reconditioning of louvred external shutters is made more difficult by their elaborate construction, as paint-stripping of the complicated profiles can be very time-consuming. It is much easier to remove the shutters temporarily from the building's elevation and to have the old paintwork quickly removed by a specialised process in which the complete unit is immersed in a bath of sodium hydroxide. Repainting of the bare timber surfaces and refitting of the overhauled components is then a much less formidable prospect. Neither is paint-stripping with a blowtorch a sensible way to prepare dowdy shutters for restoration. The heat of the blowtorch will almost certainly char the thin wooden louvre sections in your attempts to lift old paintwork from the multitude of corners and crevices contained by the shutter framing.

louvres are fixed and the panels are invariably (and mistakenly!) fixed back-to-front on external wall surfaces. To allow room for these overlapping louvres and the integral wooden vertical control rod which is located behind them, the wooden frame was never less than 28mm (1⅛in) thick. Therefore, external

9
Outside the House

The walls, fence or railings enclosing the site on which your house stands may have as much aesthetic impact as the building materials exposed on the outside of the house itself.

Garden walls were often of the same construction as the main house walls – generally 215mm (8½in) thick brickwork with impervious copings of stone or terracotta where a creasing tile course below a brick-on-edge coping was not adopted. The modern method of building single-skin (102mm [4in] thick) brick garden walls reinforced with frequent brick piers was unheard of, though small panels of single-skin brickwork were sometimes incorporated in dwarf walls which were otherwise 215mm (8½in) thick.

Despite their apparently robust construction, Victorian garden walls were usually erected in continuous ranges without expansion joints and with poor or inadequate foundations, so that many examples have suffered badly from subsidence of the supporting ground. The piling of garden earth behind the inside face of a garden wall on the boundary is also a common cause of problems, the wall being induced to overturn, often on to a neighbouring public footpath, posing a risk of injury to passers-by and consequent legal problems! Short of complete demolition and rebuilding, there is little that can be done to salvage such substandard construction, although it may be possible to renew only the most defective sections of such a wall by rebuilding them from the foundation upwards, the sound sections of masonry being left intact. Where a considerable length of wall is to be rebuilt, it is wise to incorporate expansion joints at about 6m (20ft) intervals, as modern cement mortar is not as tolerant of thermal movement in the structure as the lime mortar used by the Victorians. Various compressible joint fillers made from foam plastic and bitumen-impregnated fibre-board, and varying in width from 3–30mm (⅛–1⅛in) are available for insertion in expansion joints. In a brick wall it is usually most convenient to break a continuous surface with a 10mm (½in) wide vertical gap. This open joint is then sealed over the joint filler and in the plane of the wall surface with a proprietary water-excluding polysulphide mastic. These mastics are available in a range of colours so it should be possible to achieve a close match with the brickwork.

RAILINGS AND GATES

Architectural metalwork has a long history, but the exploitation of the decorative potential of cast and wrought iron in architecture has never been taken further than the range of effects which was tried in the nineteenth century.

Cast iron was rarely the sole material used in an iron railing. It tends to be brittle and consequently there are clear limitations upon the slenderness of cast-iron balusters. When used in railings, cast-iron components were often framed by a grid of wrought-iron members of superior tensile strength.

Wrought iron is obtained by the elimination of carbon and other impurities from the basic 'pig iron' which is the original product of the iron-smelting process. It reached the blacksmith's shop in the form of bars, ready for working. Ornamental features were formed by hammering red-hot iron into the form required, or by bending or twisting it, when cold, into the desired shapes. The first technique, known as forged work, was the superior method. Only in this way could the metal be controlled so that delicate ornament, such as flowers, could be formed. In the present day, wrought iron has been almost entirely superseded by mild steel which is easily formed when cold and is ·more readily welded than the traditional material.

Outside the House

Wrought-iron Railings

A railing is formed from many separate components which are joined together in two distinct ways: by welding, or by mechanical connections – usually collars and bolts. The simplest form of railing is an assembly of upright bars, 22–25mm (⅞–1in) in diameter, spaced at 150–175mm (6–7in) centres, passing through the top, and rivetted to the horizontal bottom rail, and forged in the form of spikes at the top. The horizontal rails are likely to be about 50mm (2in) wide and 13mm (½in) thick. Less basic was a railing which incorporated a third horizontal rail, sited about 215mm (8½in) above the bottom rail. In the space between these two rails, metal scrolls or dog bars were inserted, increasing the strength of the railing and preventing the intrusion of dogs.

Where railings were unusually high, or masonry piers giving firm fixings were not provided, or the spacing of the piers was too great to secure the railings properly, it was necessary to provide back stays. As the name implies, these are merely 'props' placed at the back of the railing to give lateral strength. The bar or standard to which the back stay is attached carries the horizontal rails and is generally made a feature of the design. A favourite means of incorporating such back stays and achieving a decorative effect was to arrange two vertical bars, strengthened by back stays, about 375mm (15in) apart, the space between them being filled in with bold scroll-work and foliage hammered from heavy bar iron. This ornamental panel was often complemented by a scrollwork finial surmounting the railing (Fig 127).

The vertical standards or supports to iron railings were placed in holes of dovetail section formed in a continuous sill of stone blocks, a

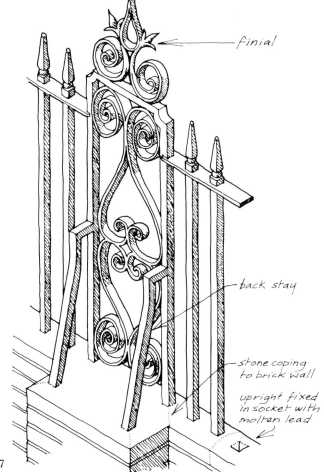

finial

back stay

stone coping to brick wall

upright fixed in socket with molten lead

Fig 127

148

stone coping, or a hard brick coping to a brick dwarf wall, and were secured by 'running' the holes with lead or Portland cement after the uprights had been located. Lead carefully caulked after having been poured is the best fixing material, except in a very damp location, where corrosion of the iron at the point where it meets the lead is likely to occur. In such a case ordinary Portland cement should be used for refixing dislodged railings.

Although bar steel is readily available in a range of shapes and sizes, some of which are almost identical to the 'standard' sections found in wrought ironwork, it may be impossible to obtain an exact match for an incomplete iron railing in the 'stock' steel sizes. To achieve a completely inconspicuous repair it may be necessary to replace an entire range of balusters with simple steel uprights.

Wrought-iron Gates

The simplest form of gate is a rectangular metal frame filled in with vertical bars. Contemporary garden gates in 'wrought iron' are, like modern railings, invariably fabricated from sections of mild steel strip and bar bent to shape and welded together, usually in a very ornate and highly untraditional form!

Victorian iron gates were often taller than the familiar hip-height garden gates which close the driveway entrance between the dwarf walls of a modern suburban garden. A tall gate had to include one or two horizontal lock rails fitted about 900mm (35in) above the bottom of the gate to provide a fixing for the lock and to strengthen the gate's structure. The parallel top and bottom rails of the gate are joined, like the lock rails, to the vertical side members. The bar from which the body of the gate is hung is called the back standard or hanging bar, and the opposite upright is called the front bar. In the case of double gates without any fixed post between them, the front bars are called meeting bars; a slam plate rivetted to one of these enables the gates to engage on each other and to be securely fastened together.

As the back standard bears the whole weight of the gate, the bar used in this position can vary from 32mm (1¼in) to 100mm (4in) square according to the size of the gate. The bottom rail is then of the same width but much less thick. The top rail may be thinner than the bottom rail, but it is often of equal width, as it

must be sufficiently wide to allow the vertical bars forming the 'infill' of the gate to pass through without seriously weakening it. In the case of a gate with 25mm (1in) square section uprights, the top and bottom rails must be 50mm (2in) wide.

Although iron gates can be hung on butt hinges like internal doors, this method was rarely adopted. A looped hinge or *hanger* at the top of the back standard and a pivot at its foot on which the whole weight of the gate is imposed, were generally used. The back standard of the gate is rounded where the hinge clasps it, and the hinge is formed from a loop of thick metal bar bolted around a short piece of bar iron, one end of which is formed in a semi-circle, the other end being 'ragged' (finished with jagged edges) for the purpose of fixing the hinge into the flanking surface of brickwork or masonry (Fig 128). In careful construction, the inside of the hinge was lined with a gunmetal collar. This arrangement prevented the hinge

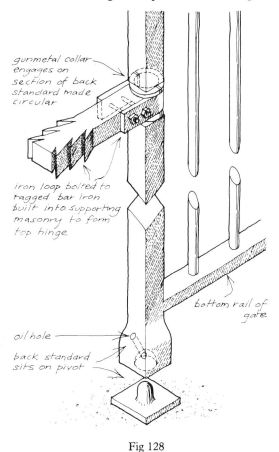

gunmetal collar engages on section of back standard made circular

iron loop bolted to ragged bar iron built into supporting masonry to form top hinge

bottom rail of gate

oil hole

back standard sits on pivot

Fig 128

149

and back standard from coming into contact and thus reduced the risk of rust forming at this point. It was rarely suitable simply to hang a heavy gate on two or three hinges.

The cheapest means of providing a pivot at the foot of the back standard involved locating this member in a dished metal socket set firmly in the ground. As many householders will know, this method suffers the disadvantage that accumulated dirt eventually clogs the socket and the gate becomes difficult to move. A neater detail which should be built into restored wrought-iron gates places the dished profile in the underside of the back standard, the projecting pivot on which it engages being set into the ground. The joint between the two components is thereby raised above ground level and the risk of jamming is consequently reduced. If a small oil hole is drilled through the flared end of the back standard (which sits on the pivot), it is a simple matter to lubricate the joint periodically, so preventing squeaks (Fig 128).

Wooden Gates

The original wooden garden gate to a Victorian house is unlikely to have endured to the present day. Continuous use and continuous exposure to the weather quite quickly take their toll on wooden gates, particularly if they are not carefully repainted fairly frequently. When renewing a decayed wooden gate, it is advisable to have its replacement made in hardwood, even if it is to be painted, as the hardwoods normally used in building are much more impervious to moisture than any of the generally available softwoods. Most large DIY outlets stock a range of 'standard' garden gates in hardwood, but the authentic Victorian look of a gate resembling a ledge-braced and battened external door in which voids alternate with the vertical wooden slats, to give a semi-transparent surface, will be obtainable only if you either make it yourself or commission a 'special' from a joinery workshop. When your gate arrives, it should be hung on metal strap hinges fixed to a stout hardwood post set firmly in a mass concrete foundation sited considerably below ground level.

BALCONIES, VERANDAHS AND PORCHES

Balconies located on the street elevation of expensive town houses provided another opportunity for a display of elaborate wrought-iron railings. Small projecting balconies below individual windows were normally formed from single slabs of stone built into the street elevation, and propped by triangular cast- or wrought-iron brackets also built into the external wall thickness; in the time-honoured way of fixing any iron railing, the balustrade surmounting the balcony was then fixed into mortices in the top of the stone slab by running lead into the joints between the metal balusters and the stonework. To give greater strength and rigidity, the integral iron handrail of the balustrade was 'fish-tailed' (formed in a 'Y' shape in plan) at each end and built into the external wall thickness.

More modest suburban houses are unlikely to boast panels of wrought-iron balcony railings, but for these dwellings, elaborate carpentry was a usual form of construction for balconies, porches and verandahs, and the decorative treatment of the timber complexities of these features became an essential quality of the architecture of the suburban villas erected in the late nineteenth and early twentieth centuries.

A verandah which is roofed by an upper storey of a house or a projection of the main roof is sometimes termed a 'loggia', even if it is open only on its main elevation and not at the sides, as the description strictly requires. However, the principles of the construction of the timber floors and wooden balustrades frequently found in these features are the same.

Just as the carved stone slabs used for the balconies of city dwellings were shaped to throw water off the balcony surfaces, so the wooden floor of a verandah or timber balcony was made to slope at about 1 in 50 from the main house elevation to its front edge. Because of this, the floor boards were laid from the front to the back of the projecting verandah or balcony and not across its width, thus discouraging rainwater from lodging in the joints. Joists running parallel to the main elevation rather than perpendicular to it resulted from this arrangement, and support for these joists was obtained by notching them into stout timber girders built into the house elevation and the brick or timber structure supporting the verandah's outer edge (Fig 129). In a long verandah these girders would be sited at intervals not exceeding 3m (10ft), but a conventional domestic balcony might require only two girders, one supporting each end. To give the required outward slope to the verandah floor, these girders could be laid at the necessary inclination or their top surfaces could be sloped to the desired pitch. In either case, the joists were installed so that their top surfaces were flush with those of the girders, the flooring being laid directly on to this common surface.

To be enduring, verandah flooring was at least 32mm (1¼in) thick, of tongue-and-groove profile, and laid in white lead; that is, the joint between any two boards was thoroughly filled with a paste composed of white lead and linseed oil. This was believed to seal the joint. Where the timber was carefully selected from the suitable types of wood, namely redwood, red pine or teak (a very durable hardwood), this treatment may still be standing the test of time.

Although verandahs which cover nothing more than a shallow basement or ventilated crawl space may be satisfactorily finished with a boarded surface, wooden boards alone will be penetrated eventually by rainwater, and any balcony surface required an impervious finish. As a balcony is meant to be walked on, the sheet metal covering conventional for roofs of bay windows was not a suitable finish, and asphalt was normally laid over the boards to give a level, watertight surface. If the original installation did not incorporate a membrane of bituminous felt separating the poured asphalt from the boards, differential movement of the timber and the wearing surface may have introduced cracks into the asphalt which serve to draw water into the building construction, causing serious deterioration. In any renewal of an asphalt surface laid on boarding (including plywood and chipboard, the modern substitute for 'T&G'), insist upon the molten asphalt being laid on a continuous separating membrane of bituminous felt.

Wooden balustrades screening verandahs, balconies, loggias and porches were framed up as panels of vertical slats located in continuous timber top and bottom rails, themselves fixed to the main supporting posts of the verandah structure. In this way, a multiplicity of joints between individual balusters and an almost continuously damp floor finish was avoided, and the risk of wet rot penetrating the ends of the spindly – and thus very vulnerable –

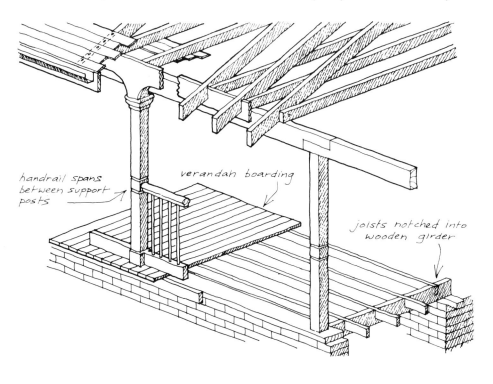

handrail spans between support posts

verandah boarding

joists notched into wooden girder

Fig 129

151

Outside the House

wooden balusters was much reduced. For the same reason, the undersides of the main supporting posts of a verandah or porch structure were sometimes set above the floor by means of metal shoes or cast-iron buttons 25mm (1in) thick and 50mm (2in) in diameter. Four such buttons were placed under a square post, the metal pins which projected from the top and bottom surfaces of these components being let into the floor and the underside of the post, and bedded in white lead. Another method was to rivet the buttons to an iron plate which was itself secured to the underside of the post. A simple but effective decorative treatment of the main verandah uprights was achieved by chamfering the supporting posts on their corners, the octagonal cross-section resulting from this chamfering being returned to a square profile at the ends by terminating the splay faces on oblique-cut chamfer stops (Fig 130).

A verandah which is not integral to the house must have a separate roof, and where this roof was added to obscure as little as possible of a main elevation, a low pitch was employed which necessitated a sheet metal roof covering on a substratum of tongued-and-grooved

boards. In good-quality construction, the ceiling of the verandah was formed from narrow strips of pine or hardwood, laid on and secret-nailed to the ceiling joists. A better appearance resulted if the ceiling boards were installed at right angles to the building, in which case blocking or firring strips had to be run at right angles to the ceiling joists to carry the boards. In cheaper work, the verandah roof was left open on the underside, exposing the timber construction of the rafters and roof boarding, the narrow, planed tongue-and-groove boards being laid with their finished side downwards.

CONSERVATORIES

The vagaries of the English climate encouraged those Victorians with a passion for the newly discovered tropical plants to extend their houses with glasshouses, which provided conditions congenial to these specimens. A celebrated example of a purpose-designed iron conservatory attached to a quite compact country mansion survives at Flintham Hall in Nottinghamshire, where a decorative central fountain complements the glistening foliage of numerous rare and exotic plants. Conservatories attached to more modest houses were rarely constructed exclusively of cast and wrought iron, though the glass roofs of 'lean-to' outhouses quite commonly consist of a type of patent glazing which incorporates lead-covered steel glazing bars. The remainder of such a structure is almost certain to be painted woodwork on the lines of balcony balustrade construction, with panes of clear glass replacing the balustrade panels, the whole framework being erected on a dwarf wall of single-skin brickwork. This choice of largely wooden structure for most Victorian conservatories explains the ramshackle appearance of many surviving examples. Timber is prone to shrink or swell with changes in temperature and humidity, and posts or sole plates in contact with the ground will have rotted over the years, causing sections of the structure to subside, bulge and sag. Where such decay is well advanced, nothing less than the complete replacement of the shaky structure with modern rot-resisting materials will suffice, but a sagging roof slope can be instantly improved by substituting aluminium patent-glazing bars for the original wooden sections.

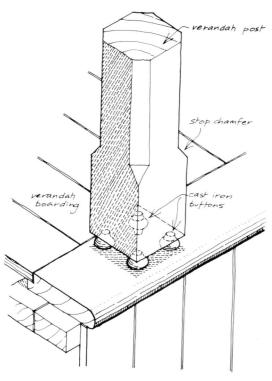

Fig 130

152

The interiors of conservatories were often elaborately decorated. Patterned encaustic tiles provided the floor finish, whilst coloured glass in leaded lights contrasted with the large sheets of clear glazing to provide privacy and add interest to the views from inside and out (Plate 25).

YARD AND PATH SURFACES

The use of quarry tiles for external pavements such as garden paths and terraces has been touched on already. It may be difficult to find replacement tiles which exactly match the size and colour of broken Victorian items, but at least various types of quarry tile continue to be manufactured today. The same cannot be said for the many varieties of Staffordshire blue clay pavers which were also used for yard surfaces. These hard tiles, or brick-shaped pavers, normally displayed a top surface patterned with rectangles or diamond shapes thrown into relief by a grid of incisions made in the clay. This incised surface reduced the risk of pedestrians slipping in wet or frosty weather. Because many of the old patterns of blue-brick pavers and

Plate 25 A small 'lean-to' conservatory. Its roof is of sloping patent glazing. The glazing of the elevations shows the common arrangement of large panes of clear glass bordered by smaller panes of coloured or patterned glass (*Author*)

channels are no longer made, you may have to advertise for replacements though it should be said that they are extremely hard-wearing and are not easily damaged.

Maximum durability was also the main reason why granite setts (sometimes erroneously called 'cobbles') were used to pave stable yards and mews areas. The iron shoes of horses quickly wore away softer surfaces than those of dense Scottish or Cornish granite. In the same way, most Victorian city streets were paved with these blocks. Indeed, in most British cities the highly patterned road surfaces of granite setts criss-crossed by tram lines disappeared below tarmac surfaces only in the 1950s.

Less enduring than the granite setts, which you may find as the surface of a yard adjoining your house, and widely used as a street surface in Victorian thoroughfares where it was import-

153

ant to restrict the noise of horse traffic, were wooden setts – square blocks of hardwood packed tightly together to form a continuous pavement. Such a surface is unlikely to have survived intact to the present day, and as the Victorians acknowledged, it can be treacherous in wet weather.

Pavements formed from a continuous surface of slabs are more common than surfaces laid with setts. Before the advent of the pressed concrete paving slabs which provide the wearing surfaces of most contemporary urban footpaths, York stone was the most popular pavement and it may survive as the surface of private pathways serving Victorian houses. As it is still quarried today, it is simple, if expensive, to replace. Though it may be a better match with retained slabs, second-hand York stone is in such demand for restoration projects that it is likely to be as costly as the new material if bought in bulk.

10
Services and Fittings

The availability of piped main services to most dwellings is really a development of the twentieth century. The humblest Victorian houses were devoid of even the most rudimentary means of bringing water and fuel into the home. Water had to be brought in buckets from a communal pump or well, cooking was done over an open fire which also served as the source of heat, artificial lighting was by candles and oil lamps, and sewage accumulated in privies or in infrequently emptied communal pails.

However, street lighting by gas-fuelled flames had made an appearance in London before even Victoria's reign, and by the end of the nineteenth century many houses had the facility of artificial light provided by burners consuming locally manufactured gas. From the 1880s electricity also became available for lighting house interiors, although the general availability of electricity had to await the establishment of the National Grid electricity distribution network. Partly for this reason, many dwellings even in urban areas remained unconverted to electric lighting until the 1930s or 1940s. Piped and purified mains water distributed from local reservoirs was introduced from the middle of the nineteenth century in parallel with the development of municipal sewerage, and the telephone was the last modern service to be introduced into dwellings, the proliferation of domestic 'phones really occurring only after World War II.

HEATING AND VENTILATION

Just as it is used for this purpose today, so in Victorian times gas was sometimes employed for heating the home as well as for lighting it. Formidably ugly, cast-iron gas grates incorporating a mat of asbestos fibres as the heating surface were superseded after 1918 by equally ugly fires fitted with the more familiar ceramic honeycomb burners. Yet the burning of solid fuel – and this almost invariably meant coal burnt in open grates – was the staple means of heating Victorian houses.

The construction necessary in a wooden-floored house to accommodate an incombustible fireplace hearth has already been described. Certain other constructional features were essential to ensure the efficient operation of an open fire. The hearth opening in the chimney breast was usually constructed with splayed sides to maximise the flow of combustion air from the room into the grate. The opening above the fireplace into the chimney flue was constructed as an inverted funnel in order to guide the ascending current of heated air and smoke towards the bottom of the flue. This throat to the chimney was formed by drawing over the brickwork which flanked the fireplace opening, each course of bricks adjacent to the opening being corbelled, or made to advance slightly in front of the course immediately below it. The projecting lower corners of the bricks were then cut off with the edge of the bricklayer's trowel and the corbelling produced a curved profile leading to the neck, or inlet, of the flue proper (Fig 131).

The effectiveness of the flue depended upon the temperature of the gases flowing through it, and therefore the height of the opening over the fire was often restricted to about 750mm (29½in), so that cold air from the room would not readily pass up the flue without first coming into contact with the fire.

It was preferable to build flues curving rather than straight, because this policy prevented rain and sleet from falling vertically on to the fire, and also tended to check the downward passage of currents of cold air or *down-draughts*. To be effective, the divergence of a flue should be such that daylight cannot be seen by a person

Services and Fittings

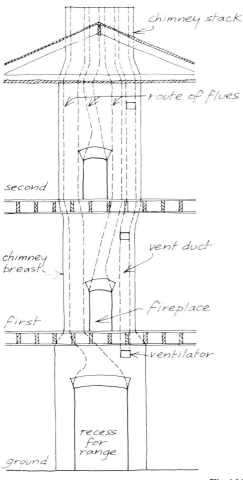

chimney stack

route of flues

second

chimney breast

vent duct

first

fireplace

ventilator

recess for range

ground

Fig 131

looking up the flue from the fireplace recess. The normal size of a flue for an ordinary fireplace was 225mm × 225mm (9in × 9in), whilst for larger fireplaces and kitchen ranges a continuous 337mm × 225mm (13½in × 9in) void was used. Fireplaces serving the same storey were often placed back-to-back so that their separate flues could be carried up together. Where hearths were situated immediately over each other (as in upper storey rooms) it was necessary to divert the upper parts of the lower flues to one side of the upper storey hearth to avoid the niche of this fireplace. To ensure the efficiency of such flues in carrying away smoke and fumes, this divergence had to be gradual, as friction in the flue caused by sharp angular offsets would drive smoke back down the chimney. A gently curving route for a flue was usually achieved by

building in large-radius curves formed in corbelled brick construction (Fig 131).

The grouping together of several fireplaces serving the same storey and the consequent grouping of the flues had one particular advantage for the builder – it minimised penetration of the roof finish by chimney stacks and thus simplified roof construction and weatherproofing. Grouping the flues also increased their efficiency as an updraught of combustion air in one flue induced a similar movement of air in adjoining flues. This phenomenon was sometimes exploited as a means of improving room ventilation. A vertical air duct about 150mm (6in) square was built in alongside the chimney flue, terminating at its upper end in the roof space of the house, with its lower end terminating at high level in the room served by the related chimney flue and fireplace. When the fire was lit, combustion gases in the chimney flue heated the surrounding brickwork and the air in the neighbouring ventilation duct and induced it to move upwards, thus drawing stale air out of the room. To minimise the draughts induced by the burning fuel from badly fitting doors and windows, fresh air was sometimes fed directly to the fireplace through a 50mm (2in) diameter iron pipe connecting it with the outside air. Cold down-draughts in the ventilation duct were obviated by a fabric flap over the grille venting the head of the duct into the roof space.

Even chimney flues which have not served a solid fuel fire for many years are likely to contain large deposits of soot, and they must be swept clean if a chimney fire is to be avoided when a new fire is lit in the grate. This accumulation of soot occurs in spite of the fact that most flues incorporate smooth internal surfaces. This finish was achieved by applying parging to the flue walls. An ancient practice which survived into the nineteenth century was the coating of these surfaces with cow-dung parging, but by the end of the century this method had been superseded by the application of a continuous cement-mortar lining (albeit often containing ox hair). If the parging was omitted, soot could settle in the open mortar joints of the flue walls, creating the risk of repeated chimney fires.

The location of the chimney stacks in relation to the roof surface was crucial to the efficient operation of fireplaces. When the wind blows horizontally, air compressed against the surface of a chimney pot flows up over its top edge in such a way that a zone of still air is created directly over the chimney opening, allowing the chimney gases to pass over the pot's leeward edge into an area of low pressure. As the windspeed increases, the pressure of this area is reduced and the chimney draught is correspondingly augmented. When the wind blows upwards, the area of low pressure is formed closer to the top of the chimney and the escape of flue gases is greatly assisted. When the wind blows downwards, the escape of chimney gases is cut off, and unless there is sufficient pressure behind the gases to deflect or lift the wind at the mouth of the chimney, a down-draught results.

A chimney sited at or near the ridge of the main house roof which is not in the lee of higher roofs will invariably function well, because the wind deflected upwards by the inclination of the windward roof slope assists the escape of chimney gases as it passes over the chimney pots. Chimneys sited below the ridge of the main roof on the leeside will be adversely affected by wind driven down the roof slope on which they are located, as indeed will chimneys crowning the apex of lower roofs on the leeside of the main roof. A traditional remedy for the down-draughts created in such chimneys involved extending the chimney pot with a metal pipe, fitted at the top with a conical cowl (Fig 132). Thus the top of the chimney was removed from the zone of downward air currents. Yet the fitting of the 'protective' cowl might prove counter-productive. By partly blocking the chimney opening it excludes down draughts, but it is equally likely that it will inhibit the escape of flue gases. An alternative modification to chimneys which was believed to be an effective cure for the smoking fireplace which resulted from down-draughts, was the fitting of a circular deflector to the top of the chimney pot. The curved top surface of this deflector caused that part of the wind which it blocked to be lifted well above the top of the chimney. Thus the chimney gases were given an opportunity to escape over the leeward edge of the modified chimney-pot terminal (Fig 132). To prevent chimney pots from being dislodged by strong winds, each pot was usually secured to the supporting stack by building in its bottom rim behind an oversailing course of corbelled brickwork situated at least one course below the

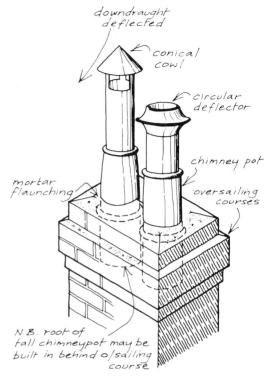

Fig 132

top of the stack, and surrounding the lower part of the pot with a sloping profile of cement mortar flaunching, bedded on the top surface of the chimney-stack brickwork (Fig 132).

Grates
For heating the habitable rooms of a house, three types of open fire, grate or stove were used by the Victorians: register grates, several forms of fire-on-the-hearth stoves and the dog or basket grate.

Ordinary register grates consisted of a metal frame (usually cast iron) which closed in the fireplace opening and which was fitted with a receptacle for the fuel, comprising front and bottom furnace bars and a fireclay or metal back and sides, over which was fitted an adjustable flap valve, damper or hinged canopy. The most efficient types of metal register grate were combined with a fireclay lining about 75mm (3in) thick which directly surrounded the fire on three sides. This pattern of grate was introduced after 1780, and from about 1840 the Carron Ironworks, the most famous manufacturers of cast-iron fittings, manufactured a

Plate 26 A cast-iron register grate surmounted by a semi-circular arch embellished with cast-iron mouldings. Many thousands of grates of similar design were mass produced during the nineteenth century (*Ashby & Horner*)

register grate incorporating a semi-circular arch (Plate 26) which remained a very popular fitting throughout the Victorian period.

In a fire-on-the-hearth stove, the fuel was burnt at or below floor level, the front furnace bars of the register grate were replaced by a small lip of fireclay or metal, and practically the entire surface of the stove in contact with the fire was formed in fireclay. This brittle receptacle was carefully placed in position in the fireplace recess, the whole space behind and at the side being filled with concrete or brickwork.

Register grates and fire-on-the-hearth stoves were sold in two forms: as fireplace interiors (in which case they were fixed into a separate chimney piece) or as combined mantel register grates or stoves, in which the entire fitting was in one piece or assembled *in situ*.

The dog grate or basket grate consisted of a fuel container mounted on legs forming a raised and portable fire-basket which was simply placed within the fireplace recess.

Kitchen Ranges

Before the advent of gas and electric cookers, cooking was invariably carried out on a solid-fuel stove integral to a kitchen range. Even the most humble terraced houses incorporated such a cast-iron fitting containing an oven, hot plate and register-grate open fire. A more sophisticated range incorporated a fire with a high-pressure 'boot' pattern boiler at the rear, roasting and baking ovens to either side of the fire, hot plates over these ovens and a plate rack spanning across the full width of the fitting at high level (see also later section on Hot Water Supply). The heat of the fire was concentrated upon each oven and upon the boiler by an arrangement of horizontal and vertical flues controlled by dampers. The normal condition was to have the central fire burning below the hotplate and hinged canopy. If a fiercer open fire was wanted, the central top plate would be slid back and the hinged canopy with its supporting side cheeks would be drawn out. Combustion was also controlled by a hinged adjustable fire bottom which could be raised or lowered according to the desired size of the fire (Fig 133).

As the overall height of the kitchen range might easily be 1500–1800mm (59–71in) and its width could be 1800mm (71in), a very large fireplace recess had to be provided for it in the chimney breast. The great heat generated by the cast-iron construction necessitated the building-in of a solid brick horizontal lining grouted with fireclay or fire cement on the floor of the fireplace recess below the ovens. This lining was normally at least 120mm (5in) high, although its thickness varied with the pattern of range used and its height was also determined by the level of the soot door or the front of the range. A similar lining was built vertically at the back of the recess, the flues being formed in this material, two to suit the outlets adjoining the baffle plates under the ovens, and one continuing the arched opening below the back boiler. Baffle plates were inserted below the ovens to break the flow of hot air under these chambers and to prevent it going directly up the flue before it had properly circulated around, and thus warmed the ovens. The seating for the boiler was solid brickwork built up from the floor. Soot doors were always provided in the brick lining of the range to give access to the flues which required frequent sweeping.

Surviving cast-iron kitchen ranges are few and far between. The promise of cleaner cooking with modern equipment and the association of the old fittings with grim times, has prompted many householders to dismantle and demolish these characterful Victorian devices in spite of their massive and heavy construction. Where the enlargement of a tiny room by the removal of range is not a pressing need, please give consideration to preserving the fitting, if only to exploit its decorative potential!

Central Heating

Modern domestic central heating generally comprises a gas or oil-fired boiler supplying hot water at low pressure to metal panel radiators via metal pipes. So it was in the late nineteenth and early twentieth centuries, though in the absence of oil and North Sea gas, solid fuel was used to heat the water in the boiler, the fuel generally being coke. Neither could Victorian central heating systems incorporate the control devices, including electronic programmers, electric pumps and motorised valves, which are conventional fittings in a contemporary domestic central heating installation. The circulation of hot water was achieved by the water attaining the proper pressure to raise it to the highest radiators, and gravity was relied on

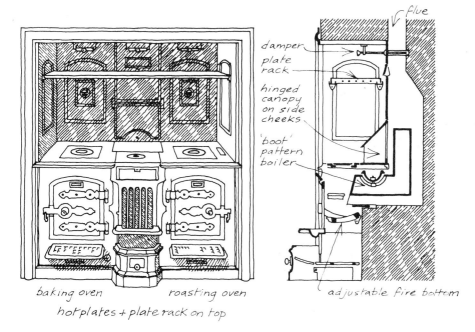

baking oven   roasting oven
    hotplates + plate rack on top

flue
damper
plate rack
hinged canopy on side cheeks
'boot' pattern boiler
adjustable fire bottom

Fig 133

159

to return it to the boiler. For this reason the small diameter pipes used today were unknown, and radiators were served by 38mm or 50mm (1½in or 2in) diameter steel pipes of the type familiar to visitors to old 'Board' schools and Victorian hospital buildings.

A conventional Edwardian central heating system for a six-bedroomed villa would include fourteen radiators fed from a 50mm (2in) diameter main, although flow and return branches to each individual radiator would be 19mm (¾in) in diameter with a 25mm (1in) return main to the solid-fuel-fired boiler sited in the cellar or basement furnace room. The slender panel radiators used today were then unheard of, the standard Victorian equipment being heavy and bulky 'column' radiators consisting of grouped elliptical-section 'hoops' of cast iron. Where it was impractical to install these heavy radiators in upper-floor rooms, the main heating pipe could be arranged simply to perform a horizontal circuit around the accommodation to take the chill out of the enclosed air.

Ducted Heating Systems

Although such a system of heating and ventilation would be highly unusual in a speculatively built house, a type of centralised room heating which was sometimes installed in 'bespoke' residences by Victorian experimenters was ducted warm-air heating. Two types of ducted system relying on steam heating were employed: indirect radiator and fan-assisted installations.

In the indirect radiator arrangement, cast-iron radiators connected to a steam-heating system were suspended in the cellar space below the joists of the ground floor rooms. Each radiator was enclosed in a duct which ended externally in a grille fitted flush with the outside wall, and internally in a metal grille fitted flush with the floor or wall surface. In this way, the heat of the radiator drew in the colder external air, which was raised to a suitable temperature as it passed over the radiator surfaces before being introduced into the room. The heating system thus operated also as a means of ventilation. A damper fitted below the internal grille gave the option of closing off this supply of heated air; the floor-mounted grilles were sited separately from the radiators so that dust or dirt accidentally swept from the floor surface into the *register*, or duct terminal underneath,

could be easily cleaned out if a grille was temporarily removed, without impairing the efficiency of the indirect radiator.

As it was difficult to heat upper-floor rooms equally well with such a system (extended ducts and bends in ducts inevitably compromising its efficient operation), where an extensive warm air system was installed, it was normal for the flow of incoming air to be fan-assisted. This involved the installation of a large centrifugal fan fitted in a duct in the basement of the house and powered by an electric motor or small steam engine. The fan was connected by a duct to a grille in the outside wall which admitted fresh air. It forced some of this air through a spiralling coil of steam-filled pipes, thus raising its temperature. The other part of this fan-assisted airflow bypassed the heating coil. Further along the system a mixing damper was provided to vary the temperature of the ducted air by mixing the hot and cold air streams in differing proportions. From this point the heated air was distributed to the rooms through metal or masonry ducts built into the floors and walls, terminating in metal grilles sited close to the ceilings. Each outlet incorporated hot and cold air ducts and its own mixing valve. To ensure good ventilation by an efficient exchange of fresh and stale air, exhaust ducts with grilles located at low level, venting to the outside air via the roof, were also fitted in all heated rooms.

Clearly, this fan-assisted system was an expensive feature of even a new house, as it required the inclusion of many ducts in the basic structure which could not be so conveniently grouped together as the battery of chimney flues around which a conventionally heated dwelling might be planned. The extra construction cost resulting from this consideration was additional to the expense of purchasing, installing and maintaining the necessary mechanical plant. For these reasons, the fan-assisted system found greater favour in countries which experience greater extremes of climate than Britain – notably the USA.

ARTIFICIAL LIGHTING

Gas Lighting

Artificial lighting by gas has fallen almost entirely out of use today except in some older houses in country areas where mantles have been kept burning by the use of bottled liquid petroleum gas. Yet in the nineteenth century the greater part of the pipework installed by a gas fitter was intended to serve the gas lighting.

Many of the Victorian iron gas supply pipes (or 'mains') located below the streets and pavements carry North Sea gas today. A gas supply to an individual house was traditionally made with a cast- or wrought-iron pipe, of smaller diameter than the street main, but the connection to the main is nowadays carried out in a flexible plastic pipe colour-coded in yellow to identify it visually as a gas pipe. This service pipe always terminates at a meter – a practice unchanged from the days of the Victorian town gas companies. Connections from the meter to fittings were formerly made with plain wrought-iron tubing with screwed joints. These joints were sealed with red lead compound and the pipes were fixed to internal walls with hooks or patent pipe clips. The service pipe was never less than 19mm (¾in) in diameter, but a large gas stove might require a supply from a distributing pipe 25–38mm (1–1½in) in diameter. The distributing pipes or branches of a modern installation are usually of copper, precisely like those used to distribute hot water throughout the central heating system. The antique wrought-iron branches used to supply gas lighting burners could be as small as 6mm (¼in) diameter, so it is not unusual to find sections of defunct gas supply pipework embedded in the 25–32mm (1–1¼in) of plaster which was the normal internal wall finish of a Victorian house. The surface of a chimney breast over the mantel shelf often obscures narrow, dropping vertical branches of the gas supply, because an eye-level location over the fireplace was a favoured fixing point for gas lighting brackets.

Looking back to the nineteenth century from our age of efficient electric artificial lighting, it is difficult to comprehend the complicated measures the Victorians adopted to obtain low-quality gas-fuelled lighting. Although from about 1880 electric lighting seemed to promise improved illumination, the earliest light bulbs produced only a dim glow and were very unreliable. It was only after World War I that technical developments radically improved the quality of electric light, and it is clear from contemporary comments that the Edwardians greatly desired improvements in domestic illumination.

An example of the care that was necessary in installing gas lighting to ensure an even moderately efficient system was the slight inclination of the pipes and brackets, so that the small amount of water vapour which condensed in the pipes and flowed back to the lowest points could be drained off, instead of impeding the gas supply. Sometimes a whole system of house pipes was arranged to drain back into a siphon at the meter position. Because a flame burns upwards, pendant (suspended) gas light fittings had to be arranged so that the burners pointed upwards. Naturally this factor imposed limitations on the size and efficiency of reflectors sited above the burners, because not even a metallic reflector could be so arranged that there was a risk of contact between it and the naked flame. Similarly, the burning flame could discolour ceilings or other surfaces too close at hand. For this reason, naked pendant fittings were usually suspended about 900mm (35in) below the ceiling, and this restricted them to high rooms. If they were fitted closer to the ceiling, a metal deflector was often installed over the flame. In no circumstance was a pendant burner sited closer than 450mm (18in) below a ceiling. A property of the gas flame which was turned to decorative effect was its similarity to a candle flame. Many wall-mounted gas brackets were made in the form of candelabra, cylindrical porcelain mouldings in imitation of candles enclosing vertical, brass candle-tube supply pipes which terminated in the hemispherical tips of the burners. Such fittings were often located on chimney breasts, complementing the ornate carved woodwork or cast-metal features of the mantel shelf and grate.

A technological development introduced around the turn of the century which did much to improve the performance of domestic gas lighting was the incandescent mantle. This was an open-ended cylinder of woven fabric saturated with a chemical solution. It was fitted over the gas burner, and when lit, produced a much brighter light than that of the naked burner flame. A further advantage of these conspicuously fragile mantles was the option of inverting the burners so that their flames burnt downwards. This arrangement made it possible to fit to gas brackets shades and diffusers of the type used to shield electric lamps. Surviving and functioning gas brackets are almost certain to be the mantle-mounted type, as the mantle

Services and Fittings

gave a light output greatly improved over the earlier 'bat's wing' and 'fishtail' naked flame burners.

Electric Lighting

Before 1918 electricity supplied to houses was used only for the purpose of artificial lighting. The demand for circuits supplying electric current through power points was a need engendered by the proliferation of electric-powered domestic appliances during the inter-war period.

Victorian and Edwardian designs for electric light fittings tended to reproduce the style of fittings adopted for domestic gas lighting. For this reason there was a preponderance of bracket fittings. The pendant fittings which monopolize the electric lighting installation of a modern speculative house were generally out-numbered in an electrically lit Victorian house by bracket fittings incorporating a single lamp. These were cantilevered off the walls on curved or 'swan-neck' metal brackets. Sometimes the lamps were simply hung on the flexible electric supply cable which was itself suspended from an ornate projecting bracket (Fig 134).

A plain Edwardian pendant would consist of a ceiling rose, a supply cable suspending a brass

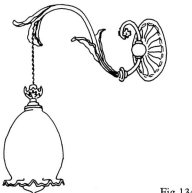

Fig 134

lampholder, a clear glass light bulb and a conical opal glass shade which gave a 'finished' appearance and reflected the light downwards. More 'Heath Robinson' in appearance and characteristically Edwardian were counterweight pendants which allowed the height of the lamp to be adjusted. This type of fitting consisted of a plain pendant with a counterweight added and

Fig 135

pulley wheels fixed both to the ceiling and to the counterweight. The cable serving the lamp passed through an eye attached to the counter-weight, so that lowering of the lamp and reflector causing raising of the counterweight did not induce the weight to rotate around the supply cable (Fig 135).

Much less common except in grand houses were *electroliers* or electric chandeliers. A simple form of electrolier consisted of a rigid tubular metal stem containing the supply cable, which ended in a circular cast-metal body to which the tubular arms of the electrolier were connected, and a spun metal shell and pendant knob respectively enshrouding the body and 'finishing off' the underside of the fitting. The enclosed cast-metal body of the electrolier included holes in its top and bottom surfaces to connect it to the tubular stem and to accommodate the wire securing the pendant knob. The sides of the body also contained threaded holes into which the arms of the electrolier were inserted and secured with setscrews. The arms of such an electrolier could be curved upwards or downwards, or they might be at right angles to the stem.

Library and dining-room pendant fittings often boasted a gilded chain stem through which the cable was threaded and an 'art-glass' shade finished with a silken fringe. This impressive form of fitting, like the ornate oil lamp it replaced, was sometimes installed as a low centre-feature over a dining-table. The art-glass shade was constructed in sections held in position by a gilded or nickel-plated metal frame, and the silken fringe was sewn to a sheet-metal band which was connected to the shade with setscrews. Similar pendant fittings, adjustable in height by means of a complicated system of pulleys, ornamental counterweights and suspension cords and clad in highly patterned or scintillating fabrics, were also installed in expensive houses. Be warned that they have become prized collector's items!

Victorian ingenuity was stretched almost to its utmost in contemporary designs for combination fittings; that is, wall or ceiling-mounted light sources which operated on gas *and* electricity. This arrangement is not as unlikely as it sounds because these devices took advantage of the property of a gas flame to burn upwards and the policy of suspending electric light bulbs by siting the burners and lamps respectively above and below the stem of each fitting. It was only necessary then to ensure that the electric cable-ways and gas supply tubes were kept completely separate. This type of fitting enjoyed only a short period of popularity, because the advantages of reliable electric lighting over gas brackets soon became apparent and there was then no point in installing 'combination' fittings which were more expensive than the simple components of a purely electrical system. For this reason alone, it is highly unlikely that many fittings of this type have survived to the present day. Indeed the continued existence of many Victorian and Edwardian light fittings outside museums is questionable because contemporary electrical wiring which has survived until today is likely to represent a safety hazard. The rubber-coated cables which were used to wire new houses even as late as the 1950s are liable to perish after a few decades, introducing the risk of short circuits and disastrous fires resulting from the contact of exposed wires. Therefore a Victorian house which was fitted with electric lighting at the outset may have been rewired once or twice in its lifetime, the period fittings having been 'retired' at each rewiring.

The reconditioning of old electric light fittings to the high safety standards of modern appliances is better undertaken by a skilled electrician than an enthusiastic amateur, but the increasing availability of reproduction items makes it a simple matter for the diligent restorer to obtain new fittings which will harmonize with the surviving Victorian features of an interior.

WATER SUPPLY

In the final decades of the nineteenth century, municipal and private enterprise began to meet the requirements of the new city buildings for reliable supplies of fresh drinking water. The corporations of Birmingham and Liverpool constructed reservoirs in Welsh valleys from which drinking water was conveyed to the two cities in underground aquaducts, whilst Manchester met its needs from the natural lakes of the Lake District. In London, the New River, an initiative of the seventeenth century, brought fresh water to large reservoirs in Finsbury from its source at Amwell in Hertfordshire. The distribution of the purified water from local surface or subterranean reservoirs was accomplished by cast- or wrought-iron water-main pipes located below the streets. A supply to an individual house was arranged by forming a hole in the street main – the supply having been isolated from this section – and a screw thread was then formed in this hole. Into this opening a hollow brass or iron ferrule was screwed. The plain end of this ferrule was then soldered to the lead service pipe with a wiped joint in which the solder uniting the two materials was made to encase the joint completely. If a wrought-iron service pipe was used, a threaded socket finished the 'house' end of the ferrule so that the iron pipe could be screwed into it. A valve or *stopcock* was then attached to the pipe near the ferrule or where the service pipe entered the building. Such stopcocks are often found in cast-iron boxes with hinged covers fitted flush with the earth in a garden area close to the front boundary with the street. They enable individual houses to be isolated from the main without disrupting the water supply in that important pipe.

In addition to the stopcock sited close to the connection to the main, an identical valve was usually fitted to the service pipe in a convenient spot close to the point of entry of the pipe into the house, so that repairs to pipes within the house could be made without the water company's stopcock near the street needing to be closed. A still more sensible arrangement placed a draw-off tap on the rising main (the domestic cold water supply pipe rising to the storage tank) on the house side of this stopcock so that the house pipes could be emptied to prevent them freezing in a severe frost. Water expands as it freezes and soft lead piping is notorious for its susceptibility to split under the increased internal pressures which result from freezing water.

Where a service pipe passed through a foundation wall, allowance was usually made for the possible settlement of the wall by leaving a space of 50mm (2in) or more on all sides of the pipe. Good practice called for the lead pipe to be enclosed in a 'thimble' of iron pipe two or three sizes larger than the service pipe, which was built into the foundation wall. Such underground pipes were as likely to be adversely affected by frost as the integrity of internal pipes was to be threatened by freezing conditions. For this reason they were often located about 750mm (29½in) below ground level which was safely below the frost line. To ward off corrosion of the pipework from the soil, iron pipes were normally painted with a protective compound, or lagged with a special pipe-covering applied when the pipe was heated. Lead pipes were sometimes protected by encasing them in rough deal tarred boxes filled with bitumen. It is unlikely that this protection will have endured to the present day. In any case, lead pipes are much less likely to corrode in most soils than is iron piping. The pipes used by the current water authorities to provide new buildings with a drinking water supply are invariably flexible tubes made from corrosion-free plastic compounds.

Water Storage

Even today in some areas, the water supply system cannot be relied upon to provide water at a pressure which will guarantee the consistent supply of fresh water to the highest sanitary fitting in the house. Partly for this reason the route of the rising main has for many years been arranged so that a high-level water storage tank is almost the first device to be fed from the supply pipe. The one exception to this rule is the direct connection to the kitchen sink, which is tapped off the main before it rises to the storage tank in order to ensure at least one source of uncontaminated mains water. An equally important reason for the adoption of a system in which most of the fittings received their cold water supply by gravity from a high-level cistern was the consideration that negative pressure in the street main should not suck back potentially contaminated water contained in the domestic fittings. The supply of mains water to the cistern was regulated by a floating ball valve attached to the incoming pipe. When the tank was filled and the ball valve floated almost level with the supply pipe, it cut off a further supply of water until some stored water was drawn off. To guard against the malfunction of the ball valve and consequent overfilling of the tank, an overflow pipe sited a little below the tank's top level and discharging into the outside air through an external wall was incorporated. The operation of this pipe gave clear notice of a defective ball valve. The pipe was fixed a little below the inlet level of the supply pipe so that stored water could never rise to the level of the inlet, sending possible contaminents back down the rising main (Fig 136).

Nowadays, domestic water-storage tanks are invariably of moulded plastic construction and they tend to be available in metric capacities equivalent to the old 50 gallon, 100 gallon and 200 gallon sizes (227, 454 and 909 litres). Victorian water storage tanks were commonly made of metal – galvanized wrought-iron cisterns being available in a range of standard sizes. They were made from 3mm (⅛in) thick plates rivetted to iron corner reinforcing angles with 10mm (⅜in) rivets. Such cisterns were quite light and durable but the water in some districts tended to attack the zinc coating of the iron with the consequence that the metal underneath corroded, fractures developed and a leak ensued. The modern moulded plastic cisterns entirely avoid this problem. It was normal to fit a removable wooden cover to the top of an iron cistern to prevent 'foreign bodies' from falling into the stored water. A tank of this type was most suitably sited in the roof space directly above the bathroom, thus economising on pipe runs, but in some circumstances shortage of space caused the cistern to be mounted on heavy wooden bearers sited at high level in the bathroom itself.

Alternative types of storage tanks which may have survived down to the present day include

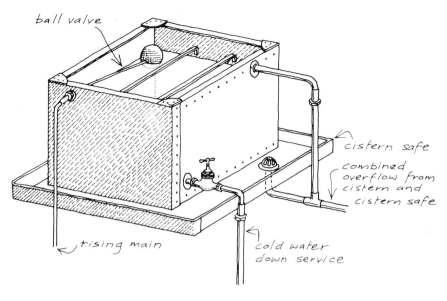

ball valve

cistern safe

combined overflow from cistern and cistern safe

rising main

cold water down service

Fig 136

slate cisterns and lead- or copper-lined wooden cisterns. Slate slabs 25mm (1in) thick were sometimes used to form the complete carcase of a cistern, the side slabs being housed into the end pieces, tie bolts being passed along the outside to secure the projecting parts of the end slabs. Joints between the slabs were sealed with neat Portland cement. Though clean and durable – providing the cement was not washed out of the joints, inviting leaks – slate cisterns could not be of large capacity because of the difficulty of obtaining large unblemished slabs. Their considerable weight demanded that sizeable slate-slab cisterns were sited outside the house on masonry piers or in a substantial integral water tower. Small domestic cisterns were also available in stoneware or glazed fireclay. Lead-lined wooden cisterns were not used to store soft water as it dissolves the lead, the water is quickly polluted with lead compounds and is consequently dangerous to drink. Copper was believed, quite erroneously, to be equally dangerous and so its water-resisting surface was coated with tin when it was used to line a wooden cistern. Wooden cisterns could develop leaks because the filling of the tank caused the wooden walls to bulge and its emptying prompted them to return to their original shape. This movement injured a lead cistern lining because the metal has little elasticity and will not withstand repeated bending at the same point. To counteract this

problem, various measures were taken to reinforce wooden tanks. Large tanks made from 50mm (2in) thick deal boards were reinforced with side posts or stiffeners housed into the bearers below the tank and braced across its top with iron tie rods. Small cisterns not exceeding 1200mm (47in) long, 900mm (35in) wide and 600mm (23½in) deep were made from single boards 25mm (1in) thick, connected at the corners with dovetailed joints reinforced with nails. The boarded bottom of the tank was spiked on to the prefabricated 'box' of sides and ends, thus preventing the lower sections of the sides and end from spreading, and preserving the metal lining.

It would be unusual to discover in an average Victorian town house an original cistern with a capacity of more than 150 gallons (682 litres) (a common overall size for this tank capacity being 1200mm × 900mm × 750mm [47in × 35in × 29½in]) although sometimes sufficient water was stored to cater for the needs of the household over two days on the basis that each person would use 25 gallons (114 litres) of water per day. The water storage capacity of modern domestic tanks tends to be smaller than this, as not only can space taken up by large tanks be put to better use, but also a reliable and continuous supply of mains water is now more likely than it was in the nineteenth century. The minimum capacity acceptable today for a tank providing a cold water service only is 50

165

gallons (227 litres), but a storage tank supplying the hot water service too should contain at least 80 gallons (363 litres).

The standard galvanized wrought-iron cistern favoured by the Victorians not only suffered the drawback that rusting of its seams was likely eventually to lead to leaks, but also that in humid weather the metal construction caused condensation to form on its outer surface, from which it would drip on to the supporting building construction. To protect absorbent materials from saturation by the dripping water, a *cistern safe* or shallow tray of sheet copper, sheet lead or thin galvanized steel was sometimes installed below the tank. The inclusion of this 'drip tray' necessitated an overflow pipe from the safe itself which could be combined with the tank overflow before it passed through the wall to discharge into the outside air. A small cistern required a 32mm (1¼in) diameter safe waste pipe and a larger installation would be fitted with a 38mm (1½in) pipe. To prevent rust or sediment clogging the pipe, in the best work the end connected to the safe was protected by a convex brass grating soldered over its open mouth and fitted with a removable rim so that the grating could be extracted in order to clean out the pipe (Fig 136).

Modern plastic cisterns are almost equally likely to create condensation in humid weather, but this tendency can be checked by insulating the tank with a jacket of glass fibre quilt or expanded polyurethane or polystyrene slabs. In any case it is wise to insulate water storage tanks located in a roof space otherwise uninsulated from the outside air, to prevent the stored water from freezing in severe winter weather. All connecting pipework which is similarly exposed must also be insulated. Preformed sections of tubular foam polyurethane which fit over the small-diameter copper pipes currently used to carry a cold water down service are generally available for this purpose. Less efficient Victorian attempts to prevent exposed lead or iron pipes from freezing included covering the pipes with hair felt and a continuous canvas jacket which was stitched tightly over the felt or secured with copper wire. Where pipes ran horizontally between ceiling joists, a measure of insulation was obtained by filling up the surrounding void with sawdust or slag wool.

Cold Water Down Service

The delivery of cold water to fittings was effected by a delivery pipe which connected with the storage cistern about 50mm (2in) above its underside, so that any sediment which collected in the tank would not be sucked down the pipe as the water was drawn off. Apart from the tap over the scullery sink which drew drinking water direct from the rising main, all the fittings, including water closets, bathtubs, lavatory basins (wash-hand basins), showerbaths and bidets (rarely fitted in Victorian houses but nevertheless available in the nineteenth century), were supplied from the cistern via a lead or iron delivery pipe.

Where a lead water supply pipe ran horizontally, hooks or lead tacks were used to support the pipe at intervals not exceeding 900mm (35in). Though the policy was not often adopted, it was good practice to set pipes in sleeves where they passed through walls and partitions in order to prevent their expansion and contraction from cracking the plaster. To conceal the resultant open space between the pipes and the wall surface, small circular shields or *escutcheons* sleeved on to the pipes were used. Such horizontal runs were generally distribution branches taken off the dropping delivery pipe of the cold water down service at each floor level to serve a group of fittings. Each fitting in the group was supplied through a branch taken from the distributing branch. In a well-installed system, valves were provided off the down-service supply pipe at the head of each distributing branch so that the supply of water could be shut off from each group of fittings. In a very expensive installation, valves might be provided on each branch so that individual fittings could be isolated from the supply.

The unreliability of the metals used for water supply pipes prompted Victorian plumbers to expose the pipes in rooms rather than to conceal them below floors or in partitions. Where they were concealed and fixed over expensive ceilings, potentially leaky pipes were sometimes placed in lead-lined safe boxes to prevent drips or condensation from staining the wall and ceiling construction beneath.

A common size for the main supply pipe dropping from the tank in the roof space was 38mm (1½in) diameter; distribution branches springing from this pipe might then be 25mm

(1in) diameter, with individual fittings being served by 19mm (¾in) or 13mm (½in) pipes.

SANITARY FITTINGS

Metal, marble, slate and pottery were all used in the manufacture of Victorian sanitary fittings. Cast iron was the metal most generally used because it was hard (if brittle), dense and impervious and was readily cast into intricate shapes in large sizes. Its surface could be painted, galvanized, japanned (coated in dense and shiny black lacquer) or finished with a metallic or vitreous enamel. Certain alloys were used to make accessories such as taps and gratings to waste outlets, notably brass, which is an alloy of copper and zinc, bronze which is composed of copper and tin, and gunmetal from copper and tin with a little zinc added.

Fine-grained slate was used for large areas of impervious slabs such as draining surfaces adjacent to laundry sinks, but it was not used in the best class of work. Marble slabs were used in a similar way in connection with expensive washbasins of the type installed in the dressing-rooms and *en suite* bathrooms of opulent houses.

Three varieties of pottery were used in the manufacture of sanitary fittings, namely earthenware, stoneware and porcelain. Earthenware is made from various clays mixed with powdered flints and other ingredients to give a quality of finished material varying from a porous terracotta-like texture to a strong, dense, semi-vitrified product. Stoneware is made from refractory clays burnt at higher temperatures and is close-grained, hard and impervious. It was usually glazed by a process in which the main ingredient was common salt, and thus went under the name salt-glazed ware. Porcelain is made from china clay mixed with powdered flints, powdered bones, sand, etc. So-called porcelain sanitary fittings were usually manufactured from a very carefully prepared earthenware composed of fireclay, covered with an enamel of porcelain. The finish of this high standard of pottery in many ways resembles the fine china of a dinner service.

The moulded plastic or pressed steel baths and basins and chromium-plated fittings which proliferate today were unknown, and naturally appear out-of-place in an otherwise authentic Victorian interior.

Sinks

Long before the advent of the moulded stainless steel sinks which are standard equipment in the kitchens of modern houses, Victorian sculleries, kitchens, pantries and housemaids' cupboards were provided with sinks in porcelain-enamelled moulded cast iron, glazed stoneware or porcelain-enamelled fireclay. They were supported on pedestals, standards, brackets or corbels. It was not the custom to mount the sink on a range of cupboards as is usual with a contemporary lightweight stainless steel unit. Even in the nineteenth century it was possible to obtain a moulded fireclay sink with an integral sloping grooved surface adjacent to the sink and draining into it, but separate draining boards of hardwood, edged in non-corrosive metals and fixed alongside the sink on cantilever brackets projecting from the rear wall were equally prevalent.

After many years' use, glazed fireclay sinks become unhygienic because the glaze wears thin and the porous earthenware begins to absorb waste water. Fireclay 'Belfast' sinks are still obtainable, but the retention of clay sinks in kitchens in preference to the adoption of completely impervious stainless steel basins cannot be recommended. This is an area where the maintenance of hygienic conditions should, perhaps, override the desire to recreate an authentically Victorian arrangement.

Wash-hand Basins

Wash-hand basins or lavatory basins continue today to be of the two basic types which were familiar to the Victorians. They were either formed in one unit, the basin, slab, skirtings and apron being made from one moulding of cast metal or pottery, or they were built up from two or more pieces and often two or more materials. This second type consisted of a basin of sheet metal, cast iron or pottery, with the lavatory top or slab and skirting being made of slate or marble perforated with an opening which was sited centrally over the basin. In the present day, this latter type of fitting is called a vanitory unit, and an impervious top slab surface of plastic laminate (often patterned in imitation of marble) usually replaces the genuine marble slab used in Victorian work in all but the most expensive installations.

The cheapest form of lavatory basin which was installed in many pre-1918 speculative houses was the plain wall lavatory on brackets. It was made of white enamelled earthenware, the basin, top and skirtings being in one piece. It was supported on two plain enamelled iron brackets and fitted with 13mm (½in) diameter gunmetal taps, strainer waste and overflow (Fig 137). Although this fitting seems primitive by the standards of modern sanitary ware, it is worth remembering that in many Victorian households washing was accomplished in a large ceramic dish filled with cold water from a large clayware jug or ewer which had been filled with water the previous evening!

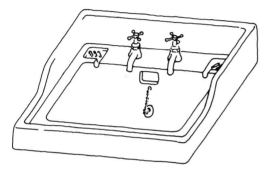

Fig 137

Antique built-up basins incorporated a carved marble top encircling a round or elliptical opening over the basin, and a low carved marble splashback or skirting fitted against the wall surface at the rear of the basin. This skirting would be extended along the sides of the basin where it was built into a full-depth recess. Where basins were built into corners, a basically triangular shape of slab with a curving front rim was often adopted. However, this space-saving arrangement tended to look cramped, and even if a corner location for the basin was inescapable a rectangular slab might be employed, not only to give a more generous appearance, but also to give more space to the user. The slab was supported at the back by a cleat or shallow bracket built into the wall and at the front by metal legs or brackets. Common sizes for such slabs ranged from 600mm × 475mm (23½in × 16¾in) to 900mm × 550mm (35in × 21½in). The thickness of the slabs was 32–78mm (1¼–3in) and the skirtings were 19–25mm (¾–1in) thick. Contemporary vanitory units are best sited in a full-depth recess so that the unattractive and potentially

unhygienic joints between the plastic laminate cladding sheets can be minimised. From many large DIY outlets it is possible to obtain laminate-clad blockboard suitable for accepting the vitreous-enamelled steel washbasins which are today's equivalent of the cast-iron products used by the Victorians. As it benefits hygiene as well as a neat appearance to exclude joints from the plastic laminate-clad surround to a recessed washbasin, handymen intending to install built-in vanitory units may wish to order from a joinery workshop 'post-formed' profiles of laminate-clad board which incorporate smooth curves at changes of plane rather than butt joints between plastic sheets joined at right angles. The limitation of the post-forming process is the condition that jointless curves in the plastic may be made in only one plane of the material, granting a further advantage to a recess location for a vanitory unit. Where the top surface of the unit is curved downwards and upwards by post-forming at the front and rear respectively, a 'monolithic' appearance results which is sufficiently impressive not to need a surface patterned in imitation of marble (Fig 138).

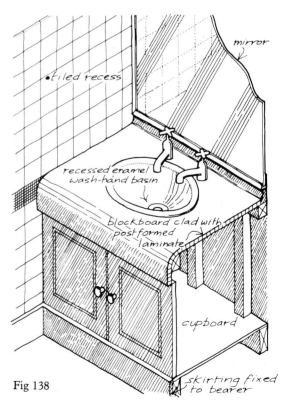

Fig 138

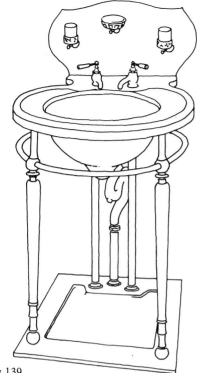

Fig 139

The most elegant type of Edwardian lavatory basin was an 'open' lavatory consisting of an elliptical basin fixed below an onyx marble slab supported on its front edge by two slender metal legs. A matching marble splash-back of very decorative shape complemented the slab, and the waste and water supply pipes, legs, soap tray, towel rail and taps were nickel, or even silver-plated (Fig 139).

Baths and Showers

For the Victorians the most popular bath was a cast-iron tub, coated inside with white porcelain enamel and outside with metallic or vitreous enamel. The rim of the bath was made in the form of a roll, cast in one piece with the bath. The rounded head, square foot, parallel or tapering sides and deep bulbous form carried on cast-iron feet are hallmarks of the traditional bathtub which is only now regaining some appeal after decades of unpopularity. If the original bathtub in your house has survived in good condition, and you do not object to the appearance of an exposed tub (a marked contrast with the 'encased' arrangement favoured for over fifty years), it may be possible

to recondition the fittings by repainting its discoloured interior with bath enamel and renewing the taps and waste grating, because good copies of ornate plated Edwardian taps are increasingly available.

Much of the technology exploited in modern bath accessories was also available to the Victorians. The predecessor of the modern 'mixer' tap was the combination bath tap, through which water was supplied to the bath via a single discharge nozzle containing the shut-off valves for the hot and cold water. Similarly, a combined shower and plunge bath equivalent to many modern installations was also available to turn-of-the-century households. A standard, cast-iron tub was modified to this arrangement by adding a vertical U-shaped metallic-enamelled zinc or steel shield to the foot of the bath, accommodating vertical supply pipes from the side spray and for the overhead shower nozzle, the supply of water through these pipes being controlled by a tier of valves on the edge of this

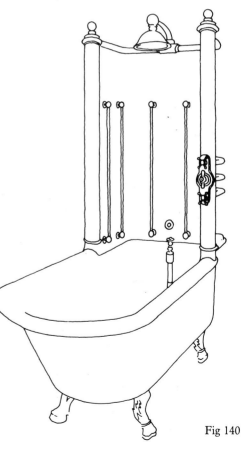

Fig 140

canopy (Fig 140). A cheaper type of combined plunge and shower bath substituted for the zinc shield a flexible rubber curtain hung on rings sliding on a circular tube around the shower nozzle. The inclusion of a side spray from vertical supply pipes was impractical in this 'budget' arrangement.

Purpose-made, independent shower baths were rarely installed in pre-World War I houses, though they were standard equipment in many institutional buildings like the Public Slipper Baths which the many Victorian tenants who lived in bath-less houses were obliged to frequent. Many ingenious shower fittings and complementary compact shower trays in porcelain-enamelled fireclay or moulded plastic are available today to make the inclusion of a shower bath in a refurbished house more of a standard feature than a luxury. A new shower bath is best built into a fully tiled recess so that the impervious surface of the tiles protects the other components of the local building construction from the detrimental effects of steam and hot water.

Water Closets

As with lavatory basins, so with water closets: the basic types still installed today were familiar to the Edwardians. The pedestal wash-down closet is perhaps the most common type of wc. Some Victorian houses in London and the south-east still retain their original wash-down wc pans which were made in the Chelsea works of Thomas Crapper, pioneer of the modern flushing wc. The essential features of this fitting are: 1) an impervious basin of suitable shape and area to be completely drenched by the flushing water, 2) the retention of sufficient water in the trap at the base of the fitting to ensure the immediate immersion and dilution of excreta and to prevent the pan from venting the soil pipe, 3) the provision of a flushing rim which thoroughly distributes the flushing water, and 4) a trap which refills immediately with fresh water when the foul water has been evacuated. The proprietary fittings available at the end of the nineteenth century which incorporated these features were so clearly recognised as superior in every way to the foregoing 'hopper' and 'wash-out' closets that they had entirely superseded these devices in the buildings being erected at the end of Victoria's reign. A standard installation incorporated a cast-iron flushing cistern fixed about 1800mm (71in) above the closet, the ball valve which released the water in the cistern being operated by a pull chain. The manufacturer's name was often embossed on the front face of a metal cistern or sealed into the glaze coating the fireclay in the case of a ceramic cistern.

The syphonic type of flushing wc was sometimes installed in expensive houses. It tends to be quieter in operation than the simple wash-down closet as it operates on the principle that the syphonic action of its deep-seal trap draws the contents of the pan down to the soil pipe as fresh water flushes the basin. The fireclay moulding for this type of wc is much more complicated than that of the wash-down closet and a larger capacity cistern giving a minimum 3 gallon (14 litres) flush was necessary. Again, the flushing cistern was generally sited at high level, an arrangement ensuring efficient flushing which is rarely employed in contemporary houses. Yet the low-level cisterns which proliferate in the modern and modernised dwellings were known to the Victorians, and even a type of low-level cistern with push-button flushing apparatus similar in its operation to contemporary compact 'flush panel' cisterns was available. Like many later builders of semi-detached suburban houses, some nineteenth-century contractors realised that where space was limited, the great advantage of a low-level cistern was the option of siting it below a window. In order to compensate for the less efficient flush of a low-level cistern, the Victorians fitted a large diameter flush pipe between it and the pan (minimum 63mm [2½in] diameter). Modern low level wc suites rarely incorporate a flushing pipe greater then 32mm (1¼in) diameter. It should be added that injection-moulded, self-coloured plastic wc seats first appeared only about thirty years ago. In Victorian times and for many years afterwards, wc seats were of painted or enamelled wood.

HOT WATER SUPPLY

In a modern centrally heated house where low-pressure hot water is the heating medium, a supply of hot water is normally provided by utilising a branch of the heating system to warm cold water stored in an insulated cylinder or *calorifier*. Water in this tank is heated by a coil of copper pipe integral to the central heating system, which passes through the vessel. Cold water from the high-level storage tank refills the cylinder as the hot water is drawn off. This system is easily assembled from the small diameter copper pipes which are invariably used in modern, hot water, radiator central heating, but these components were not available to the Victorians and domestic water heating was usually achieved by a more direct method (though a calorifier system formed from cumbersome iron pipe was sometimes installed in large buildings provided with steam heating). The standard domestic installation comprised the 'back boiler' of a cooking range or living-room grate, which received heat from an open fire when a damper was operated. The heated water, becoming less dense, ascended a flow pipe into a large storage cylinder, thus displacing cold water already in this tank which was induced to enter the boiler, there to be heated, until hot water filled the entire system. Hot water for washing could then be drawn off at the bathroom and kitchen taps. These storage cylinders were often built into the internal brickwork of the house – normally at high level within the chimney breast, which also enclosed the cooking range, thus economising on the connecting pipework. This arrangement ensured good insulation of the cylinder and conserved the heat of the stored hot water not immediately required. By siting the system at the centre of the house, the heat radiated also helped to keep the rooms warm. Where the parts of such a system remain in good condition although they have fallen into disuse, it may be possible to return the storage cylinder and supply pipes to working order, even if the original heat source of the open fire is obsolete, by installing an electric immersion heater in the tank. This device effectively heats stored water when it is energised by throwing a switch.

The condition of the pipework which connects the 'back boiler' with the cylinder may be the chief factor in bringing a Victorian hot water supply system back into use. Four main types of tube were used for this purpose and to supply hot water to the taps: lead, galvanized iron, and brass or copper tube. Though copper pipe was highly valued because the metal is not corroded by pure water and is sufficiently elastic not to be adversely affected by the expansion caused by carrying hot water (factors which account for its almost universal adoption in modern central heating systems) it was rarely used by the Victorians because of its high price. Similarly, brass pipework was uncommon, not only because of its high cost, but also because it was more likely than copper to split in service. Galvanized iron pipe was most generally used for cold and hot water distribution, yet it is prone to corrode at joints and bends where the protective galvanizing can be eaten away by friction or maintenance. This defect alone may militate against the recommissioning of a disused back-boiler system. Equally liable to fail, but by reason of their poor elasticity rather than any special susceptibility to corrode, were lead hot water pipes which were very widely used in the north of England.

Range boilers were made in various shapes and sizes from cast iron, wrought iron and copper. Cast iron, being the cheapest material, was very widely used in speculative houses and if a cast-iron boiler was imperfectly made or in any way misused, the brittle nature of the material might result in an explosion and serious injury to people. Used with soft water, cast-iron boilers very soon rusted and discoloured the water. Wrought-iron boilers were usually made from 6–10mm (¼–⅜in) thick plates welded together. Popular shapes for these back boilers included the boot, arched and saddled forms, all of which were arranged to arch over a horizontal duct of the flue leading from the open fire (Fig 133).

In larger houses and blocks of flats, the simple domestic range boiler was not adequate to meet the water-heating needs and an independent boiler had to be installed for this purpose. Normally constructed from 8–10mm (⁵⁄₁₆–⅜in) thick wrought-iron plate in the same way as good-quality back boilers, they were much more powerful than the 'built-in' type. A chamber for burning the solid fuel fed in through an iron fire door was surrounded by water contained in a wrought-iron 'jacket'. When heated, the water ascended into the pipework of the hot water system through a flow pipe on top of the boiler and was displaced by colder water returning from the system through a pipe entering the boiler casing at low level. An independent boiler had to include two basic features unnecessary to a back boiler; namely, its own flue or pipe connection to a conventional chimney flue, and a connection on top of which a high-level steam pipe with a safety valve was fitted.

DRAINAGE

Drainage Below Ground

The method of disposing of soil and waste water from a house depends upon the availability of a public sewer. Even in the late nineteenth century many urban and suburban areas were provided with a system of public sewers. Indeed, little modification or renewal of the original extensive Victorian sewer network has been undertaken in the ensuing decades, as many local authorities are now discovering to their cost.

RURAL HOUSES

A small, cheaply constructed Victorian country house having no access to a sewer would have drains only for the disposal of waste water from the scullery sink. This drain would connect with a sump or cesspool built with open joints which allowed the water to soak away into the surrounding soil. Because water closets were ruled out on grounds of cost, primitive earth closets had to meet human needs.

The principle of the earth closet was that dry, loamy earth, freshly applied, would deodorize excreta which could then be dug into the top surface of the garden earth. The fitting which operated on this principle consisted of a perforated hinged seat on brackets, which extended over and held in place a portable pail. At the rear of the seat was a wooden box containing the dry earth which was released into the pail by pulling a stirrup-shaped handle alongside the seat. When the pail was close to full, its contents were emptied into the garden earth and the empty disinfected pail was refixed below the hinged seat.

Better quality rural houses were provided with water closets which demanded the installation either of a watertight underground cesspool to collect the sewage or a septic tank for its treatment, the latter device being effectively a small sewage disposal works. Until the end of World War I and for some years afterwards, the septic tank system of sewage treatment was employed only in connection with the largest rural houses.

Cesspools intended only to drain waste water

from washing and food preparation were also called *soakaways* because they were built 'dry' in stone or brickwork with open joints, allowing the accumulated waste water to soak into the surrounding earth. Such underground chambers were usually cylindrical with a domed roof, which might incorporate a circular opening in the crown fitted with a cast-iron airtight cover lying flush with the garden surface. Soakaways of this type functioned well only in certain types of earth. They were never located in clay soil which is virtually impervious. Watertight cesspools used in clayey soil where the liquids would not filter away, or in loose soil where pollution of the earth from sewage was unacceptable, were built of bricks laid in cement mortar, and a ventilating pipe was provided. The inside of the cylindrical chamber was finished with a coat of Portland cement in an attempt to make it watertight. Although good-quality construction demanded a 215mm (8½in) thickness for the enclosing wall and vaulted roof of a 'tight' cesspool, if the supporting soil was dense and stable, the cement-rendered floor of the chamber was simply applied over a single thickness of bricks rather than a more solid concrete slab base. Sometimes a cesspool was split into two separate compartments, the first, smaller chamber being a settling tank for the solid waste, and the second, larger vessel being the liquids chamber. In this arrangement the build-up of potentially explosive gases in both compartments would be avoided by the provision of piped outlets to a common air vent above ground. The neatest type of cesspool currently available is a prefabricated two-piece grp (glass reinforced polyester) chamber which is simply buried in a large hole in a garden area adjoining the house. Local authorities covering rural areas generally provide a cesspool-emptying service which involves pumping the accumulated waste into a mobile tank. This service was available in some areas even in Victorian times, though cesspool emptying was then effected by a horse-drawn van fitted with a vacuum pump rather than the purpose-designed motor vehicles which are used today.

Apart from the foul drainage system discharging into a cesspool or septic tank, and the gutters and downpipes draining rainwater from roofs into water butts or an external tank so that it might be used for washing and garden watering, land attached to rural houses was often safeguarded from flooding by installing a separate system of field drains. These consisted of short sections of earthenware pipe about 75mm (3in) in diameter, laid with open butt joints to allow the percolation of the subsoil water through the joints. The pipes were placed about 1m (3ft) below the surface in parallel lines from 1.8–2.4m (6–8ft) apart, the trenches in which they were housed being partly filled with loose stones to assist the drainage of the subsoil water into the pipes. In sparsely populated areas, such field drains were run to a convenient ditch, but in suburban locations, where field drains were used to drain otherwise marshy garden paths, the drain was usually terminated at a soakaway sited in porous ground.

Though digging in the garden may bring to light a broken length of pipe which seems to suggest that the field drainage is defunct, this is unlikely to be the case. Many Victorian systems continue to drain waterlogged land efficiently and you are not advised to dig them up!

URBAN HOUSES

Much speculative housing was erected in the major British cities long before knowledge and concern about bad sanitation caused comprehensive systems of underground sewers to be built. The only sanitation available to these impoverished dwellings were pails emptied at intervals as a service of the local authority. However, the health hazards which accompanied this arrangement were clearly recognized and consequently the building of the sewers which are the key features of sewage disposal in our towns today continued throughout the late nineteenth and early twentieth centuries.

Two types of public underground drainage system exist in urban areas, namely combined and separate systems. The latter arrangement provides separate drains for foul water emanating from sinks and wcs, and surface water drained from roofs, yards and gardens. As its name suggests, the combined system discharges both types of drainage into a single sewer, its chief shortcoming being the risk of flooding at the sewage treatment works following a downpour. Where separate systems apply, the local authority will insist upon the installation of entirely separate foul and surface

water drains in any modification of the existing drainage to cater for the enlargement or rearrangement of your house. In an area where separate systems do not exist but are contemplated, the local authority may require new domestic drains to be kept separate to the line of the site boundary, beyond which they may discharge through one pipe into the existing combined sewer.

Current building regulations require that drains below ground shall run straight between manholes or inspection chambers giving access to the pipes. Indeed, this was reckoned to be good practice even before 1900, and the advent of national building regulations prescribing a unitary standard, but the proliferation of local by-laws laying down differing requirements caused the details of underground drainage to differ from area to area. Therefore, do not be surprised if you find wholly inaccessible curves built into drains below ground! Principles which *were* generally observed included discharging kitchen sinks into a waste pipe separate from that serving the bath, washbasin and wc, providing trapped gullies for the waste water discharged from scullery sinks, and avoiding locating drains beneath the house. In many provincial towns, rainwater pipes and sink, basin and bath wastes were required to discharge into the open air over a gully, and some districts even permitted the discharge of bath wastes into rainwater hopperheads, but this practice is prohibited in new work. In London the arrangement of rainwater or bath and basin waste pipes discharging into a gully above the level of the water in the trap was allowed, and this concession prevented dead leaves, etc, which were carried down the rainwater pipes from fouling the gully gratings.

British sanitary regulations traditionally required underground drains to be disconnected from the house at one end and from the sewer at the other, causing the internal house drainage to be doubly disconnected from the public sewer. Disconnection at the house end was effected by the traps fitted below the sink, washbasin and bath and incorporated in the wc as well as by the gullies over which the wastes discharged. Disconnection at the other end of the drain was achieved by means of an intercepting trap or *interceptor*. In many areas, ventilation of the drain by at least two untrapped openings sited at its opposite ends

Fig 141

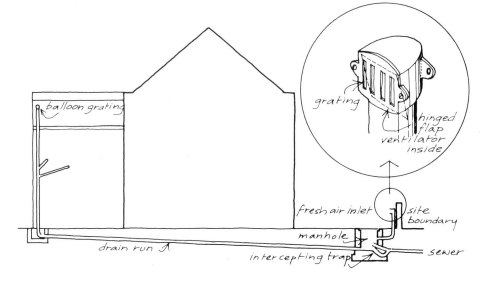

was a supplementary requirement. This condition was usually satisfied by providing at the foot of the drain a fresh-air inlet which vented the manhole nearest the sewer with a single short length of vertical pipe, sited against the back of the front boundary fence. This boundary manhole provided access to the interceptor. At the top of the fresh air inlet a mica flap valve was fitted, which was intended to admit fresh air and to prevent foul air escaping. At the head of the drain a foul-air outlet was provided by extending the soil pipe serving the wc above roof eaves level and covering the open end of this soil and vent pipe with a balloon-shaped wire cage, preventing the ingress of birds and dead leaves (Fig 141). Modern regulations require a minimum distance between this outlet and any nearby window.

Although every attempt was made to avoid laying drains below the house for fear of the damage to the pipes which could be caused by differential settlement of the house foundations and surrounding ground, in terraced houses drained to the front the location of drains below the structure could not be avoided. In best-quality work the portion of the drain which passed beneath the house was carried out in cast-iron pipes, giving a very rigid construction which was not susceptible to distortion or collapse. However, the high cost of this arrangement caused many builders of suburban houses to rely instead on encasing conventional salt-glazed stoneware pipes in about 150mm

(6in) of concrete where they passed below the building. To protect the drain further from damage caused by settlement, a space was left between the top of the pipe and the brickwork or masonry of any foundation wall through which it passed. An arch turned over the drain leaving a 50–75mm (2–3in) air space over the encased pipe gave a satisfactory detail. Pipes 100mm (4in) in diameter (the conventional size) laid to a fall of 1 in 40 were sufficiently large to cater for the combined foul and surface water drainage emanating from even a large detached house. Medium-size terraced and semi-detached houses draining to the front or rear may utilise only two manholes – one in the rear yard which accepts connections from the soil stack, waste and rainwater gullies, and one by the boundary which gives access to the interceptor. In contrast, large, square, detached houses may require six or seven separate manholes to cater for a multiplicity of waste and rainwater gullies sited in several locations around the external walls, and to accommodate the sharp changes of direction in the pipe necessary to carry the drain round the perimeter of the house.

DRAIN CONSTRUCTION

Only two types of pipe for underground drainage were available to the Victorians: cast-iron pipes and salt-glazed stoneware pipes.

Cast-iron pipes were made in stock lengths of 900mm, 1800mm and 2700mm (36in, 72in and

108in) exclusive of the *socket* or swelled end, into which the plain, or *spigot* end of the next pipe was fitted. Pipes were available from 50–250mm (2–10in) internal diameter, increasing in 25mm (1in) increments. Cast-iron pipes used below ground were bedded on concrete and the joints between sections were always caulked with lead. They are still widely used today for high-quality underground drainage, but the old method of caulking the joints with lead has been entirely superseded by quicker and more reliable patented jointing systems.

Much more widely used in nineteenth- and twentieth-century underground drainage systems than cast-iron pipework were salt-glazed stoneware pipes. These were made with internal diameters of 50mm, 75mm, 100mm, 150mm and 225mm (2in, 3in, 4in, 6in and 9in) for domestic use. Pipes of 50mm and 75mm (2in and 3in) diameter were used only for surface water drainage. Stoneware pipes were 685mm (27in) long, 75mm (3in) being taken up by the socket so that a standard distance of 610mm (24in) between sockets resulted. Joints between pipes were made with Portland cement mortar composed either of neat cement or cement and sand in equal proportions. To help the drain layer to centre the spigot of an upper pipe correctly in the socket of a lower section in a slightly inclined drain, a gasket of tarred yarn was sometimes inserted in the socket. However, this technique was frowned on by some local authorities who insisted on the joint being formed only with cement. A circular cement joint of consistent thickness was the correct result of this method of joining pipes, the cement being finished with a splayed profile on the pipe's outer surface, to form a collar around the upper pipe (Fig 142). The drain layer accounted for excess cement being squeezed into the pipe as it was laid, by drawing a semi-circular wooden scraper or *badger* through the sections of pipe in which a joint had been freshly made. In most districts it was common practice simply to bed a run of such pipes directly on the earth. Even in the nineteenth century, this was regarded as a defective arrangement and in good-quality work the pipes were laid on a continuous bed of concrete.

However, the inclusion of a concrete bed was far from common even in twentieth-century installations and it is most likely that this feature was omitted from below the underground drainage of the majority of houses, with consequent problems for the integrity of the drains (see Defects in Underground Drainage on page 177).

This method of drain-laying prevailed until the 1960s, but since that time technical developments have revolutionized underground drainage installations. A type of fireclay pipe is still commonly used for buried drain runs, but instead of the rigid installation resulting from the use of cement-jointed socket connections – which are susceptible to fracture with settlement of the supporting ground – a flexible system is adopted, the connections between pipes being formed with a moulded plastic

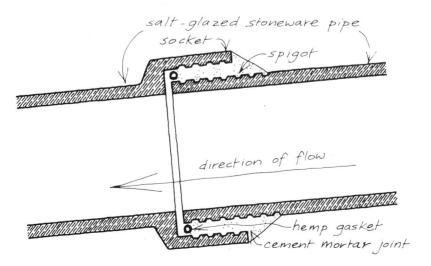

Fig 142

collar containing gaskets which prevent the joints from leaking. As a flexible drain run will tolerate small movements without fracturing, the rigid base essential to a traditional installation may also be dispensed with, and the pipes are often run in a trench partly filled with carefully graded gravel or *pea shingle* which spreads rather than concentrates any loads imposed over the drains, thus minimising distortion and deflection of the pipes. These flexible systems include the pipe sizes and standard accessories such as clayware trapped gullies, which are conventional in traditional stoneware drainage, so it is quite possible to modify or extend an existing rigid installation with pipes joined by flexible connections if the necessary adaptors are obtained. Robust upvc (plastic) pipes are also increasingly used for underground drainage in new work.

MANHOLES

It is always recommended that manholes should be built from 215mm (8½in) thick brickwork on a base of 150mm (6in) thick concrete, but in older domestic drainage manholes enclosed by 102mm (4in) single-skin brickwork proliferate. The internal dimensions of even shallow manholes are rarely less than 750mm × 600mm (30in × 24in) which is usually matched by

a cast-iron cover of equal size. In the present day it is necessary to build the walls out of hard, impervious brick of semi-engineering quality, but this requirement is quite recent and common bricks were often used in old construction. Where such soft bricks were used, it was customary to render the internal surface of the brickwork with cement. This, however, did not protect cheap bricks from the frost damage to which they are susceptible.

The internal arrangements of manholes differed radically according to the pipework adopted for the drainage. In cast-iron drainage, the channels and bends used in manholes are of full circular section. They differ from those used in less accessible locations only by incorporating openings in their top surfaces for inspection purposes. These openings are fitted with screw-down iron covers and thus the openings to the manhole from the drain are entirely closed. In stoneware drains the drain is wholly open to the manhole, the channels being of half-round section and the connecting bends from branches being of three-quarter-round section. For a 'standard' manhole of a domestic system, built in the time-honoured way, the following construction sequence applies: the circular-section main drain and branches from the sanitary fittings are built into the chamber walls at precise levels above the concrete base slab to

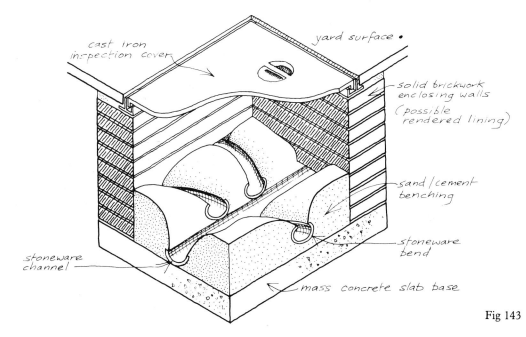

Fig 143

176

ensure the correct fall of the drain, and these outlets are then connected up with the semi-circular and three-quarter-round sections of channel and branch bends which are cut to lengths and profiles which will guarantee an unimpeded flow of solids and waste water. Even today, these components may be of the traditional salt-glazed stoneware. The spaces left between the sides of the channels and the manhole walls are then filled with dense concrete finished to a sloping profile with an absolutely smooth surface. This benching ensures that in a drain which overflows because it has to cope with a sudden torrent of rainwater, the excess water will always return to the main channel and not lodge in a low area where it can become stagnant and infectious (Fig 143). For this reason, fractured or damaged benching should always be restored to a smooth, impervious finish without delay. Sub-standard benching is usually the most easily noticed defect when a manhole cover is lifted for an inspection of a drain. Where a deep manhole was necessary, as on a steeply sloping site, it was usual to arch the enclosing brickwork over the outlet to the drain, to protect the drain connection from any settlement of the brick chamber.

DEFECTS IN UNDERGROUND DRAINAGE
Some of the problems which may be encountered in old rigid drainage have already been indicated. Defective joints are probably the most common cause of blockages in stoneware drains. Where the original drain-layer failed to centre the spigot of the upper pipe truly in the socket of the lower section, the internal moulding of the socket may project above the general invert (flow) level of the pipe, thus causing an obstruction which will trap sediment and eventually block the pipe. This defect was made worse if excess cement from the badly formed joint was allowed to fall on to the offending stoneware projection. Not only was the risk of blockage increased, but also the danger of sewage seeping into the surrounding earth through an incomplete cement joint was introduced. In a case where sewage percolated out of a pipe, public health was endangered by contaminated soil and the lower reaches of the pipe were not secure from blockage, because liquid sewage flowing out of the incomplete joints formed a current under the pipe which

worked sand and mud into lower open joints, ultimately blocking the pipe at a point where its slope was not great enough for the sediment to be washed forwards. A further problem invited by cracked or incomplete cement joints is the tendency of the leaky construction to attract tree roots. All tree roots and particularly those of the willow, grow towards water. The fine roots furthest from the tree then enter the pipe through very small holes, ultimately choking the drain by the growth of small fibrous roots inside the pipe. Where a leaking drain is not in danger of blockages from tree roots but occupies a narrow gangway alongside the house, greater problems are posed by the adverse effect of the constantly saturated soil on the adjoining foundation. A previous owner may have ignored a leaking drain carrying only waste water or rainwater because it did not seem to represent a health hazard, but as the ground below the adjacent footing becomes more and more marshy, it is less and less able to support the foundation, and if this condition arises at a corner where the footing is unable to span over this 'soft spot', collapse of the foundation and the wall it supports will eventually ensue.

Almost all defects in old underground drainage are due to the inflexibility of the pipework. Settlement of the surrounding earth imposes stresses on the pipes which cause the hard cement joints to fracture. This shortcoming has been largely eliminated from contemporary drainage by the adoption of flexibly jointed pipework.

The wide range of possible defects in underground drainage points to the wisdom of conducting a thorough inspection of this aspect of the building construction before purchasing a Victorian house.

Drainage Above Ground
Lead and cast iron were the two materials from which pipes carrying drainage above ground were made. Lead was preferred to cast iron not only by architects, but also by local authorities, as late as 1914, though in imitation of American practice, cast iron was increasingly adopted in the late nineteenth century for low-cost buildings, and by the inter-war period it had entirely superseded lead downpipes on city buildings.

Cast-iron soil and waste pipes were lighter than underground drain pipes in the same material, and those used to carry rainwater were of lighter section still. Soil and waste pipes were invariably of circular cross-section, as indeed were 'standard' rainwater pipes, but pipes of square, rectangular or even octagonal section were often used in prestige buildings. Circular and square-section pipes continue to be available today, but environmental health officers in inner London boroughs may disallow the use of square cast-iron rainwater pipes if they also vent a drain because it is difficult to form impervious joints between square-section pipes. The connection of vertical cast-iron pipes was by the method earlier described for joining underground drainage. The accessories of an exposed cast-iron rainwater drainage system are its most attractive features. Sections of pipe with ears already cast on for fixing the vertical assembly to the wall were manufactured, but often separate ornate pipe clips or *holderbats* were used for this purpose, each clip being secured to a horizontal brick joint with two 100mm (4in) long wrought-iron rainwater pipe nails. Where the roofs drained to a lead-lined internal parapet gutter, openings lined in lead

had to be formed at suitable intervals in the parapet to carry the accumulated rainwater out into hopperheads, which were often of quite elaborate design, and sometimes incorporated the date of the building's erection and the initials of its owner (Fig 144). These details were borrowed from the traditional forms of lead drainpipes and hopperheads. Lead, because it is easily moulded, is much more able than cast iron to be formed into highly ornate and even fanciful shapes. The clips or tacks securing old lead pipes are invariably more elaborate than the mass-produced, cast-iron holderbats.

Whether of cast iron or lead, the sizes of the soil and waste pipes which were carried externally to the vent stack connecting with the drain were fairly consistent. The vertical soil and vent pipe itself was usually at least 88mm (3½in) in internal diameter, a pipe approximately 100mm (4in) in diameter being a widely employed size in cast iron. Soil pipes feeding into this stack from wcs were of equal diameter. Naturally, bath and sink waste pipes were of smaller sizes – usually in the range 38–63mm (1½in–2½in), lead being the favoured material for these thinner pipes. The difficulty of connecting lead to iron pipes was overcome by sleeving the end of the lead in a brass ferrule, to which it was joined by a wiped solder joint, and securely caulking the ferrule into the socket of the iron pipe with molten lead. Where a lead stack pipe had to connect to a stoneware socket at the head of the underground drainage, Portland cement rather than caulked lead filled the joint around the brass ferrule.

Houses which were fitted with 'overground' drainage entirely in cast iron and had overhanging eaves also used cast-iron gutters. Though these could be of half-round section, the 'ogee' profile was a popular and decorative pattern (Fig 145). This gutter profile is once again in vogue after years of obsolescence, the reason for its revival being the wide availability of a portable machine which forms colour-coated strip aluminium to ogee shape. Contemporary aluminium ogee guttering avoids the chief defect of the cast-iron product: namely, rusting of the flat backplate of the moulding around the fixing nails, which causes leaks and the eventual collapse of entire lengths of the gutter. Since the aluminium product is thin-

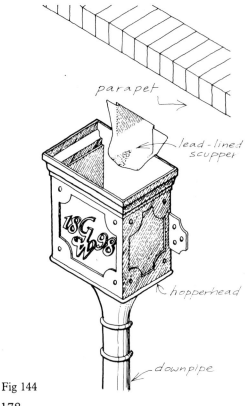

parapet

lead-lined scupper

hopperhead

downpipe

Fig 144

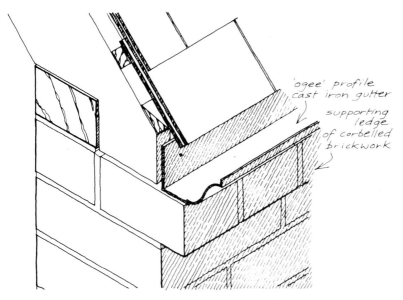

'ogee' profile
cast iron gutter

supporting
ledge
of corbelled
brickwork

Fig 145

walled (unlike the cast-iron guttering), a less attractive feature of the modern version is its insubstantial appearance, which is particularly noticeable at the end of a run because the gutter profile is usually blanked off with a shaped piece of sheet aluminium. It is to be hoped that the manufacturers will produce a purpose-made 'stop end' moulding of robust appearance so that each completed installation can more closely resemble the erstwhile cast-iron fittings.

The continued availability of cast iron for soil and rainwater pipes has led to its use in many restoration projects, but the high cost of the material and its susceptibility to fracture when roughly handled rules it out for low-budget repairs and renovations. Moulded plastic upvc piping is almost universally used in new work and in the rehabilitation of old houses, its standard colours being white, black and light grey. Black is perhaps the most suitable colour for replacement gutters, as a line of guttering in

black when seen against the background of a pale-coloured painted fascia tends to look slighter than it is. Also the carbon black which is a constituent of the plastic 'mix' safeguards the material against rapid degradation by the ultra-violet wavelength of sunlight. Various patent systems of half-round, deep half-elliptical and trapezoidal-trough section black plastic guttering are available for easy fixing by the moderately skilled handyman. Light grey seems to be the finish favoured for new external upvc wastes and soil and vent pipes. This neutral colour is fairly inconspicuous in the context of most of the traditional building materials. Joints between sections of pipe are made with a plastic solvent cement. A full range of fittings for the various patented systems, including the moulded plastic versions of all the accessories germane to cast-iron drainage, is available through the larger DIY stores.

179

11
Alterations and Improvements

STRUCTURAL ALTERATIONS

'Knocking Through'

Although there exist many types of Victorian houses displaying countless permutations on a wide range of floor plans, mid-twentieth-century ideas on planning are entirely alien to all types of Victorian house. The primitive nature of Victorian building services and structure meant that there was no contemporary appreciation of 'open planning'. This concept was realised only when framed structures and central heating were introduced into domestic architecture. Victorian houses tend to be cellular – the plan of each floor is an aggregation of separate rooms, individually heated by their own grates, their walls providing support for the timber joists of the upper floors. Not until the twentieth century was the potential of steel or concrete floor beams spanning long distances between columns fully exploited.

The general availability of central heating systems and the widespread awareness of the daring effects achievable in modern structures are factors which have encouraged the opening-up of individual cellular rooms into adjoining spaces to give grander apartments. This alteration is usually achieved by installing a rolled steel joist (RSJ) on the line of the partition wall which formerly supported the upper-floor joists, and then removing the partition. The steel beam spans a wide opening between brick piers which replace the extreme ends of the original wall. In this way, many householders have converted adjoining small rooms into continuous through lounges up to 10m (33ft) in length. It is true that there is a Victorian precedent for this treatment. Ground floor front 'parlours' or sitting-rooms of Victorian houses of all but the smallest types were sometimes arranged to open into rear living-rooms through double or 'folding' doors. Yet the omission of the double doors and their framing from a new opening often underlines the fact that the enlarged space which has been created is only an amorphous, irregularly shaped room which is completely out of sympathy with the cellular spaces of the rest of the house. Each case must be looked at on its own merits because larger houses may absorb 'knocking through' without the character of the accommodation being destroyed. On the other hand, where this treatment is applied to small houses, the fitting of panelled folding doors to a less-than-full-width opening which links both rooms is an arrangement in character with the scale and details of the house (Fig 146). Be warned that the double doors which replace a heavy brickwork or timber partition will not give equally good sound insulation! The joinery is light in weight and gaps at the joint of doors and frame cannot be completely sealed against airborne noise.

Loft Conversions

A second rearrangement of the original Victorian accommodation which is often carried out is the conversion of vacant roof space into additional rooms. That this is a popular policy is proved by the rash of bulky dormer windows which continues to spread through suburban streets, often disfiguring the neat roof slopes of the affected houses. The insistence upon making such dormers very large in relation to the roof planes from which they spring is the main cause of their disfiguring effect. The policy is understandable as an attempt to maximise the usable volume of the house, but its potentially disastrous aesthetic consequences should not be ignored. There are few precedents for flat-topped dormers in Victorian houses, except those of the Arts and Crafts Movement period, and even in these

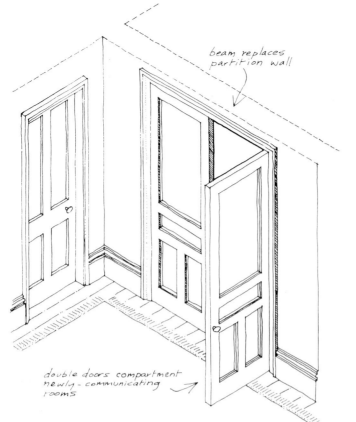

beam replaces partition wall

double doors compartment newly-communicating rooms

Fig 146

'cottage' dwellings the dormer structure was kept quite small – perhaps up to 2m (6½ft) wide and 1.5m (5ft) high at most. The use of mass-produced softwood windows which do not correspond in overall size, configuration of lights or frame thicknesses with the original purpose-made windows, further underlines the alien character of an over-bulky dormer. Modern 'standard' windows invariably display a far greater proportion of glass to framing than the Victorian items, with the result that their mullions and transoms look worryingly insubstantial. This unattractive flimsiness is emphasized in a flat-roofed dormer because the mullions of a multiple-light window appear to 'support' the roof structure (Plate 27).

Even worse than an oversized dormer leaning out of a small roof slope is a flat-topped dormer, the upper part of which visually breaks the roof ridge or 'severs' the hip of a pyramidal roof. Most local planning authorities are in any case opposed to this type of domestic extension, but they tend to turn a blind eye to overlarge dormers located on roof slopes surmounting

rear elevations. However, if you really intend to preserve and enhance the character of your Victorian house you would be well advised to avoid the 'king-size' dormer altogether! Where new dormers cannot be avoided, try to add a form of window which uses the claddings and fenestration patterns adopted by the Victorians and which relates to existing openings in the main wall surface below (Fig 147).

Where a roof slope is sufficiently steep for the low space behind the eaves to be converted to living accommodation, it may not be necessary to enlarge the roof volume with a dormer. A modern product which has replaced the old-fashioned skylight is the roof window. This device is fixed in the plane of the roof with its protective weathertight flashing projecting slightly above the surface of the surrounding tiles or slates. These factory-produced, prefabricated units are invariably double-glazed so that condensation on the underside of the glass is obviated. The window pivots at its centre to admit fresh air and allow cleaning of the external glazing from the inside. An inde-

181

Plate 27 The enormous new dormer window is completely out-of-tune with the small-scale features of this semi-detached Victorian shop/dwelling (*Author*)

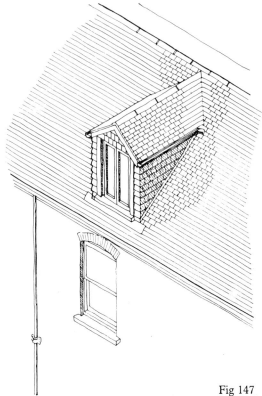

Fig 147

pendent ventilator is also often incorporated so that it is not essential to pivot the window (and thus admit wind-blown rain in bad weather) in order to draw in fresh air. As it lies in the plane of the roof, a roof window is much less conspicuous than a dormer window, although a rash of these windows is almost as disruptive of the otherwise calm appearance of a broad roof slope as an ill-sited dormer.

Many dormers are made very large because a current building regulation requires a minimum height of 2.3m (7ft 6in) over 50 per cent of the area of rooms in the roof, and the addition of a high flat-topped dormer window is a simple way of satisfying this requirement. Yet equal consideration should be given to lowering

the level of the joists which will support the new floor so that the mandatory headroom can be achieved. This may be a practical policy which brings benefits in other areas. Certainly a lower level for the topmost floor will ease the installation of the new stair flight needed to link the former top floor with the converted roof space, because a reduction in the storey height also reduces the floor area required to accommodate the new stair. Furthermore, a reduced intermediate storey height may make it more possible for a new upper level to be reached via a staircase which complies with the building regulations than does the existing floor-to-floor dimension. Providing a minimum internal height of 2.3m (7ft 6in) in habitable rooms is achieved (bathrooms and wcs are not classified as habitable rooms and may therefore be lower), lofty Victorian storey heights can be considerably reduced.

Rear Extensions
Where a roof void or other unused internal space is not available to provide space for expansion, the option of extending the plan

182

outwards is usually considered. This normally means adding space to the house either at the side or at the rear. In the case of terraced houses, extensions are almost always restricted to the rear elevations. Planning officers are not normally too concerned about the appearance of rear extensions but this indifference should not excuse houseowners from trying hard to build something in sympathy with the original structure! A conspicuous exception to the planning officer's 'blind eye' approach arises when the house is sited in a Conservation Area. This is a district whose visual amenity has been officially acknowledged by the local planning authority. Consequently, special notice is taken of any external modification proposed for a building sited therein and planning consent may be required for quite tiny alterations. Leafy suburban areas containing well-preserved Victorian houses are increasingly candidates for designation as Conservation Areas.

The standard design for a new back extension comprises a flat roof surmounting a three-sided one or two storey 'box' of brickwork or rendered blockwork, the walls of the box being perforated by standard-pattern painted softwood-framed windows. As additions to very utilitarian houses, such extensions may be aesthetically acceptable, but they normally stand in stark contrast to the quite elaborate detailing of Victorian dwellings. Yet it is not difficult to see where modifications can be made to this formula, which will result in a more harmonious blend of old and new. If the flat roof is replaced by a pitched roof which reproduces the slope and covering of the main roof, some affinity between the two structures is automatically achieved. The use of matching materials for the extension's external walls is also a prerequisite if a strong visual unity of the old and new is sought.

The very first problem likely to be encountered in the construction of a rear extension is the necessary depth of the new foundations. The footings of Victorian houses are often quite shallow and new foundations of identical depth are unlikely to comply with the requirements of contemporary building regulations. Thus the foundations of a new extension may need to go down deeper than the original footings and this circumstance introduces the risk that the old work will be undermined. In some cases it may be necessary to underpin a section of the old

footing to reconcile its founding level with that of the new work. Building Inspectors in Greater London have become particularly concerned about shallow foundations following the dry summer of 1976 when clay subsoils dried out and shrank, reducing the support given to superincumbent footings and in some cases causing their collapse. The proximity of mature trees to the new structure also gives building control officers some cause for concern, as trees draw much moisture out of the adjacent soil. In some instances builders have been asked to take the underside of foundations for simple single-storey extensions down to 1.5–2.0m (5–6½ft) below ground level. As this requirement habitually emerges only when the original footings have been exposed it is quite likely to cause a doubling of the foundation work originally anticipated and a proportional increase in its cost.

Where the external walls of the house are of brickwork and a matching appearance in the walls of the extension is desired, this element cannot be of solid construction and still comply with the weatherproofing requirements of the national building regulations unless it is at least 327mm (13in) thick. This is an expensive and space-consuming form of construction which provides only a poor standard of thermal insulation. Hence, most modern brick-faced external walls are cavity walls in which the external leaf is of facing brick and the internal leaf is of 100mm (4in) thick aerated concrete blockwork. Despite the good insulating properties of the 50mm (2in) wide cavity which separates the two leaves, this construction does not achieve a standard of thermal insulation adequate to satisfy the current building regulations. Its insulating properties can be improved either by adopting thicker blocks for the inner leaf or building some insulating material into the cavity. A neat and satisfactory way of implementing the latter policy places 25mm (1in) thick polystyrene slabs against the outer face of the inner leaf in a widened (75mm [3in]) cavity (Fig 148).

Where late Victorian or Edwardian houses have their external walls coated in roughcast or pebbledash render, an inexpensive form of solid construction can be adopted for extensions. Lightweight concrete blocks at least 190mm (7½in) thick and rendered externally, satisfactorily exclude wind-driven rain and provide

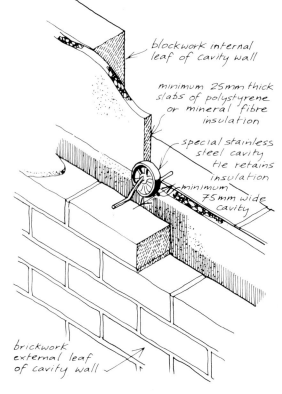

blockwork internal
leaf of cavity wall

minimum 25mm thick
slabs of polystyrene
or mineral fibre
insulation

special stainless
steel cavity
tie retains
insulation

minimum
75mm wide
cavity

brickwork
external leaf
of cavity wall

Fig 148

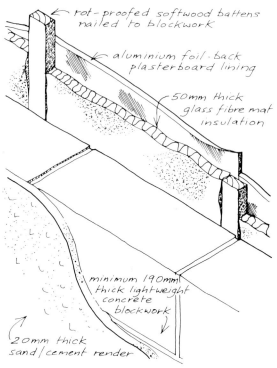

rot-proofed softwood battens
nailed to blockwork

aluminium foil-back
plasterboard lining

50mm thick
glass fibre mat
insulation

minimum 190mm
thick lightweight
concrete
blockwork

20mm thick
sand/cement render

Fig 149

a reasonable level of thermal insulation. Their insulating properties can be greatly enhanced by lining the blockwork's inner face with a 60mm (2⅜in) thick glass-fibre quilt contained between vertical wooden battens, on to which the internal wall finish of aluminium-foil-backed plasterboard is nailed (Fig 149). This construction grants almost twice the level of thermal insulation required by the building regulations. It is not possible to achieve the mandatory 'U' value of 0.6 W/m² °C without adding some highly insulating material to the blockwork either externally or internally. A type of plasterboard laminated with polystyrene sheet is as satisfactory an insulator as the glass-fibre quilt, but on no account should the aluminium-foil backing or similarly impervious membrane be omitted, as this vapour barrier prevents troublesome condensation from forming within the walling material.

Few details are as unsympathetic with the appearance of the average Victorian house than a bituminous felt flat roof finished at the eaves

in a boarded fascia, yet because of its low initial cost, this formula is almost universally adopted for small domestic extensions. Roofs of this type are prone to leak unless the roof finish is well maintained and periodically renewed. The 'roof space' – or voids between the joists – is difficult to ventilate, an exercise made worse by the necessity of including a continuous insulating layer in this zone if the construction is to meet current building regulations standards. The most serious consequence of poor ventilation and damp penetration is, of course, the establishment of dry rot. If the use of a flat roof is inescapable, in aesthetic and constructional terms it is preferable to site a roof deck of solid construction (such as a reinforced concrete slab or pre-cast concrete trough floor) behind a continuous parapet. The top surface of the dense slab may then be securely waterproofed with a poured asphalt roof covering.

Far superior in its capability of throwing off rainwater and providing an easily ventilated roof void (itself an insulating medium) in which

184

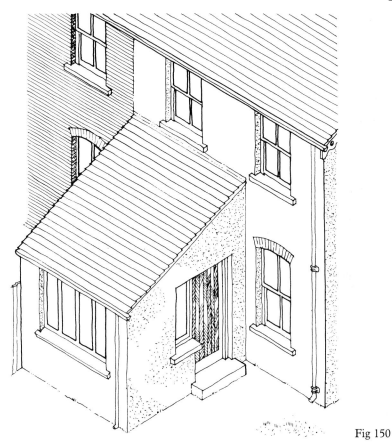

Fig 150

it is a simple matter to install additional insulation, is the pitched roof. The lean-to roof is endemic to the back extensions of small Victorian houses of the provinces, so that the integration of small rear extensions into the shapes of these houses is actively assisted by its adoption (Fig 150). Where a 'back extension to a back extension' is contemplated, the customarily narrow plan of the second extension may militate against the use of a simple lean-to roof and a monopitch or double-pitched roof has to be adopted. Monopitch roofs were used over the original back extensions of many Victorian houses, though if the span of the ceiling joists of the added section exceeds 3m (10ft), the external volume of the roof begins to look oversize. Broader extensions which cannot be roofed satisfactorily with a lean-to should be capped by a conventional double-pitched roof. Small double-pitched roofs are simply constructed on the 'couple close' principle (Fig 57). The width of a pitched roof required over a new rear extension – or even a pair of new

extensions – is unlikely to approach the 6–7m (20–23ft) dimension which is most economically spanned by mass-produced prefabricated timber trusses as used in modern house construction.

A further option opened up by the pitched roof is the possibility of exposing the rafters to give an 'open roof' appearance appropriate to a 'cottage kitchen'. In this event, it is still necessary to incorporate a layer of thermal insulation in the plane of the roof slope. Thus the spaces between the rafters should be framed up to give fixing surfaces for foil-backed boarding fitted tightly between the sides of the rafters. This boarding then helps to retain the insulating quilt of glass fibre or mineral wool on top, which is wedged between the rafters.

Replacement Windows

The design and positioning of new and replacement windows in extensions to the structure or the original accommodation is crucial to a successful restoration of a Victorian house.

185

Alterations and Improvements

Many nineteenth-century houses – including thousands of modest terraced dwellings – were fitted with French windows giving direct access from a living-room to a garden or yard. The modern equivalent of this feature is the sliding aluminium 'patio door' which is everywhere installed in new or enlarged openings in the walls of old houses with no consideration of its visual effect on the adjacent architecture. Yet there are few modern building products which are more alien to the original window detailing of Victorian houses. Contemporary mass-produced softwood-framed French doors hardly represent an improvement over the metal versions because the thickness of the timber used for the doors and the fixed frame is so slight that it causes a disproportionately large area of glazing to contrast with a small and mean-looking area of wooden frame. The restorer seeking complete authenticity is therefore obliged to commission purpose-made joinery to replace an unserviceable Victorian installation. 'Bespoke' replacement frames are best made entirely in hardwood, but if this material cannot be afforded for all the parts, it is essential that the sill at least is of hardwood to resist premature rotting caused by rising damp and saturation by driving rain. The recent introduction by one national manufacturer of a range of hardwood-framed sliding patio doors suggests that the reconciliation of carefully restored Victorian houses with an external sliding door which meets modern standards of draught-proofing and ease of operation may not be far away.

If the most familiar modern versions of large Victorian French windows display too much glass and too little frame to 'fit in', this quality is no less marked in the smaller sizes of mass-produced wood windows. Apart from the very smallest standard-pattern softwood windows incorporating top hung vents, the width of the fixed frames of these units is always unconvincingly narrow and for this reason, as well as the common discrepancy between the sub-division of a modern frame and a Victorian installation, it is always easy to identify modern wooden windows in an antique façade. Paradoxically, purpose-made aluminium windows of the type installed by most double-glazing contractors generally display more frame area in relation to glass than do wood-framed windows. The automatic objection to

aluminium windows – that their silvery metal frames contrast badly with an otherwise 'period' elevation – can be overcome by obtaining frames finished in enamel paintwork. White is the most satisfactory colour coating as it helps to expand visually the width of the frames to an authentically Victorian dimension.

The most enduring and appropriate window frame material of all is hardwood. Its use is generally restricted to purpose-made windows, though middle-price, mass-produced hardwood windows in a range of sizes are increasingly available. Clearly, the commissioning of purpose-made hardwood windows, although expensive, admits the possibility of an exact match with the surviving Victorian frames. Those who succumb to the temptation to leave the hardwood surfaces unpainted sacrifice a close affinity between the new work and the old!

Softwood is far less durable than hardwood as a material for the manufacture of purpose-made window frames, and in view of the longevity of much Victorian softwood joinery, there naturally arises the question of why this is so. The cause of the disparity between the performance of modern softwood and its Victorian equivalent lies in the difference between the way freshly cut timber is treated today and the way it was treated in the nineteenth century. In Victorian times, the roughly squared logs were often carefully stacked and allowed to 'season' in the open air for several years before being machined into joinery sections. In contrast, modern softwood is invariably kiln-dried quite soon after it is felled. The accelerated drying-out quickly makes it suitable for shaping but thereafter the wood is more prone to distort and decay than the well-seasoned timber of yester-year.

Front Entrance Canopies and Porches

Probably the most modest alteration made to commonplace houses by new owner-occupiers is the addition of an external 'storm porch' to reduce draughts admitted through the front entrance door. In houses with an integral porch this improvement is often achieved by fitting an outward opening door in the plane of the street elevation, thus creating a 'draught lobby' in front of the original entrance door. In many cases this alteration has the architecturally unfortunate result of reducing the area of shadow contained by the front elevation and

consequently reducing the interest of the 'composition'. The radical change in the appearance of the elevation caused by this modification can be reduced if the new external door shows a generous area of glass in relation to a minimal frame area, thereby 'hiding' itself in the existing architecture. Various patterns of double-glazed, aluminium-framed outward opening doors which include efficient integral draught seals largely meet this requirement, but such a door is even less conspicuous if it is obtained colour-coated with a dark paint or in a bronze-anodized finish so that it will more successfully hide in the shadows.

Houses lacking an integral porch which are entered through a door in the plane of the front elevation are notoriously draughty. Devices traditionally adopted to exclude draughts include curtains hung over the internal door surfaces and small lobbies formed in the affected corners of front rooms. Yet quite naturally, many owners have seized on a more radical solution to this problem – the addition

Plate 28 The pleasing unity of materials and details in a short terrace of small dwellings is easily destroyed by ostentatious additions or alterations to an individual house (*Author*)

of an external porch. There is a great temptation to finish such a feature with imitation random-rubble walling or varnished boarding, etc, as if it is a significant independent structure, rather than to recognise that often its real impact is upon the architectural coherence of a range of houses which are fundamentally identical. The pleasing unity of a short terrace of modest houses is easily disrupted by overly individualistic additions (Plate 28). Therefore it is advisable to aim for the simplest possible shapes and finishes in an added entrance porch. The materials used in the roof and wall construction ideally should reproduce those of the main house roof and external walls. For houses sited in Greater London this often demands the procurement of second-hand stock bricks for porch wall construction.

187

Alterations and Improvements

There is no doubt that it is aesthetically as well as financially advantageous for adjoining owners to erect simultaneously a pair of porches serving neighbouring terraced houses, because the size of the resulting structure is likely to integrate more successfully with the front elevation than a single 'sentry box'! Where the exclusion of draughts is not as great a need as gaining a dry threshold, a simple canopy is almost as efficient as a fully enclosed porch, and is much easier to construct. There are many precedents for cantilever or bracketed front entrance door canopies in late Victorian houses. Their sloping tiled or slated roofs were commonly supported on carved wooden brackets springing from padstones or corbelled brick courses built into the street elevation, and it is a simple matter for a bricklayer to modify small areas of existing front elevation brickwork to provide end bearings for the triangular timber support frames of a new entrance canopy. Stout softwood sections (100mm × 100mm [4in × 4in]), pressure impregnated against rot, give a suitable structure if they are supported on this masonry 'shelf' and also secured to the super-incumbent brickwork with expanding bolt fixings. The whole assembly may then be roofed with felt, battens and slates or tiles matching the main roof finish.

Added Bathrooms and WCs

Rear extensions are often added to existing ground-floor accommodation – or to ground and first floors – to house a much-needed bathroom. Even in 1981 almost a million dwellings lacked basic amenities, such as a wc accessible from the inside, a fixed bath, a sink, or hot and cold water supply to three points (sink, bath and wash-hand basin). Victorian houses represented the larger part of these 'unfit' dwellings and for many new householders the building of extensions to enclose these essential services is more of a functional necessity than a self-indulgent design exercise. Where the living rooms of the house are conventionally disposed (ie the occupants sleep upstairs), a chief disadvantage of siting the bathroom and wc on the ground floor is the extended distance from the bedrooms to these amenities. However, the pipework for the above-ground drainage is minimised by this arrangement, and providing the vent pipe of the wc is not terminated too close to an upper-storey window, this aspect of the work may well be more acceptable to the building inspector than an upper-storey installation in which the new sanitary fittings are remote from the soil and vent pipe.

The plan of the archetypal late nineteenth-century terraced house incorporated a two-storey back extension flanking a yard. Where the upper storey of this extension contains a third bedroom accessible only from the central upstairs room, it may be sensible to convert this space into a combined bathroom and wc or a bathroom and separate wc. As the route to this rear room quite commonly takes a diagonal line across the central bedroom and houses planned in this way invariably have a central staircase, reversal of the stair may be necessary to make sense of this arrangement (Fig 151).

It must be emphasized that bathrooms and wcs are not classified as habitable rooms and therefore they can be accommodated in otherwise 'uninhabitable' areas which hardly extend to door head height. Understairs spaces commonly fit this description. As the ceilings of Victorian houses are rarely less than 2.5m (8ft 3in) above floor level, there is sometimes scope for installing mezzanine levels over staircases and the resulting low spaces may be ideal locations for *en-suite* bathrooms.

As bathrooms have recently become the vehicle for flights of fancy in interior design and decoration, something should be said about the finishes which are suitable for bathrooms newly integrated into Victorian houses. Full or half-height wall tiling is appropriate for new or refurbished bathrooms, but it should be said that the impressionistic floral patterns and pastel shades of many Italian ceramic tiles which are currently imported into Britain are entirely alien to Victorian precedent. Naturalistic or floral patterning in genuine Victorian wall tiles was much more conventionalized than the images applied to most modern products, though it may be possible to find contemporary tiles which approximate to the more mechanical appearance of the nineteenth-century article. Patterns in Victorian tiling also tended to be regular; it was not the custom – as often applies today – to insert patterned tiles in apparently arbitrary places in areas of plain tiling. Cork tiles are a modern floor covering which happily complements the other finishes of a restored

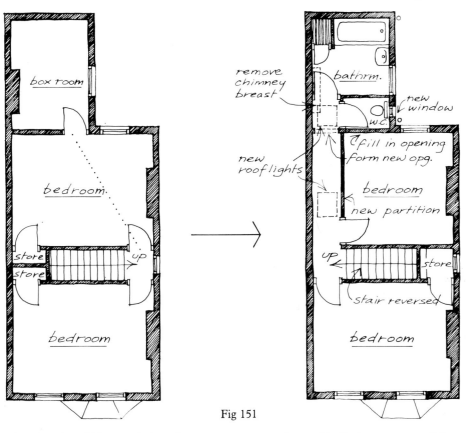

Fig 151

Victorian interior. When sealed against water penetration, they provide a warm-feeling, low-maintenance floor finish in bathrooms. Highly patterned vinyl tiles are less appropriate. There is a precedent for boarded ceilings, but Victorian softwood surfaces were always painted and not allowed to shout 'knotty pine'!

Grant Aid

There is now a comprehensive structure of grants to assist the repair and improvement of sub-standard houses. Very full information on grants is freely available from local authorities and you would be well advised to apply for the relevant advisory leaflets if you are contemplating making major changes to a previously neglected dwelling. Improvement grants for the improvement of older properties to a good standard are made at the local authority's discretion, but a council is obliged to make an intermediate grant to an applicant who is the owner of a property lacking the basic amenities of fixed bath or shower, wc, wash-hand basin, sink or the hot and cold water supplies which serve them. Similarly, owners of houses in Housing Action Areas or General Improvement Areas are eligible for repairs grants in respect of works of repair or replacement not associated with works of improvement or conversion, if the council is satisfied that the applicant could not, without undue hardship, meet the cost of the work without a grant.

DAMP-PROOF COURSES

Probably the most conspicuous defect in many surviving Victorian houses is the failure of the original damp-proof course to resist rising damp and the consequent deterioration of the building construction. Very few surviving Victorian houses are likely to have been built without a dpc because national legislation required this feature from about 1875, but the original asphalt membrane is likely to have worn out. There exists a range of measures for keeping rising damp at bay.

A modest method of limiting the effects of rising damp – it is essentially a 'damp alleviation' technique – consists of atmospheric siphons which are installed at specific intervals in the external walls. Moisture contained in the base of a wall is reduced by drawing it through this series of porous tubes which are permanently inserted in the brickwork. The distance between the tubes and their angle of inclination has to be carefully calculated according to the type of wall and the local ground conditions. The tubes terminate in small circular gratings fitted flush with the outside face of the wall. The system is useful for reducing the amount of water contained in a wall without necessarily succeeding in eliminating it.

A second type of 'tentative' installation which aims to combat rising damp without causing major disruption to the structure or finishes is the electro-osmotic system. The principle of its operation is that if an electrical potential can be set up between a building and the adjoining earth, moisture can be encouraged to flow from the former to the latter. Only a small amount of current is used, but results 'from the field' suggest that the method is not always successful.

At the opposite extreme from these quite modest attempts to discourage rising damp is the classical procedure for renewing a dpc; the affected wall is shored up and alternate sections of the lowest brickwork course are removed and rebuilt, a damp-proof course of slate or other impervious material being incorporated in the new structure. When these renewed sections are complete, the retained sections are demolished and these, in turn, are rebuilt, thus completing the continuous 'barrier' which is the new dpc. This operation is extremely expensive and in recent years other methods have been developed in order to achieve an almost equally effective result.

Insertion

A modern method of inserting a new physical dpc uses a chain saw to cut out a continuous slot in a mortar joint of the affected wall, into which the new polyethylene dpc is fitted a section at a time. The dpc is inserted in approximately 1m (3ft) lengths. It is wedged in place with pieces of slate and the part of the slot unfilled by the dpc is filled with mortar. It is not normally practical to make the cut below the internal floor level, but the type of saw developed by the Building Research Station and now in general use allows the cut to be made in the horizontal mortar joint closest to the internal floor level. The shallow strip of wallface left below the dpc and above the floor surface should be finished with two coats of bituminous paint to seal out dampness. As a defence against rot, skirtings refixed over this vulnerable area ideally ought to be of plastic or some similarly impervious material which is not affected by moisture. The innumerable contractors who specialise in the installation of new physical dpcs usually insist that any adjacent wall plaster which has been affected by dampness is removed, and the hacking off of a continuous 1m (3ft) depth of plaster from the affected wall is standard procedure. Following the insertion of the dpc the denuded brickwork is given some time to dry out before new plaster containing a water-repellent ingredient is applied. A non-corrosive metal dpc such as sheet lead provides the very best barrier against rising damp, but the cheaper polyethylene or pitch polymer damp-proof membranes used by most companies are almost equally durable.

Injection

Plainly, the sawing of a wall for the insertion of a damp-proof course may be a practical treatment for rising damp in detached houses and in some semi-detached houses, but terraced houses in which the party walls rather than the easily accessible front elevation provide the main route for rising damp pose a different problem. Unless neighbouring owners jointly resolve to install a new physical dpc for their mutual benefit, sawing of the party wall is out of the question. However, impregnation of the lowest brick courses of the affected wall with a silicone water-repellent fluid provides a solution. To be fully effective, an injected chemical dpc, like any new physical barrier, requires the removal of a 1m (3ft) high band of plaster from the internal surface of the affected wall. Small holes at 150mm (6in) increments in a horizontal row are then drilled down into the heart of the wall and the proprietary liquid is poured into these openings or injected under pressure until the foot of the wall is saturated with the water repellent. Just as the plaster which is applied after the installation of a physical dpc must include a water repellent, so the plaster coating a wall which has been impregnated with a chemical dpc must be equally damp-resisting if the installer's guarantee is to hold good.

The history of chemical dpcs reaches back only to the late 1940s and their general application to house renovation work is of even more recent date, so there is little evidence to show whether they are reliable in the long term. Yet most firms which offer this treatment guarantee their work for a thirty-year period. Only if it is offered by the long-established companies is this warranty to be taken seriously. It is doubtful if the business lifetime of some of the smallest and newest firms will extend to thirty years!

Easily-cured Causes of Rising Damp

Conditions quite separate from the breakdown of the original dpc can help to propagate rising damp. Where the dpc of a solid external wall remains effective, the appearance of rising damp inside is often due to the piling of garden earth against the wall and above the dpc. This defect is very simply corrected by lowering the external ground surface below dpc level. Quite conventional to the external treatment of late Victorian and Edwardian houses was the application of a continuous cement render plinth to the foot of the external wall, the chief purpose of which seems to have been the concealment of the 'ugly' dpc. It was not appreciated that this plinth 'bridged' the dpc, thus providing a route for ground water to permeate the brickwork above its level. To be effective, a dpc must extend through the whole thickness of the wall and not stop short of the external face, be pointed up with mortar, or be concealed by a rendered plinth. The removal of an offending rendered plinth above the line of the dpc markedly improves the efficiency of an original damp-proof layer which is otherwise intact.

Concealment of Rising Damp

In earlier times, the discovery of the effects of rising damp does not seem to have prompted its cure so much as its concealment. A favourite technique for concealing the defect involved stripping the internal wall surface of plaster and fixing to the brickwork a patent, corrugated bitumen-impregnated lathing which was concealed behind the new plaster. A decorative surface free of blemishes resulted if the corrugated lath was fixed and lapped exactly as specified by the manufacturer, because the

dampness was thereby prevented from penetrating the joints of the lathing and affecting the new decorations. Of course, the brickwork or masonry behind the lath continued to suffer the effects of damp penetration. More elaborate still was the installation of a continuous blockwork inner skin built just inside and parallel to the affected wall. Neither technique can be recommended where the opportunity exists instead to install a new damp-proof course which will dry out the *entire* building construction.

ENERGY CONSERVATION

Thermal Insulation

In the course of earlier chapters, something has been said about adding thermal insulation to uninsulated wall and floor surfaces, yet the part of the house which is most frequently associated with installing insulation is the roof. It is true that most of the energy used in heating a house quickly leaks out through an uninsulated roof space, and local authorities, as the agents of central government, have acknowledged this shortcoming by providing grants to applicants whose houses lack any form of loft insulation. Types of insulation which are eligible for grant aid include glass or mineral wool mats or quilts at least 80mm (3in) thick, exfoliated vermiculite at least 130mm (5in) thick or cellulose fibres of 80mm (5in) minimum thickness, the two latter products being 'loose fill' materials.

The installation of glass-fibre quilts is extremely simple. Unrolled between the ceiling joists to form a continuous insulating layer, they are effectively held in place by the sides of the joists. It is often more difficult to obtain a consistent thickness of loose fill material between the joists. This applies particularly at the point where the joists terminate against the rafters which are descending to meet the back of the eaves fascia. To prevent the loose fill from spilling over this edge and filling a void which should be kept open to ensure good ventilation of the roof space, it is necessary to 'dam' the ends of the 'channels' between ceiling joists with bricks or wooden blocks cut to size (Fig 152).

This emphasis on the necessity of maintaining permanent ventilation of the roof space naturally provokes the question of how roofs which enclose habitable rooms may be satisfac-

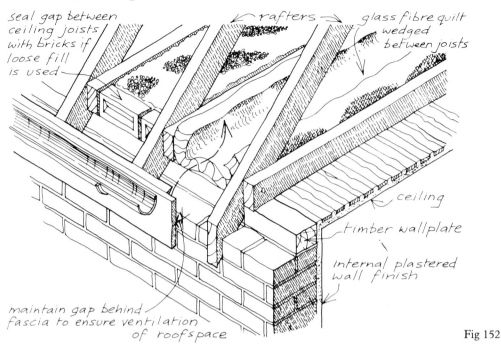

seal gap between
ceiling joists
with bricks if
loose fill
is used

rafters

glass fibre quilt
wedged
between joists

ceiling

timber wallplate

Internal plastered
wall finish

maintain gap behind
fascia to ensure ventilation
of roofspace

Fig 152

torily insulated, because there is often very little space between the external roof surface and the internal plaster finish. Clearly, it is unwise to fill the whole of this cavity with insulation, excluding ventilation and introducing conditions conducive to dry rot. Ideally, some void space should be retained below the roofing felt which lies underneath the tiles or slates, but to discourage interstitial condensation (condensation of moisture *within* the insulating material) it is necessary to introduce an impermeable vapour barrier on the warm side of the insulation. If other 'uninhabited' parts of the roof are being insulated with glass fibre, the inclusion of a vapour barrier is a simple matter because a glass-fibre quilt laminated with impervious polythene sheet is readily available and the composite material is easily installed in the sloping plane of the roof by stapling the polythene sheet to the sides of the rafters. Where there is scope to line a raking roof structure with plasterboard, the vapour barrier is equally simply incorporated by adopting either the aluminium foil-backed or polythene-backed versions of this material.

Exploitation of Solar Energy

Installing extra insulation is only one aspect of energy conservation in the home. In the design of new houses the relevance of 'active' or 'passive' solar design techniques to energy conservation is now quite often acknowledged. These procedures respectively exploit the contribution of solar energy to house heating and recognize that a new dwelling can be sited and constructed in such a way that its energy needs will be reduced. Most existing houses were erected with slight consideration for the optimum orientation of living rooms and with no concern at all for a good standard of insulation, so it is only the techniques of 'active' solar design which are of interest to their owners.

An attached conservatory on the south side of the house acts as an effective sun trap in winter as well as in summer, and some of the heat generated can be vented into the house through an opening fitted with doors which prevent heated air in the main accommodation from leaking into a glazed room made cold by a cloudy sky. Solar panels fitted on a south-facing roof slope are a less cumbersome means of harnessing the sun's energy. These black-painted panels are connected by pipework passing into the house to a tank, through which passes a section of the pipework of the hot water system. The panels, their connecting pipes and tank are filled with an oil which responds quickly to a change in temperature. An increase in the temperature of the oil caused by sunlight striking the panels is rapidly transferred to the section of hot water pipework which passes through the tank, and thus the cylinder is charged with hot water quite independent of any action of the immersion heater or central heating boiler. Even intermittent sunshine may be adequate to ensure a constant supply of hot water from a very well-insulated cylinder. The winter season is not entirely sunless and the small amount of heat generated by watery sunlight striking the solar panels will at least reduce the amount of conventional fuel required to raise stored water to a temperature suitable for washing. In summer, hot water requirements can be met entirely by exploitation of the sun's energy. Against these savings has to be set the capital cost of installing the system which can exceed £1,000. Nevertheless, solar panels are installed increasingly in existing houses as a worthwhile means of reducing energy costs.

Central Heating

Most new owners of unmodernised Victorian houses will be more concerned to discover how a chilly interior may be made warm than to cut down on heating bills. The remedy to this condition which springs to most people's minds is central heating – a method of house heating which has probably been oversold by commercial interests in recent years. For most householders central heating means a system of panel radiators fed through copper pipes with hot water under low pressure. The boiler which heats the water to the required temperature may be oil, gas or solid-fuel-fired. However, before the merits and demerits of this standard arrangement are described, something should be said about 'central heating' by electricity.

Local electricity boards have bid for a share of the central heating market by promoting the use of night storage heaters. These units store heat built up from the consumption of cheap rate night-time electricity in a dense concrete core and emit this heat when it is wanted during the day. Yet they are not 'central heating' in the true sense as each unit is effectively independent of the other heaters in the system. A second type of electric space heating which can be installed in existing houses, though it causes more disruption than night storage heaters, consists of a continuous quilt containing thin wire heating elements which is installed above the ceiling finish. When a small electric charge is passed through the wires the quilt acts as a radiant heating panel. The propensity of heated air to rise and the low power of this system suggest that it is really only suitable as 'background' heating and not as the main heat source. The installation of underfloor electric heating in an existing interior demands even more radical modifications of the construction and this system is best restricted to new dwellings where its integration into the design has been considered from the outset.

The disruption caused by the installation of piped, hot water central heating which the adoption of electric night storage heaters avoids includes the lifting of carpets and floor boards for the integration of the pipework. It is possible to visit countless houses where this job has been clumsily or insensitively carried out. Pipes hurtle out of stair risers and career across walls and through cornices; no regard is shown for the coherence of the original architecture. Yet this is not the natural result of a new central heating installation in an old house. Like any other craft, plumbing can be carried out well or badly, and if you are not able to undertake the work yourself there is no substitute for employing a skilful plumber who will respect the views of his client on the proper location of pipes, etc, in relation to prized interior features. The introduction and general availability of small-diameter easily worked microbore and minibore pipes and simple 'solder ring' connections has encouraged many householders to tackle the installation of domestic central heating systems.

What about the types of boilers used to heat the water for low-pressure hot water heating? Boilers fuelled by gas are more compact than those that burn either oil or solid fuel, but in many country areas the option of using a gas-fired boiler may not exist. Even in urban areas traditionally well served by gas mains it may be difficult to obtain a gas supply for a house currently unprovided with gas. This circumstance has arisen because the present high demand for gas as a heating fuel has put much extra pressure on many very old gas mains. Thus local gas boards are loth to increase the strain by tapping additional branches from an already highly stressed pipe.

If gas cannot be obtained, the adoption of an

oil- or solid-fuel-fired boiler is conditioned only by the ready availability of the particular fuel. Space must be available for storing the fuel consumed by either type of boiler. Heating oil is conventionally stored in a tank of 500–600 gallons (2273–2727 litres) capacity which is always sited outside the house, the oil being supplied to the boiler's burner through connecting pipework either by gravity or under the pressure provided by an electric pump. Solid-fuel boilers are now much more compact and lightweight than the colossal cast-iron devices which occupied a part of many a Victorian basement. Coke is no longer the favoured fuel. Instead the solid fuel is obtained in the form of pulverized coal 'pellets' which are fed into a hopper at the top of the boiler. This fuel guarantees a consistent temperature and efficient burning reduces it to a small amount of ash which must be removed periodically from the pan at the foot of the boiler. Unlike oil, the storage space needed for the solid fuel need not be sited outside, although it must be covered so that the coal remains dry.

Gas boilers create no waste apart from the combustion gases which must be exhausted to the outside air. If an existing and otherwise unused chimney flue is nearby, the fumes from the boiler may be ducted into it, but the absence of such a flue places no limitation upon the siting of the gas-fired boiler. If it can be located on an external wall, the flue gases can be ducted into the open air via a balanced flue, which is fitted on to the side or rear of the wall or floor-mounted boiler to discharge outwards rather than upwards. The appeal on behalf of the architecture which must be made here is that you should find a location for such a flue which is inconspicuous in the context of the elevation. The 'balanced flue option' is not open for the venting of oil- and solid-fuel-fired boilers because the sulphur contained in the fumes they produce cannot be diluted, and this demands the boiler's direct connection to, and exclusive use of, an existing or newly constructed chimney flue.

The radiators of a typical low-pressure hot water heating system served by an oil-, gas- or solid-fuel-fired boiler are features of most modern interiors as familiar as the washing machine or refrigerator. Their pressed metal construction attempts to maximise the radiant area. The cheapest types are manufactured in a way which ensures that a continuous welded flange finishes the top of the radiator. This profile collects dirt and dust and is very difficult to keep clean, but at least one manufacturer produces an otherwise conventional radiator which incorporates a 'roll' profile at this level, giving a neat and easily cleaned top surface. In addition to this basic type, a wide range of models is available, from radiators presenting a completely flat vertical surface to shallow fittings formed from continuously corrugated thin steel sheet. Radiators should be sited in positions where the heat loss is greatest – this usually means below the windows. However, it is quite likely that no model from a range of standard radiators will exactly suit the size and shape of an under-sill location. Do not rule out the possibility of obtaining a radiator to suit each individual circumstance. Providing an adequate manufacturing period is available in advance of the installation, even the largest of manufacturers will produce individual radiators to suit particular locations. Thus cranked or curved panels can be obtained to fit snugly into splayed or segmental bays. As they will combat cold radiation from the related window surfaces much more efficiently than standard panels conveniently sited elsewhere, these 'specials' may be well worth waiting for.

Double Glazing

High on the list of energy conservation measures familiar to contemporary owner-occupiers comes double glazing. The widespread awareness of this product and the general good opinion of its qualities must be due in no small part to the great amount of advertising which has been devoted to it in recent times. Yet in the league of cost-effective energy conservation measures it ranks fairly low. The saving on energy costs made by installing double glazing in a formerly single-glazed window is not nearly so marked as the saving which results from installing insulation in a formerly uninsulated roof space. The vast majority of Victorian houses were built with 215mm (8½in) thick solid brick external walls which gave poor thermal insulation, so that double-glazing the small proportion of these surfaces which is occupied by the windows may save only 5–10 per cent of the heat lost through the fabric. To leave the windows single-glazed and to insulate the walls further could be much more worthwhile.

Innumerable companies offer the service of installing double-glazed replacement windows and the quality of the products offered varies very widely. Some of the large companies offer a good specification for this work which requires the installation of the anodized aluminium window frames in hardwood sub-frames. Sometimes an overly heavy appearance results from this combination of materials, but the hardwood can be painted to relate it to the colour of adjacent surfaces and it is virtually rotproof. For the installer this arrangement is particularly advantageous because it grants a 'tolerance zone' around the standard-section aluminium frames. Where new metal windows are being fitted into irregularly shaped Victorian openings, the scope for fitting the new precisely into the old which is granted by the wood may be indispensable. Also the hardwood can be machined in the joinery works to the general profile of the jambs, head and sill of an individual window. This option is particularly helpful where, for instance, a rectangular aluminium frame has to be fitted into an opening spanned by a segmental brick-work arch.

It may be argued that since a good speci-fication for aluminium-framed replacement glazing requires fixed hardwood frames to ensure a tight fit with existing construction, might not the aluminium be dispensed with altogether? There is much strength in this argument. Purpose-made hardwood windows can easily be fabricated to accommodate pre-manufactured, sealed double-glazed units and they do not require subframes. The oppor-tunity to shape the wood on site means that they can be fitted precisely into existing openings. Even if they are entirely unprotected by paint or varnish, many types of hardwood will endure at least as long as the aluminium alloys used in most commercially available replacement windows, and wood, unlike metal, is a good insulator. The special and possibly short-lived 'thermal break' now included in many aluminium frames to ensure that condensation is prevented from forming on the internal frame surfaces is unnecessary in a timber window.

Modern, mass-produced softwood windows are much less durable than any hardwood frame and it is true that they are unlikely to last as long as aluminium windows, even if their external paint protection is quite carefully maintained. However, softwood frame sections are produced which will accommodate sealed double-glazing units and at least one national joinery supplier markets a type of double-glazed unit which incorporates a stepped profile at its edge so that it can be fitted into standard-section softwood frames.

NEW FITTINGS AND FURNISHINGS

In recent years there has emerged a host of manufacturers and suppliers who specialise in the production and sale of imitation 'period' domestic fittings. The services offered range from the manufacture of previously discon-tinued patterns of metal staircases and ironmongery to the reprinting of antique wallpapers. Such is the diversity of architectural styles visible in Victorian and Edwardian houses that it is almost impossible to give any general guidance on furnishing in the 'authentic' Victorian manner. The only meaningful general point which can be made concerns the materials used in any fitted item. Avoid synthetic materials and finishes. The Victorians knew nothing of nylon, polystyrene or pvc. Internal door handles were of 'bright' metal (such as brass) or metal and china; window and external door fittings were usually of 'black' (wrought) iron; carpets and rugs were woollen; ceilings were invariably of painted plaster, wall and floor tiling was carried out in fireclay products, etc. Fittings and finishes in synthetic materials naturally proclaim their modernity when they are seen in association with the original features.

If you accept these prohibitions and really desire an authentic restoration, the next step is to establish the style and the period of your house. For those who are not expert at spotting architectural styles, the date of its construction usually gives some clues about the style likely to have been adopted. Between 1830 and 1850 the neo-classicism of the late Georgian period continued to be practised, the hallmarks of this style being the plain painted 'stucco' render surfaces of the street elevations and the high-level parapet which rides above them, largely hiding the roof slopes. After mid-century the more agitated forms and variegated materials of

Alterations and Improvements

Gothic Revival architecture began to influence the appearance of even cheap, speculative houses. Carved stone capitals appeared alongside porches and bays; large, plate-glass windows replaced the multi-panel lights characteristic of Regency houses, and 'polychromatic' brickwork exploiting the varying colours and textures of different types of bricks displaced the vast expanses of unmoulded stucco which had been favoured by the Georgians. From about 1880 the reaction of the Aesthetic Movement against the almost intentional clumsiness of the Gothic Revival reintroduced some daintiness into everyday domestic architecture. Pale-painted woodwork lightened interiors and elevations, where it was contrasted with soft red brickwork and tile-hanging. Many suburban houses boasting this combination of materials were still being erected at the start of World War I but two further stylistic influences which almost exclusively affected Edwardian houses should be mentioned.

An aspect of the 'aesthetic' reaction against Gothic coarseness was a new appreciation of 'vernacular' architecture – the unselfconscious traditional buildings of the countryside. This interest of the 'domestic revival' architects engendered the simple, picturesque domestic architecture of the Arts and Crafts Movement which quickly popularized visually dominating roofs, small windows and roughcast render as an external wall finish – features which continued to appear in suburban housing even into the 1930s. A concurrent, if weaker influence, came from continental *art nouveau* and as this mode seems to have been viewed as a sophisticated urban style, it was often fused with details introduced by the Aesthetic Movement, so that few of the rustic motifs favoured by the Arts and Crafts Movement appear in turn-of-the-century, city-centre houses. Nevertheless, leaded lights incorporating swirling patterns of coloured glass (influenced by *art nouveau*) representing plant and flower forms, are as much a feature of the front entrance doors of the pebbledashed villas of the suburbs as they are of the entrance glazing of the red-brick Edwardian mansion blocks of the inner city.

From this brief outline of the stylistic changes and the pointers to the age of specific details made elsewhere in the book, it may be easy to identify the period and 'pattern' of your house.

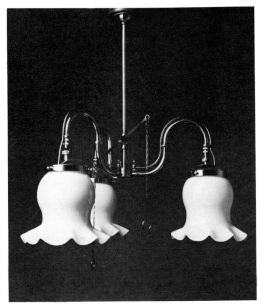

Plate 29 A reproduction late-Victorian three-arm pendant light fitting. This model is fitted with inverted incandescent mantles which operate on natural gas or 'bottled' liquid petroleum gas. Electric fittings of similar design are also available (*Sugg Lighting*)

Plate 30 An Edwardian-style brass basin tap. The range of 'period' fittings in the brass or nickel-plated finishes which preceded today's ubiquitous chromium plate is expanding rapidly (*Sanitary Appliances*)

196

From here it is a short step to finding fittings and furnishings which harmonize with the architecture. The salerooms of most towns are crowded with the commonplace 'brown' furniture of the late nineteenth and early twentieth centuries, and good pieces often can be bought at prices far lower than those of modern mass-produced furniture. Similarly, many rugs and carpets (often of oriental origin) which nicely complement this older furniture are commonly offered for sale in the same auction rooms. In this connection, it is worth remembering that any item more than 100 years old is classified as an antique and this status is usually reflected in its price. Victorian prints and paintings also appear at auction sales. Be warned that nineteenth-century water-colours are becoming sought-after items with the result that many poor-quality paintings of this period are often hugely overpriced.

Finding authentic fittings presents a greater problem because few Victorian light fittings and little sanitary ware has survived *in situ*. Several manufacturers and retailers of antique patterns of light fittings are now operating.

Brass is invariably used for the construction of these products, though it was by no means the only metal used to make the bodies of the Victorian fittings. However, the opal, coloured and etched glass shades characteristic of Victorian pendant and bracket lights have been faithfully reproduced in many 'period' fittings (Plate 29).

Few would wish to revive Victorian patterns of sanitary ware, for the nineteenth-century fittings were almost uniformly hideous and sometimes unhygienic, but several companies offer plated bath, shower and basin taps which closely resemble their Edwardian prototypes. Thus a surviving cast-iron bath tub can be quite easily reconditioned by adding new taps to complement an interior freshly recoated with bath enamel (Plate 30).

Plate 31 A late-Victorian interior survives intact at Linley Sambourne House, 18 Stafford Terrace, Kensington, London. It is cared for by the Victorian Society as a museum of Victorian domestic design. Appointments to tour the house may be made by telephoning the society (*National Monuments Record*)

Alterations and Improvements

Several wallpaper manufacturers offer a small range of paper in patterns designed by the notable Victorian artists, including A. W. N. Pugin, Lewis F. Day and William Morris, but these fabrics may be 'hand-printed', only available to order, and therefore very expensive. Something like the same conditions apply to textiles suitable for curtains and loose covers, although in this area a broader range of nineteenth-century patterns is generally available. In recent years many textile designers have drawn inspiration from late-Victorian patterned fabrics and because of this a wide range of 'Victorian-style' textiles designed by modern artists is available. This is therefore an area of interior design where the desire to obtain a coherent 'Victorian' character does not *demand* the adoption of authentic William Morris patterns!

The introduction of a 'paint-mixing' service at many DIY shops has greatly extended the range of colours available for internal and external paintwork. This enlargement of the 'British Standard Range' has made it more possible to obtain colours which closely resemble the original painted surfaces of Victorian joinery and plasterwork. Yet the high-gloss paints which are used today were unknown to the Victorians. The surface of the oil paint which was commonly applied to woodwork and plaster was more similar to the currently available 'silk' finishes than to the sheen of modern gloss paint. Also, the Victorians believed that if they could not afford real oak or mahogany it was legitimate to imitate the patterns of these and other woods by graining, and even in cheap speculative houses, highly figured painted surfaces were as usual as areas of plain paintwork. Only in the late nineteenth century, when the influence of the Arts and Crafts Movement architects began to be felt, was the practice of graining called into question, because these leaders of fashion regarded the reproduction of wood grain in paint as 'dishonest'.

For those who intend to recreate a highly authentic Victorian interior, a visit to Linley Sambourne House, the Victorian Society's own museum of late Victorian domestic design at 18 Stafford Terrace, Kensington, London W8, is indispensable (Plate 31).

Perhaps the last main area of furnishing which needs to be touched on is the contribution which can be made by indoor plants. The aspidistra (or cast-iron plant) is very often associated with Victorian interiors and the reason for its preponderance in these apartments was its tolerance of gloomy conditions. Yet many other types of plant were favoured by the Victorians: cacti, ferns and exotic palms were greatly admired, but the greenhouse or conservatory conditions which were needed to sustain them could not always be achieved. Sansevieria (or 'mother-in-law's tongue') would tolerate compromise conditions and so was almost as popular as the aspidistra. The conclusion which must be drawn is that luxuriant greenery is quite appropriate to the restored interior of a Victorian house, and with the possible exception of the 'Swiss cheese plant', the fashion for which is of quite recent origin, the more exotic the vegetation, the better!

Useful Addresses

BRICKS

Blue Circle Enterprises
Brick Division
Sittingbourne Wales
Sittingbourne, Kent ME10 3TN
Tel 0795 21066

London stock bricks

Ibstock Johnsen PLC
29 Crawford Street, London W1H 1PL
Tel 01 402 1277

*Facing bricks and pavers in many colours,
handmade bricks*

W. T. Lamb & Sons Ltd
52 East Street
Horsham, Sussex RH12 1HN
Tel 0403 66201

'Red rubber' bricks

Rudgwick Brickworks Co Ltd
Lynwick Street
Rudgwick, West Sussex RH12 3DM
Tel 040 372 2212

STONE RESTORATION

Ashby & Horner Masonry Ltd
795 London Road
West Thurrock, Essex RM16 1LH
Tel 040 26 6841

*Specialise in repair and restoration of 'hard' stones
such as Portland and York*

London Stone Ltd
34 Clifton Street, London EC2A 4RU
Tel 01 247 6544

*Specialise in repair and restoration of 'soft' stones
such as imported marble*

J. Whitehead & Sons Ltd
Marble Craftsmen
Imperial Works
64 Kennington Oval, London SE11 5SP
Tel 01 735 1602

SLATES

Burlington Slate Ltd
Cavendish House
Coniston
Cumbria LA21 8ET
Tel 096 64 515

Cumbrian (Lakeland) slate

J. W. Greaves & Sons Ltd
Llechwedd Slate Mines
Blaenau Ffestiniog
Gwynedd LL41 3NB
Tel 076 881 522

Welsh (Portmadoc) slate

Penrhyn Quarries Ltd
Bethesda, Bangor
Gwynedd LL57 4YG
Tel 0248 600 656

Welsh slate

CLAY ROOFING TILES

Hawkins (Cannock) Ltd
Longhouse Works
Cannock, Staffordshire WS11 3BJ
Tel 054 35 3744

Also manufacture of hard paving bricks

Keymer Brick and Tile Co
Nye Road
Burgess Hill
West Sussex RH15 0LZ
Tel 044 46 2931

Useful Addresses

Langley London Ltd
The Roofing Centre
161–167 Borough High Street
London SE1 1HU
Tel 01 407 4444

Rosemary Brick & Tile Co Ltd
Haunchwood-Lewis Works
Cannock, Staffordshire WS11 3LS
Tel 0922 412346

Sandtoft Tileries Ltd
Sandtoft
Doncaster, South Yorkshire DN8 5SY
Tel 0427 872 696

Clay pantiles

Swallow's Tiles (Cranleigh) Ltd
Bookhurst Brick and Tile Works
Cranleigh, Surrey GU6 7DP
Tel 048 66 4100

H. F. Warner Ltd
Star Works, Star Lane
Knowl Hill, Reading
Berkshire RG10 7YB
Tel 062 882 3333

William Blyth Ltd
Hoe Hill
Barton-on-Humber
Humberside
Tel 0652 32175

Clay pantiles

CAST AND WROUGHT IRON

Albion Design
12 Flitcroft Street
London WC2H 8DJ
Tel 01 836 0151

Artistic Ironworkers Supplies Ltd
Wrought Iron Works
Unit 1
Whitehouse Road
Kidderminster, Worcestershire DY10 1HT
Tel 0562 753483

Ball Bros (Engineers) Ltd
Reliance Works
Arden Street
Stratford-upon-Avon
Warwickshire
Tel 0789 292268

Booth & Brookes
Mildmay Ironworks
Burnham-on-Crouch
Essex
Tel 0621 782109

Brittania Architectural Metalwork &
Restoration
5 Normandy Street
Alton, Hampshire GU34 1DD
Tel 0420 84427

Cradley Castings Ltd
Mill Street
Halesowen, West Midlands B63 2UB
Tel 0384 60601

Dorothea Restoration Engineers Ltd
Pearl Assurance House
Hardwick Street
Buxton, Derbyshire SK17 6DH
Tel 0298 77115

Metalcraft (Tottenham) Ltd
6 Durnford Street
London N15 5NQ
Tel 01 802 1715

Southwell Builders (Stockwell) Ltd
104A Lansdowne Way
London SW8
Tel 01 622 7970

Thurton Foundries
Thurton
Norwich, Norfolk
Tel 050 843 301

Further names from:
The Council of Ironfoundry Associations
14 Pall Mall
London SW1
Tel 01 930 7171

VICTORIAN PATTERN METAL STAIRCASES

Albion Design
12 Flitcroft Street
London WC2H 8DJ
Tel 01 836 0151

Jay Curzons
Brook Cottage
Stretton-on-Dunsmore
Rugby, Warwickshire
Tel 020 335 2308

Dorothea Restoration Engineers Ltd
Pearl Assurance House
Hardwick Street
Buxton, Derbyshire SK17 6DH
Tel 0298 77115

Safety Stairways Ltd
141 Field Road
Bloxwich
Walsall, Staffordshire
Tel 0922 77722

FIREPLACES

Amazing Grates
153 Highgate Road
London NW5
Tel 01 485 0496

Restored cast-iron fireplaces, reproduction firedogs and fenders

Kingsworthy Foundry Co Ltd
Kingsworthy
Winchester, Hampshire
Tel 0962 883776

Copies of firebacks, firebaskets, firedogs and firescreens

Mr Wandles Workshop
200 Garrett Lane
London SW18
Tel 01 870 5873

Restoration and sale of period fireplaces and mantelpieces

IRONMONGERY

J. D. Beardmore & Co Ltd
3 Percy Street
London W1P 0EJ
Tel 01 637 7041

Locks and Handles
8 Exhibition Road
London SW7 2HF
Tel 01 584 6800

Rothley Brass Ltd
Merridale Street
Wolverhampton
West Midlands WV3 0RB
Tel 0902 27532

Yannedis & Co Ltd
25/27 Theobalds Road
London WC1X 8SR
Tel 01 242 7106

GLASS

British Society of Master Glass Painters
88 Woodwarde Road
Dulwich, London SE22 8OT
Tel 01 693 6574

They keep a register of glass artists working in Britain

P.P.G. Ltd
14/18 High Street
Stratford, London E15 2PR
Tel 01 534 8011

Patent glazing for lantern lights and verandah/conservatory roofs

The Standard Patent Glazing Co Ltd
Forge Lane
Dewsbury, West Yorkshire WF12 9EL
Tel 0924 461213

Patent glazing for lantern lights and verandah/conservatory roofs

PERIOD JOINERY MOULDINGS

Ashby & Horner Ltd
795 London Road
West Thurrock, Essex RM16 1LH
Tel 040 26 6841

Manufacturers of 'bespoke' joinery

Useful Addresses

W. H. Newson & Sons Ltd
61 Pimlico Road
London SW1W 8NF
Tel 01 730 6262

FIBROUS PLASTER MOULDINGS

Aristocast
Bold Street
Sheffield, South Yorkshire S9 2LR
Tel 0742 442423

George Jackson & Sons Ltd
Rathbone Works
Rainville Road
London W6 9MD
Tel 01 385 6616

G. J. Green & Veronese
24 Edison Road
Crouch End, London N8 8AE
Tel 01 348 4462

Hodkin & Jones Ltd
515 Queens Road
Sheffield, South Yorkshire S2 4DS
Tel 0742 56121

Jonathan James Ltd
17 New Road
Rainham, Essex RM13 8DJ
Tel 040 27 56921

J. G. McDonough Ltd
347 New Kings Road
London SW6 4RJ
Tel 01 736 5146

Moran & Wheatley
Avondale Studios
Avondale Place
Batheaston, Bath, Avon
Tel 0225 859678

Thomas & Wilson Ltd
454 Fulham Road
London SW6 1BY
Tel 01 381 1161

W. J. Wilson & Son Ltd
Elm Tree Street
Mansfield, Nottinghamshire NG18 2HD
Tel 0623 23113

TERRACOTTA MOULDINGS

Shaws of Darwen (Ceramics) Ltd
Waterside
Darwen, Lancashire BB3 3NX
Tel 0254 71811

*This company has recently recommenced the
manufacture of bespoke terracotta mouldings.
They can copy salvaged pieces or make new
mouldings from full-size drawings. Contact:
David Malkin
Tel 0782 85611*

STONE CLEANING

Ken Negus Ltd
44 South Side
Clapham Common, London SW4 9BL
Tel 01 720 2938

Peter Cox Ltd
Lamberts Place
St James Road
Croydon, Surrey CR9 2HX
Tel 01 684 6646

Rominar Ltd
160 Bethnal Green Road
London E2 6DG
Tel 01 739 4168

PERIOD SANITARY FITTINGS

Barber, Wilsons & Co Ltd
Crawley Road
London N22 6AH
Tel 01 888 2041

Edwardian-pattern shower fittings and taps

Czech & Speake
88 Jermyn Street
London SW1
Tel 01 839 6868

*Edwardian-pattern shower fittings and taps, glass
fibre reproductions of antique bathtubs*

Sanitary Appliances Ltd
3 Sandiford Road
Kimpton Road Industrial Estate
Sutton, Surrey SM3 9RN
Tel 01 641 0310

Edwardian-pattern shower fittings and taps

Sitting Pretty
131 Dawes Road
London SW6
Tel 01 381 0049

Antique baths, basins, and wcs, Edwardian-pattern shower fittings and taps

PERIOD LIGHT FITTINGS

Christopher Wray's Lighting Emporium Ltd
600 Kings Road
London SW6 2DX
Tel 01 736 8434

Suppliers of period internal and external electric light fittings. Other showrooms at Bristol, Leeds and Kilkenny, Ireland

W. Sitch & Co
48 Berwick Street
London W1
Tel 01 437 3776

Manufacturers and suppliers of period electric light fittings, restorers of antique light fittings

Sugg Lighting Ltd
Napier Way
Crawley, West Sussex RH10 2RA
Tel 0293 21874

Manufacturers and suppliers of period internal and external light fittings operating on electricity or gas

WINDOWS

Boulton & Paul Joinery Ltd
Riverside Works
Norwich NR1 1EB
Tel 0603 660133

W. H. Newson & Sons
61 Pimlico Road
London SW1W 8NF
Tel 01 730 6262

ASBESTOS CEMENT SLATES

Eternit Building Products Ltd
Meldreth
Nr Royston, Hertfordshire SG8 5RL
Tel 0763 60421

T.A.C. Construction Materials Ltd
PO Box 22
Trafford Park
Manchester M17 1RU
Tel 061 872 2181

Tunnel Building Products Ltd
Motherwell Way
London Road
Grays, Essex RM16 1EJ
Tel 040 26 3322

CHIMNEY POTS & RIDGE TILES

John Caddick & Son Ltd
Spoutfield Tileries
Stoke-on-Trent, Staffordshire ST4 7BX
Tel 0782 616413

Manufacturers of chimney pots, chimney cowls and ridge tiles

Redbank Manufacturing Co Ltd
Measham
Burton-on-Trent, Staffordshire DE12 7EL
Tel 0530 70333

Manufacturers of air bricks, chimney cowls, chimney pots and ridge tiles

Stanley Brothers Ltd
Croft Road
Nuneaton, Warwickshire CV10 7ED
Tel 0682 382301

Manufacturers of air bricks, chimney cowls, chimney pots and ridge tiles

CONCRETE ROOF TILES

Redland Roof Tiles Ltd
Reigate, Surrey RH2 0SJ
Tel Freephone 2695

QUARRY TILES

Daniel Platt & Sons Ltd
Brownhills Tileries
Tunstall
Stoke-on-Trent, Staffordshire ST6 4NY
Tel 0782 86187

Red 'Crown flat' quarry tiles

Dennis (Ruabon) Ltd
Hafod Tileries
Ruabon, Wrexham, Clwyd LL14 6ET
Tel 0978 842283

Manufacturers of 'Heather Brown' quarry tiles since 1878

ENCAUSTIC FIRECLAY FLOOR TILES

H. & R. Johnson Ltd
Highgate Tile Works
Tunstall
Stoke-on-Trent, Staffordshire ST6 4JX
Tel 0782 85611

Manufacturers of bespoke encaustic tiles. They can copy salvaged pieces or make new mouldings from full-size drawings. Contact: David Malkin

SPECIALIST BUILDING CONTRACTORS

Ashby & Horner Ltd
32 Earl Street
London EC2A 2JD
Tel 01 377 0266

J. W. Falkner & Sons Ltd
24 Ossory Road
London SE1 5AP
Tel 01 237 8101

These builders are renowned for their expertise in restoring historic buildings. Countless small, local, 'jobbing builders' and individual tradesmen also offer the care and skill necessary to achieve a satisfactory result. The good opinion of a previous client is always the best recommendation of the competence of a company or a craftsman

SPECIALIST DECORATIONS CONTRACTOR

Campbell, Smith & Co Ltd
9–11 Cowper Road
Stoke Newington
London N16 8NY
Tel 01 245 8551

Very high-quality redecoration and restoration of period interiors and furnishings

DAMP-PROOFING

Peter Cox Ltd
Damp Proofing Division
Wandle Way
Mitcham, Surrey CR4 4NB
Tel 01 640 1151

Protim Ltd
Fieldhouse Lane
Marlow, Buckinghamshire SL7 1LS
Tel 062 84 6644

Rentokil Ltd
East Grinstead
West Sussex RH19 2JY
Tel 0342 833022

Many smaller companies operate in particular districts of the country

SALVAGED MATERIALS

Andy Thornton Architectural Antiques Ltd
Ainleys Industrial Estate
Elland, West Yorkshire HX5 9JP
Tel 0422 78125

Architectural Heritage of Cheltenham
Bayshill Lodge
Montpellier, Cheltenham
Gloucestershire
Tel 0242 45589

Architectural Salvage
Netley House
Gomshall, Surrey GU5 9QA
Tel 048 641 3221

They keep a register of those who have old building materials for sale and those who are seeking antique items. Small registration fee

London Architectural Salvage & Supply Co Ltd
St Michael's Church
Mark Street, off Paul Street
London EC2
Tel 01 739 0448

Related Reading

ARCHITECTURE AND HOUSING IN VICTORIAN BRITAIN

Victorian Architecture Dixon, Roger, and Muthesius, Stefan. (Thames & Hudson, 1978) A scholarly and comprehensive survey of all types of Victorian buildings, including speculative housing.

The English Terraced House Muthesius, Stefan. (Yale University Press, 1982) This book includes a fascinating and very thorough investigation of the planning and appearance of terraced housing in Victorian England.

DO-IT-YOURSELF; GUIDANCE FOR BEGINNERS

The Reluctant Handyman Keegan, Patrick, and Layzell, Ian. (Macmillan Papermac, 1982) Simple domestic D-I-Y jobs treated humorously and clearly illustrated.

The New Homeowner Manual Limon, A. *et al.* (Hamlyn, 1982) Concise, factual descriptions of the basic skills of building construction and home maintenance.

DO-IT-YOURSELF; SPECIFIC SKILLS

Central Heating Bowyer, John. (David & Charles, 1977) An examination of the virtues and vices of the different systems, their capital and running costs, and the way of assessing the size of equipment needed for a given area.

David & Charles Manual of Home Electrics Burdett, Geoffrey. (David & Charles, 1981) A thorough description of every aspect of home electrics which stresses safe methods of modifying or renewing existing installations.

David & Charles Manual of Home Plumbing Hall, E. (David & Charles, 1982) A very fully illustrated guide to domestic plumbing. Advice is given on the repair, maintenance and improvement of existing systems.

D-I-Y Guide to Natural Stonework Harrison, J. A. C. (David & Charles, 1979) For owners of stone-built dwellings, an invaluable guide to techniques of repair and renovation.

DIAGNOSIS AND TREATMENT OF DEFECTS IN OLD BUILDINGS

The Care of Old Buildings Today Insall, Donald. (Architectural Press, 1972) Special problems of old buildings and related restoration techniques described and illustrated.

The Repair and Maintenance of Houses Melville, Ian, and Gordon, Ian. (Estates Gazette, 1972) Under-illustrated and over-wordy but nevertheless informative account of defects in traditional houses, based on the extensive practical experience of the authors, both of whom are chartered surveyors.

Protecting Buildings Richardson, Stanley A. (David & Charles, 1977) Describes the symptoms, causes and treatment for all the major problems that afflict a building due to incursions of water, insects and fungi.

AUTHENTIC FURNISHINGS FOR PERIOD HOUSES

Putting Back the Style Artley, Alexandra (ed). (Bell & Hyman, 1982) A guide to aesthetic authenticity in the decoration and furnishing of English houses erected between 1750 and 1939.

Index

Index